Contents

Meet the author

This book is the one I wanted to read when I first started studying tax over 25 years ago whilst reading law and training to be a Chartered Accountant. Unfortunately, there were no books like it on the market so I had to learn my tax from some decidedly dry and dusty tomes.

Having worked with many small business people over the years, I am passionate about making difficult but essential subjects like tax accessible to everyone. We all learn in different ways so I have included detailed numerical examples and tables of information alongside the written text. The format of the book is based around the real-life decisions that business people have to make every day, so there are plenty of examples and case studies based on actual events. Each point is described using as little jargon as possible and where technical words are used, there is a glossary in Appendix 3 to help with those unfamiliar terms. Please be reassured that irrespective of whether you succeeded or failed at school maths you can grasp the basics of the tax system. As you read the book, you will find out that understanding business tax is more about your attitude to tax than it is about being able to perform complex calculations.

I hope that by regularly referring to this work you will learn to avoid some of the tax pitfalls that so often plague new ventures and come to understand the tax consequences of all the various decisions you have to make on a daily basis. Reading the book will not turn you into a tax expert overnight but it will make you aware of where tax impacts on your business, preventing potentially expensive mistakes. You will also find that your increased knowledge takes some of the fear out of dealing with your tax affairs, enabling you to have more meaningful and equal consultations with your bankers, accountants and of course HM Revenue and Customs.

I hope you enjoy this new edition. Good luck and best wishes with your business venture.

Sarah Deeks LLB FCA

Only got a minute?

Irrespective of whether you trade as a sole trader, partnership or limited company there are certain common features of the tax system that apply to all businesses. One of the most significant points to remember is that you pay tax on your business profits and not your drawings, dividends or money taken from the business. You should also be aware that the profit (or loss) in your business accounts has to be adjusted to take into account the tax rules. The most significant adjustment usually relates to the tools, equipment and vehicles used in your business. Instead of calculating commercial depreciation you have to claim capital allowances on these items instead. If you make a loss you do not have to pay tax and you may be able to claim a tax refund by off-setting the loss against other income or profits.

Understanding how the tax system is administered is important. All businesses pay their taxes to Her Majesty's Revenue and Customs (HMRC for short) under rules known as self-assessment. In order to know how much tax you owe you have to complete a tax return. Companies file a corporation tax return. Sole traders and partnerships complete the relevant pages of the income tax return. There are deadlines for filing tax returns and paying tax. Failing to meet these dates will result in fines and interest charges.

All businesses need to notify the tax authorities about their activities, keep appropriate business records, prepare accurate accounts and file correct returns. To ensure that you comply with these rules HMRC have wide-ranging powers to inspect businesses records and visit business premises.

Employing staff and paying directors has tax consequences. You have to deduct income tax and National Insurance from their salaries under the Pay As You Earn system (PAYE for short). You also have to maintain detailed records of any perks or benefits they receive and expenses they claim.

If your business is registered for VAT you have to file regular VAT returns to account for VAT paid to you by your customers. You are able to claim back VAT paid to your suppliers. In some cases you will benefit by using a special VAT scheme.

Tax affects a business from the 'cradle to the grave', so starting a new business, incorporating an existing self-employment or partnership, selling a business or closing one down, all have tax implications which require consideration if you are to minimize your tax bills.

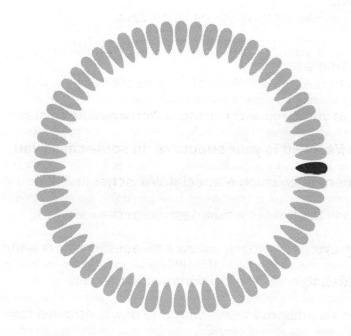

5 Only got five minutes?

An understanding of the tax system is essential for anyone involved in a small business venture – proprietors, partners and directors – if they are to avoid tax pitfalls and understand the tax breaks available to them at each stage in the business lifecycle.

Starting a business

When starting up a new small business you should first of all decide whether you want to trade as a sole trader, partnership or limited company. This will depend on a number of factors including whether you are working on your own or with other people and how risky the business is. There is no easy way to tell whether you will save tax by trading as a company rather than a sole trader because it depends on how profitable the business is and how much money you need for your personal use.

Having decided upon your trading entity you then need to notify HM Revenue and Customs (HMRC for short) about your business activities. If you fail to notify the tax authorities about your business you can be fined. If you are self-employed or a partner you will also be registered to pay monthly Class 2 National Insurance. In all cases you should consider whether you need to register for VAT compulsorily or whether you want to register voluntarily. If you have employees or you are a company director you will need to set up a Pay As You Earn (PAYE) scheme.

Two tax breaks to consider when you start up a new business are:

▶ 'Pre-trading' expenses incurred in the seven years before you start trading can be offset as a tax deductible expense in your first accounting period providing that you have retained the relevant receipts; and

▶ Capital assets such as equipment and cars owned before the business gets off the ground can be introduced into the business at their market value. You can then claim writing down allowances on them.

When you first start in business you need to make sure that you understand how much tax you will owe at the end of your first trading period so you can budget for it accordingly.

Running a business

Once your business is up and running you will be regularly involved with tax issues. If you are not registered for VAT and do not have any employees/directors you will mainly be concerned with your end-of-year tax bill. You should also keep a careful eye on your sales income to make sure that you know when to register for VAT as failing to register on time can be expensive. Once you are registered for VAT you must account for 'output' for VAT on your sales, reclaim 'input' VAT on your expenses and supply details of your taxable transactions to HMRC by completing regular VAT returns.

As soon as you take on employees or pay directors you must deduct income tax and Class 1 National Insurance from their salaries and wages via the PAYE system. You must also budget for employer's Class 1 National Insurance contributions as these are paid on top of an employee's gross salary. You must keep detailed PAYE records, pay the tax deductions over to HMRC once a month and complete various forms at the end of the tax year.

Other business transactions that have tax consequences include:

▶ buying or leasing equipment and cars;
▶ buying or renting property and working from home; and
▶ contributing to a pension.

Profits and losses

The amount of tax you owe at the end of the tax year or accounting period depends on whether your business makes a profit or a loss. To calculate your profit or loss for tax purposes you should:

- ▶ Maintain records of your income, outgoings and bank transactions. If you fail to keep your accounting records for a set period of time you can be fined.
- ▶ Choose a suitable accounting date. If you are self-employed or a partner this may be the same as the tax year end. If you anticipate that your profits will increase over time you may obtain a cash flow advantage by choosing a date that is not the same as the tax year end but over the life of your business you will pay the same amount of tax regardless of which accounting date you select.
- ▶ Draw up accounts based on your accounting records and adjust them so they comply with tax law. Some areas require particular attention. For example, commercial depreciation is ignored for tax purposes and capital allowances are claimed instead; entertaining expenses are not tax allowable; and whilst repairs are tax deductible improvements are not.

Sole traders and partners pay income tax and Class 4 National Insurance on their profits. Limited companies pay corporation tax. Profits are calculated before deducting proprietor's drawings (in the case of sole traders and partnerships) and dividends (in the case of limited companies).

If you make a trading loss you will not owe any tax. You may be able to obtain a tax refund by deducting the loss against any other income in the current year or you can carry the loss forward and off set it against your future profits so you pay less tax then. If you have only just started your business and you make a loss, you can carry the loss back against your income from earlier years in certain circumstances.

Self-assessment

The income tax and corporation tax system is known as 'self-assessment'. Once you have told HMRC that you are trading they will send you a tax return to complete at the end of the tax year (5 April) if you are self-employed or a partner. If you trade as a limited company you will receive a return at the end of your accounting period. It is your responsibility to complete the relevant pages of the return using your income and expenses records and file the form by the due date. Company tax returns must usually be submitted within 12 months. Paper returns for sole-traders and partners have to be filed by 31 October after the end of the tax year but the deadline for electronically filed forms is three months later on 31 January.

The tax return includes a self-assessment of your tax liability and this calculation becomes the basis of your tax payments. Sole traders and partners usually pay income tax and Class 4 National Insurance twice a year on 31 January and 31 July but in some circumstances payment is only required on 31 January. The due date for paying tax if you are a limited company is nine months and one day after the end date for your accounting period.

If you file your tax return late, submit an inaccurate return or pay your tax after the due date you will be liable to a financial penalty unless you have a reasonable excuse for non-compliance.

To deter abuse of the self-assessment system HMRC have to have comprehensive enquiry powers. These enable them to check your tax return if they believe it contains errors. Some returns are also investigated randomly. During an enquiry HMRC may review your business and personal records and inspect your business premises and assets. If they find errors they will discuss these with you in a meeting. Ultimately they will amend your self-assessment return although you can appeal against this if you disagree with their findings.

Incorporating your business

If you start off trading as a sole trader or partnership the question sometimes arises as to when or if you should incorporate your business and become a limited company. There are many commercial reasons for doing this including expansion of the business, the need for external investment or changes in the tax legislation which favour trading as a company. It is difficult to be certain whether you will save tax by incorporating your business as it depends on your profit trend and how much money you need to withdraw from the business for your own needs. Detailed calculations and professional advice are usually required.

The tax legislation recognizes that if you incorporate an unincorporated business the original entity simply continues in a different form. As a result you can transfer assets, losses, capital allowances and your VAT registration from the original business to the new company provided that you satisfy certain conditions.

You need to choose a suitable date to incorporate your business. This decision will mainly be based on commercial factors because from an income tax point of view there is no benefit to be obtained by selecting one date over another. Minimizing capital gains tax on the transfer of land, buildings and goodwill from your existing business to the limited company will be your main focus and the legislation provides various options depending on which assets you want to transfer and the amount of share capital you require in the new company.

Disposing of your business

The time may come for your business to be sold, closed or passed on to someone else. The tax consequence of each course of action depends on whether the business is unincorporated or a limited company. If you are selling all or a part of your trading business as a going concern the most important tax relief to consider is entrepreneurs' relief which reduces the amount of capital gains tax that you have to pay. Up to £5 million of gains are eligible for this relief and as the threshold lasts for a lifetime more than one business may qualify. As described in Chapter 13, selling a business is a complicated transaction and you will need advisers to help you to minimize your tax liabilities.

If you cannot sell your business but simply close it down there are also tax implications to consider. Shutting down a company is more complicated than closing an unincorporated business and the degree of formality required depends on whether the business is solvent. For unincorporated businesses the disposal of left-over stock and equipment has tax consequences especially if you sell items to yourself. If you make a loss in your final accounting period you may be entitled to tax relief. The tax treatment of income or expenses incurred after the business has stopped trading (called 'post-cessation' receipts or expenses) depends on specific rules. In all cases the business has to VAT de-register and the PAYE scheme has to be closed down.

If you decide to pass your business on to someone else there should not be any capital gains tax to pay because of gifts relief. There will also be no inheritance tax to pay if you are entitled to business or agricultural property relief. In order to maximize these reliefs you will require professional help.

Conclusion

If you are planning a new venture it is the decision as to whether you trade as a limited company or unincorporated business that has the most impact on your tax liabilities. If you are already running a small business you should be aware that most business decisions (such as the purchase of equipment, taking out a pension or selling up) have tax consequences and these need consideration if you are to minimize your tax bills.

Introduction

What is this book about?

You probably have a reason for buying this book. Are you about to start a new business or expand an existing enterprise? Perhaps you want to feel more confident when dealing with your advisers or the tax authorities? Does tax confuse you? If so read on. The Teach Yourself title *Understand Tax for Small Businesses* tells you how tax affects small businesses from the moment you conceive that brilliant idea, through the day-to-day routines until you eventually sell the business or close it down.

Who is this book aimed at?

This book is aimed at the smallest businesses. You are most likely to be a sole trader but you could be a partner or trade as a limited company. Often your business will just be you but you may have some help from your spouse, partner or another member of your family. As time goes by you may take on a few employees. It is a book about the average man or woman who just happens to be running a business rather than working in a job. You will not necessarily be a particularly high earner but simply trying to make enough profit to pay the bills and provide you and your family with a decent standard of living.

Using this book

Tax is a vast and complex subject but the layout of this book is designed so that you do not have to wade through irrelevant details to find the answer to your question. If you are short of time you can read the one-minute or five-minute summaries. The first four chapters are recommended reading for everyone as they introduce you to the various taxes and teach you how the tax system works, when forms have to be completed and what happens if you fail to comply. You will also learn how to calculate your taxable profit (or loss) and how to estimate your tax bill. Having mastered the basics you can then turn to the chapter relevant to the decision you are making. The book does not teach you how to fill in forms because HM Revenue and Customs produce comprehensive guidance to help you complete your returns, instead it tells you where to get the forms and the assistance you need via numerous Internet links.

The text of this book is up to date at [30 June 2010] but tax is a constantly changing subject so you should update your knowledge by periodically checking HM Revenue and Customs' website. Important numbers such as tax rates and allowances are largely confined to tables in Appendix 1. These include space for you to update them each year until 2012 with Internet links telling you where to obtain the most recent figures. There is a detailed glossary for those hard-to-understand terms as well as a calendar of important dates.

The law in Scotland and Northern Ireland differs from that in England and Wales. So if you are buying or selling property, or undertaking a legal transaction such as writing a will or securing a debt, you may find that some of the terminology differs.

This book may be suitable background reading for new students of tax, law, accountancy, business and finance but as it does not include any legislative references it cannot substitute for your student texts. I have also taken liberties with some of the jargon to make it more understandable for the tax novice.

_____

Being commercial about tax

For most people being in business is about making money. Paying tax on those profits and transactions is therefore part of business life. If you focus too much energy on saving tax rather than making profits you may take your eye off the ball and may miss a valuable commercial opportunity.

TAX IS JUST A PERCENTAGE

Would you like to pay £1 million in tax? I would! It would mean that I was making a profit of at least £2 million. This is a simple concept but one often over-looked. If you concentrate your efforts on making more money by getting that extra sale or increasing your fees, even after paying tax you will be richer. In the million pound scenario you earn £2 million, the tax authorities take 50% of it (£1 million) and you get to keep 50% of your profits (£1 million). For every extra £100 you earn, your income rises by at least £50.

SPENDING TO SAVE TAX

Please avoid the temptation to make unnecessary purchases just to save tax. Paying into a pension might be a good idea but you should be aware that to reduce or eliminate your tax liability will usually cost you more than the tax you owe and may strap your business for cash. Buying new equipment might be acceptable if you need it now and had planned to buy it, but many people make inappropriate purchasing decisions just to avoid paying tax to the government. In other words do not let the tax tail wag the commercial dog.

FAILING TO BUDGET FOR TAX

Failing to budget for tax is one of the principal reasons why businesses fail. No one likes paying tax, least of all once or twice a year in a large lump sum. If you forget to do anything about it, or like an ostrich put your head in the sand and hope it will all turn out for the best, your finances may get rocky. If however you start your business on the right footing, adopt good business practices and allocate funds to pay your tax regularly throughout the year, you should always be able to meet your tax liabilities when they are due even if it is irksome to part with the money.

If you were going to invest in a new business, you would probably want to know how risky the new venture would be. We all have different attitudes to how much risk we find acceptable in our lives and so it is with your tax affairs. Playing risk games with your tax will ultimately take up more time and effort than keeping your affairs low-key and up to date. If it gives you a buzz trying to find ways to reduce or avoid paying tax, good luck to you. You may have saved tax but you will probably have increased the risk that HM Revenue and Customs will enquire into your affairs and this in turn will have a significant cost in money and time. At the other extreme you may be someone who does not sleep unless they know that their affairs are in perfect order. If so, reduce your worry and find a good accountant. Having read this book you may also decide that doing your own tax is not for you. It all depends on whether you are someone who believes that using specialists will save you money in the long run, or whether you want to save their costs by dealing with the tax authorities yourself at the risk that you make a few mistakes along the way.

Keeping it legal

Having read this far into the book, you may be wondering why you need to bother with tax at all. Surely there must be a way round dealing with the tax authorities? Myths abound about how a friend of a friend has never had to fill in a tax return in spite of being self-employed for ten years. The simple answer to this scenario is that failing to deal with your tax affairs is illegal. It is not up to the tax authorities to send you a tax return. It is your responsibility to make sure that they know you exist so that they can send you a form to complete. Failing to pay your tax in this way is called tax evasion and you could face criminal prosecution when the tax authorities discover that you owe them tax. I say 'when' not 'if' because with increased cross-checking between different government departments, concerted 'spill-the beans' campaigns and international co-operation, it is very hard to evade tax for your whole life.

Tax evasion is a wide-ranging concept and includes understating your income or claiming a tax deduction for expenses to which you are not entitled. Tall tales frequently circulate about which expenses you can off-set for tax. If you are in doubt refer to this book, HM Revenue and Custom's guidance or seek professional advice otherwise you could find yourself with significant fines or even a criminal record.

Whilst evading tax is illegal, avoiding paying more tax than you need to is entirely legitimate. You are at liberty, within the constraints of the tax system, to organize your affairs however you wish. So if you want to pay pension contributions to reduce your tax, or claim loss relief in a certain way because it is more effective, the tax authorities do not mind. The tax legislation is however littered with provisions known as anti-avoidance measures which restrict your actions. So you cannot, for example, avoid tax by paying funds into an offshore bank account or undertaking a series of artificial transactions.

Advisers

This book is designed to help you understand more about business tax. It is no substitute for advice from an experienced accountant or tax practitioner who can take all the facts and circumstances of your business into account. If you are considering an expensive purchase or making a complex decision, you should always seek professional help.

Few businesses even small ones manage without professional advisers and most consider their costs to be a necessary expense of being in business and budget for them accordingly. Reading this book should help you to get the best out of your adviser because you will know when to ask for help and you will understand more of their advice. Importantly you will feel more in control of the relationship because you can ask for specific advice rather than paying an accountant to provide you with the background information that a book like this contains.

So how do you go about finding an accountant to help you with your business taxes? Personal recommendation is usually the best route, so I suggest asking friends and acquaintances who are also in business. Failing that, you could contact one of the professional bodies regulating accountants listed in Appendix 3. Anyone can call themselves an accountant but unless they are professionally qualified there is little recourse should things go wrong. Do not be afraid to interview several advisers when making your decision – most offer an initial free consultation so that they can assess your needs and you can find out what they can do for you. Reading this book will help you to ask them the right questions. Overall trust your instincts. You are hoping that this will be the start of a long and fruitful relationship, so personality and approachability are just as important as technical expertise.

1

Which taxes do businesses pay?

In this chapter:
- *checklist summarizing which taxes businesses have to pay*
- *your essential questions answered: who has to pay income tax, corporation tax, capital gains tax, inheritance tax and National Insurance? what is each tax charged on and at what rate? are there any exemptions or pitfalls? how is the tax paid?*
- *sample tax calculations*

Before moving on to more complicated subjects it is first of all necessary to understand the range of taxes that businesses have to pay so that you are aware of the full extent of your potential tax obligations. This chapter also introduces you to some simple tax calculations.

Taxes and duties checklist

There are two main types of taxes levied in the UK – direct taxes and indirect taxes. Direct taxes tax income, profits and gains. There are four direct taxes – income tax and inheritance tax paid by individuals, corporation tax paid by companies, and capital gains tax paid by both individuals and companies. There are also four types of National Insurance. All employers irrespective of whether they are sole traders, partners or companies pay Class 1 employer's contributions on the wages and salaries paid to their directors and employees. Indirect taxes are charged on expenditure and include VAT, Excise duties and Stamp duties.

In addition to the taxes listed above there are a number of taxes, levies and duties that apply to specific industries such as aggregate extraction, waste management, power generation, oil, shipping, air transport, haulage and insurance.

Direct and indirect taxes and National Insurance are administered by HM Revenue and Customs (see Chapter 2). You may also have to pay rates or council tax. These are administered by your local authority.

This chapter examines all the direct taxes and National Insurance. VAT is dealt with in Chapter 9. Rates and council tax are covered in Chapter 8.

The following checklist summarizes all the main UK taxes and indicates whether they apply to sole traders, partners or companies.

Tax	Sole traders	Partners	Companies
Direct taxes			
Income tax	YES	YES	NO
Corporation tax	NO	NO	YES
Capital gains tax	YES	YES	NO
Inheritance tax	YES	YES	NO
National Insurance			
Class 1 – employee's contributions	NO	NO	NO
Class 1 – employer's contributions	YES	YES	YES
Class 2	YES	YES	NO
Class 3	YES	YES	NO
Class 4	YES	YES	NO
Indirect taxes			
VAT	YES	YES	YES
Excise duties	YES	YES	YES
Stamp duties	YES	YES	YES

Tax	Sole traders	Partners	Companies
Local government			
Rates	YES	YES	YES
Council tax	YES	YES	NO

Income tax

WHO PAYS IT AND WHAT IS IT CHARGED ON?

Income tax is principally paid by individuals. It is charged on:

▶ *The trading profits of sole traders and partners (see Chapter 4);*
▶ *Employment earnings including salaries, wages, perks, tips, commission, holiday pay, sick pay and maternity, paternity and adoption pay (see Chapter 7);*
▶ *Pensions including the state pension;*
▶ *Some state benefits such as jobseeker's allowance, income support and employment and support allowance;*
▶ *Income from property (rental income, ground rents, insurances and lease premiums);*
▶ *Income from savings and investments (bank and building society interest and share dividends);*
▶ *Miscellaneous income from settlements, estates, trusts and casual and one-off receipts.*

Most sources of income are taxed but there are some that are exempt from income tax including:

▶ *Statutory redundancy and some payments for loss of your job (see Chapter 12);*
▶ *Pension lump sums on retirement (see Chapter 10);*
▶ *Some state benefits and sickness policies;*
▶ *Individual savings accounts (ISAs) and Child Trust Funds;*
▶ *National Savings certificates and premium bonds;*
▶ *Tax credits.*

The majority of people living in the UK are liable to pay tax on all their income including their business profits regardless of whether the money is earned here or overseas. If you live abroad (are non-resident) you still have to pay UK tax on your UK income. If you have been living overseas for some years (are not ordinarily resident in the UK), or come from overseas (are non-domiciled) different rules may apply and you will need to seek professional advice to ensure that you complete your tax return correctly.

PAYMENT

Income tax is paid in the following ways:

▶ *Under self-assessment for sole traders, partners, those with property income or more complicated affairs (see Chapter 2);*
▶ *Through the PAYE system for employees, directors, pensioners and the recipients of some state benefits (see Chapter 7);*
▶ *By deduction at source from bank and building society interest.*

CALCULATION

Calculating income tax can be complicated depending on the number of different sources of income that you have. Persevering with the numbers is however worthwhile because it may help you to successfully manage your income tax liabilities (see Chapters 3 and 4).

Before you start your income tax calculation you need to add together all your sources of income to arrive at your total income for the tax year. You should refer to Appendix 1 for the tax rates and personal allowances for the appropriate tax year. To calculate the tax on your business profits you must then work through the following steps:

1 *A personal allowance is deducted from your income before you calculate your tax bill. It increases slightly each tax year and is £6,475 in 2009/10 and 2010/11. Some older people receive a higher allowance. If your income exceeds £100,000 in 2010/11 your personal allowance is restricted. If it is more* *than £112,950 you will not be entitled to a personal allowance at all.*

2 *After you have deducted the personal allowance, the first part of your income is taxed at 20%. This is known as the basic rate of income tax. The amount of income charged to basic rate tax changes slightly each year and is £37,400 in 2009/10 and 2010/11.*

3 *Any further income you receive is taxed at 40% – the higher rate. If your taxable income reaches £150,000 in 2010/11 you are taxed at the additional rate which is 50%.*

EXAMPLE

Ben is a self-employed electrician. His annual profits are £46,500. He calculates his income tax liability as follows:

Tax year 2010/11	Step	£
Profits		46,500
Personal allowance	1	–6,475
Income subject to income tax		**40,025**
Tax due		
£37,400 at the 20% basic rate	2	7,480.00
£2,625* at the 40% higher rate	3	1,050.00
Total income tax owing		**8,530.00**

* Total taxable income £40,025 minus £37,400 which is the part taxable at the basic rate of tax.

Ben will also owe Class 4 National Insurance (see National Insurance).

Insight

If you run a small unincorporated business you might want to consider ways to keep your profits below the higher or additional income tax thresholds. Options include investing in new equipment (see Chapter 6) and paying into a pension (see Chapter 10).

SAVINGS AND INVESTMENT INCOME

When calculating your income tax liability it is helpful to
understand that dividends and interest are taxed differently from
trading profits, salaries and other sources of income.

UK dividends are paid with a 10% tax credit. If your total income
does not exceed the 20% basic rate limit you owe no further income
tax on your dividends even though the dividend tax credit is less than
the basic rate of income tax. If your total income including dividends
means that you have to pay higher rate tax, instead of paying 40%
tax on the dividend you pay tax equivalent to 25% of the dividend
you receive. For example, a £100 dividend will add £25 to your tax
bill if you are a higher rate taxpayer. If your annual income is more
than £150,000 a £100 dividend will add £36 to your tax bill.

Interest is usually paid with 20% income tax deducted at source. If
your employment income or self-employed profits are less than the
starting rate for savings limit (£2,440 for 2009/10 and 2010/11), the
first £2,440 of your interest is taxed at 10% and you will be owed
a tax refund. If your employment income or self-employed profits
exceed the starting rate for savings limit you pay tax at the basic rate
and you owe no further tax on your interest. If your total income
including the interest results in you having to pay higher or additional
rate tax, you can deduct the 20% tax that you have already paid on
your interest from the tax you owe.

Corporation tax

WHO PAYS IT AND WHAT IS IT CHARGED ON?

Corporation tax is paid by companies on their profits and gains
for an accounting period. Profits include all of a company's sources
of income including investment and property income. Company
profits are calculated in broadly the same way as those for sole
traders and partners (see Chapter 4) but with some important

differences in the way that financial transactions (interest paid and received and profits and losses on loans) are treated. Companies, but not sole traders or partners, can claim a tax deduction for expenditure on goodwill and intangible assets, and depending on their trade they may be entitled to tax credits for research and development and to clean up contaminated land.

Corporation tax is charged on the profits of all UK resident companies and non-resident companies that trade in the UK through a branch or agency.

If your company is a member of a group of companies it is taxed on its own profits in the usual way but groups are treated differently from companies in some respects including the treatment of their losses. If you have a group of companies you will require an accountant.

DIVIDENDS

If your company pays a dividend there is no tax to pay on it but the dividend is not a tax-deductible expense in calculating your corporation tax bill. Dividends are paid with a 10% tax credit and as you learned in the section on income tax, unless the recipient is a higher or additional rate taxpayer there is no further income tax to pay on the dividend. Dividends are also not liable to National Insurance which can make them useful in tax planning. Dividends which the company receives are not liable to corporation tax but they are taken into account when claiming marginal relief (see Calculation).

Insight

If you run a family company you should consider the National Insurance savings of paying a dividend rather than a salary – but watch out for the many pitfalls (see Chapters 3 and 10).

PAYMENT

Corporation tax is paid under self-assessment (see Chapter 2).

CALCULATION

Calculating your corporation tax liability is straightforward once you have worked out your taxable profits because there are only two tax rates; one for companies making small profits and one for others (see Appendix 1). The only complication occurs if the company's profits exceed the marginal relief limit (£300,000) but are less than the upper limit of the marginal relief band (£1.5 million). In this situation the profits are taxed at the full corporation tax rate reduced by marginal relief. This is calculated according to a set formula which is:

1 *The standard fraction (see Appendix 1) multiplied by:*
2 *The upper limit of the marginal relief band (see Appendix 1) less profits (which at this stage must include dividends received by the company plus their tax credits) multiplied by:*
3 *The company's profits charged to corporation tax divided by the profits as calculated in stage 2. If the company has not received any dividends you can ignore this stage.*

Instead of following this complicated formula you can also use HMRC's marginal relief calculator on www.hmrc.gov.uk/calcs/mrr.htm.

You must remember to claim marginal relief in the company's tax return.

EXAMPLE

Ali Enterprises Ltd made a corporation tax profit in the 2010 financial year of £390,000. The company received no dividends. The company's corporation tax liability is calculated as follows:

▶ *£390,000 × 28% = £109,200. This is reduced by marginal relief.*
▶ *Marginal relief is calculated as follows:*
   7/400 × (£1,500,000 – £390,000) = £19,425.
▶ *The company therefore owes corporation tax of:*
   £89,775 (£109,200 – £19,425) – a corporation tax rate of 23%.

Marginal relief is reduced if the company's accounting period is less than 12 months or if it has any associated companies. It cannot be claimed by close investment-holding companies. You will probably need an accountant to help you work out whether you have any associated companies.

Capital gains tax

WHO PAYS IT AND WHAT IS IT CHARGED ON?

Capital gains tax is paid by individuals (sole traders and partners) and by companies who pay it as part of their corporation tax bill. Essentially it is charged on the profit you make from selling a capital asset; the profit or gain being the difference between the price you acquire the asset for and the price you sell it for.

Capital gains tax is charged on a wide variety of assets such as:

▶ *Property used in your business including your home if you use part of it exclusively for work (see Chapter 8) and property rented to tenants;*
▶ *Shares in private companies and traded on the stock market;*
▶ *Some compensation for the loss of assets; and*
▶ *Goodwill and intellectual property.*

Not all assets are liable to capital gains tax. Those which are exempt from the tax include:

▶ *Your home but not any part used exclusively for work;*
▶ *Transactions between spouses and civil partners;*
▶ *Cars and other machinery and assets with a useful life of less than 50 years (but not where capital allowances have been claimed (see Chapter 6);*
▶ *A disposal by one trading company of a substantial shareholding (10% plus) in another;*
▶ *Personal items (chattels) sold for less than £6,000;*
▶ *Gambling winnings and prizes;*

- ▶ *Most life insurance proceeds;*
- ▶ *Assets passing on death (see Inheritance tax).*

Most people are liable for capital gains tax on all their assets regardless of whether they are situated in the UK or overseas. If you live abroad for five or more whole tax years most disposals of assets while you are overseas are not liable to capital gains tax but you have to pay capital gains tax on assets used in a UK business. If you come from abroad (are non-domiciled) you are only liable for capital gains tax on your overseas assets in some circumstances.

PAYMENT

For individuals, capital gains tax is paid through the self-assessment system on the 31 January falling after the tax-year in which you make the gain (see Chapter 2). For companies it is paid as part of the corporation tax bill.

CALCULATION

Calculating your capital gains tax can be complicated because there are a number of deductions or reliefs that you may be able to claim to reduce your liability. Your entitlement to these reliefs depends on whether you operate as sole trader or partner, or as a limited company.

Annual exemption: individuals (sole traders and partners) but not companies are entitled to an annual exemption. It serves a similar function to the personal allowance in income tax. If your gains are less than the annual exemption you do not have to pay capital gains tax (see Appendix 1).

Entrepreneurs' relief: individuals (sole traders and partners) but not companies may be eligible to claim entrepreneurs' relief on the first £5 million of gains when they dispose of a trading business or shares in a trading company. The £5 million limit is a lifetime threshold and you may claim against it on more than one occasion. For example if you sell one business for £2 million and a few years later sell another for £400,000 both gains are eligible for relief. Being entitled to entrepreneurs' relief means that you pay capital gains tax at 10% rather than 18% or 28% (see Appendix 1).

Indexation allowance can be claimed by companies. It is calculated by applying the increase in the retail prices index for the period of ownership of the asset (starting from March 1982) to the cost of acquiring it.

Rollover relief can be claimed by any business which replaces certain business assets one year before they are sold and up to three years afterwards. Rollover relief can be claimed on a number of assets including land, buildings and goodwill (see Chapter 8). The new asset does not need to be the same type as the asset being disposed of. If you are considering investing in a replacement asset professional help is advisable.

The basic capital gains tax calculation is outlined below. You will need to prepare a calculation for each capital asset you sell or dispose of in the tax year. If you make a loss on an asset you can deduct it from your gains. The steps in a capital gains tax calculation are as follows:

1 *Work out your sales price deducting any selling costs such as agents' fees.*
2 *Calculate the cost of buying and improving the asset. Add on any purchase costs to this number such as stamp duties, legal costs and agents' charges. If you owned the asset on 31 March 1982 you must use the market value of the asset on 31 March 1982 in the calculation and not its original cost.*
3 *Deduct the purchase costs or the 31 March 1982 value from the disposal proceeds. If you have made a loss there are no further reliefs to claim. Refer to Chapter 5 to make sure you use your losses effectively.*
4 *If you are a sole trader or partner claim the annual exemption (see Appendix 1) against any remaining gain.*
5 *The gain left after claiming all available deductions and reliefs is taxed at the appropriate capital gains tax rate: 10% if you*

are entitled to entrepreneurs' relief, or 18% or 28% depending on the amount of your income and gains (see Appendix 1).

6 *If you are replacing the asset and owe capital gains tax on its disposal, consider claiming rollover relief.*

EXAMPLE

In July 2010 Simon who pays income tax at the 40% higher rate sells a freehold shop which he bought in May 2000. Simon is not entitled to entrepreneurs' relief because he is selling the shop in isolation not as a disposal of part of his business as a going concern. He is not replacing the shop with another business asset so rollover relief does not apply. Simon calculates his capital gains tax liability as follows:

Tax year 2010/11	Step	£
Freehold shop sold July 2010 (after deducting selling costs)	1	150,000
Freehold shop purchased May 2000 (including acquisition costs)	2	−100,000
Gain	3	50,000
Annual exemption	4	−10,100
Taxable gain		39,900
Capital gains tax at 28%	5	**11,172**

In an alternative scenario, Simon disposes of part of his business as a going concern and sells the freehold premises as a result. In this case he is eligible for entrepreneurs' relief. He calculates his gain as follows:

Tax year 2010/11	Step	£
Sale of part of business as a going concern	1	150,000
Acquisition costs	2	−100,000

Tax year 2010/11	Step	£
Gain	3	50,000
Annual exemption	4	−10,100
Taxable gain		39,900
Capital gains tax at 10%	5	**3,990**

Insight

If you are disposing of the whole or a part of your business, check out your entitlement to entrepreneurs' relief and rollover relief. It will usually pay you to take professional advice.

Inheritance tax

WHO PAYS IT AND WHAT IS IT CHARGED ON?

Inheritance tax is charged on the value of your capital assets when you die and is paid by the executors of the estate. It is also charged on some transactions occurring during your life, for example gifts made within seven years of your death and transfers of assets into a trust. Inheritance tax is not paid by companies.

Inheritance tax is charged on all your assets apart from those listed below. There is no exemption for your home as there is with capital gains tax. Exempt assets include:

▶ *Amounts left to a spouse or civil partner unless they come from abroad (are domiciled overseas) when a limit of £55,000 applies;*
▶ *Certain business and agricultural assets (see Chapter 14);*
▶ *Amounts bequeathed to charities, heritage bodies and political parties.*
▶ *Decorations for valour and compensation paid to Second World War victims.*

No inheritance tax is due on the first part of your estate assets. This is known as the 'nil rate band' (see Appendix 1). If the total value of your assets when you die (your estate) is less than this amount you do not have to pay inheritance tax. Your nil rate band increases if you 'inherit' the unused portion of the nil rate band of your deceased spouse or civil partner.

Only a few people have to pay inheritance tax because their assets exceed the nil rate band but successful business people are likely to be amongst those who do. If you are liable to inheritance tax it is charged on all your assets irrespective of whether they are located in the UK or overseas. If you come from overseas (are non-domiciled), you are liable for inheritance tax on your UK assets. Deciding your domicile for inheritance tax is complicated and you will require professional advice.

CALCULATION

It may be useful to understand the basic inheritance calculation so that you can regularly appraise whether you have an inheritance tax liability. If you have a business you will need to make arrangements about what happens to it when you die and you may want to plan your affairs to minimize your inheritance tax liability (see Chapter 14).

The following steps demonstrate how to perform a basic inheritance tax calculation:

1 *Work out the value of the estate assets. Detailed valuations are often required for real estate, shares, businesses and personal items. Liabilities such as loans can be deducted.*
2 *Deduct the funeral costs;*
3 *Deduct the value of any bequests to spouses and civil partners, business and agricultural property qualifying for relief (see Chapter 14) and exempt gifts such as legacies to charities;*
4 *If the value of the estate is below the relevant threshold (see Appendix 1) there is no inheritance tax to pay. The relevant threshold is increased if you are a surviving spouse or civil partner who has inherited the unused nil rate band from your deceased spouse or civil partner.*

5 *If the value of the estate is more than the nil rate band, inheritance tax is calculated at 40% on the excess over that threshold.*

EXAMPLE

Paul, a wholesaler of cleaning products, dies unexpectedly in January 2011. His business is valued at £200,000 and qualifies for business property relief. He leaves the business to his brother. He owns the family home jointly with his wife. The house and his personal effects are worth £400,000 and he has shares and investments worth £30,000. In his will he leaves the house, personal items and investments to his wife. Paul also owns a flat in Ibiza valued at £100,000 which he leaves to his daughter.

There is no inheritance tax liability. The business assets qualify for business property relief and the bequests to his wife are covered by the spouse exemption. This leaves the flat in Ibiza valued at £100,000. As this is below the nil rate threshold (see Appendix 1), no inheritance tax liability arises. The unused part of his nil rate band is £225,000 (£325,000–£100,000). 69% of his nil rate band is therefore unused. His wife's executors will be able to increase her nil rate band by this percentage when she dies. For example, if the nil rate band on her death is £400,000, it will increase to £676,000 (£400,000 × 1.69).

If Paul had been a single man who had left his entire estate jointly to his daughter and brother, the inheritance tax calculation would be as follows assuming his funeral costs were £5,000:

	Step	£
House		400,000
Investments		30,000
Flat in Ibiza (Note 1)		100,000
Business		200,000
Total value of estate	1	**730,000**

(Contd)

	Step	£
Funeral	2	–5,000
Business property relief (Note 2)	3	–200,000
Estate after business property relief		525,000
Exempt threshold	4	–325,000
Taxable estate		200,000
Inheritance tax at 40%	5	**80,000**

Note 1: The flat in Ibiza is subject to inheritance tax even though it is located abroad because Paul is domiciled in the UK. There may also be taxes to pay in Spain. If so some of these may be deducted from Paul's UK inheritance tax liability but his executors will require professional advice.

Note 2: Business property relief and agricultural property relief are considered in more detail in Chapter 14. Deciding whether assets are business assets or agricultural assets is not always clear-cut and you will need professional advice.

GIFTS

You can reduce your inheritance tax bill by giving away your money while you are alive. The following gifts are exempt from inheritance tax:

▶ *£3,000 per tax year to any person or combination of people, plus a further £3,000 in the first year that you make a gift;*
▶ *Up to £250 per tax year to any number of people;*
▶ *Regular gifts out of income (not capital), for example £50 per month to your daughter;*
▶ *Amounts paid to support your family, for example maintenance settlements if you are divorced or separated;*
▶ *Gifts made upon the marriage or civil partnership of any person up to the following amounts: £5,000 from a parent, £2,500 from a grandparent or other relative and either party of the marriage or civil partnership to the other, and £1,000 from anyone else.*

You can also give away larger sums of money and provided that you survive for more than seven years after making the gift no inheritance tax is due. If you die within the seven-year period the gift may become liable to inheritance tax. These gifts are known as 'potentially exempt transfers' because they may be exempt or they may not – it all depends on when you die, the nil rate band at that time and the amount of any other potentially exempt transfers you have made in the previous seven years. If you die between three and seven years after making the gift any inheritance tax due on the gift is reduced.

You may now be thinking that it would be a good idea to give away your assets over and above the nil rate band or combined nil rate band if you are married or in a civil partnership, to your children (or other relatives) whilst you are alive and provided that you live for seven years all your inheritance tax problems will be solved. You may also be thinking that if you need the money back again or you need to use the assets you have given away at sometime in the future that this would be no problem because 'it is all within the family'.

Insight

The tax authorities prevent you avoiding inheritance tax by giving away money subject to the condition that it is returned to you if you need it by the 'gifts with reservation of benefit' rules. In some cases such gifts are liable to income tax under the 'pre-owned assets' legislation.

National Insurance

WHO PAYS IT?

National Insurance is paid by people who are self-employed and partners, employees, employers and those who are none of these but who wish to voluntarily protect their entitlement to the state retirement pension. Young people aged under 16 do not have to pay contributions even if they work and those in full-time education between the ages of 16 and 18 are credited with contributions for that period. If you are over state retirement age, no contributions are required. If you do not work because you are looking after children or severely disabled relatives for 20 or more hours per week you are entitled to a weekly credit. Special rules may apply if you come to the UK to work or you go abroad.

National Insurance is divided into four classes. The rates at which contributions are due are set out in Appendix 1.

▶ *Class 1 National Insurance is paid by employees (including directors) and employers. It is based on a percentage of the employee's salary, bonuses and some perks but it is not charged on dividends. Contributions entitle you to claim jobseeker's allowance, incapacity benefit, employment and support allowance, state pension and state second pension (see Chapter 10). Class 1A National Insurance is paid by employers on staff perks such as company cars whilst Class 1B National Insurance, also paid by employers, is charged on amounts paid under a PAYE settlement agreement (see Chapter 7).*

▶ *Class 2 contributions are paid at a flat weekly rate by those who are self-employed and in a partnership. This includes spouses and civil partners who are also business partners. The payments protect entitlement to the state pension, incapacity benefit, employment and support allowance and maternity allowance. For details about registering to pay Class 2 contributions see Chapter 3.*

▶ *Class 3 National Insurance is a voluntary weekly sum paid by those who have not earned sufficient income to make the year qualify for National Insurance purposes. Paying Class 3 contributions protects your entitlement to the state pension and other benefits in some circumstances. If you are considering paying voluntary contributions you should take advice as in some cases the payments may not increase your pension or benefit entitlement.*

▶ *Class 4 contributions are paid by self-employed people and partners based on a percentage of their profits. They give no entitlement to benefits or pensions.*

Insight

If you employ staff, do not forget that you have to pay employer's Class 1 National Insurance contributions on top of each employee's gross salary. You also have to pay Class 1A contributions on any perks you provide. Employer's National Insurance can make your employment costs higher than expected.

PAYMENT

▶ *Class 1 National Insurance is collected through the PAYE system (see Chapter 7).*
▶ *Class 2 and 3 contributions are paid by monthly direct debit or quarterly payment to the National Insurance Contributions Office (NICO), part of HM Revenue and Customs.*
▶ *Class 4 National Insurance is collected through the self-assessment tax return as part of a sole trader or partner's tax bill (see Chapter 2).*

EXEMPTIONS

If you are self-employed or a partner you can claim 'small earnings exception' which exempts you from paying Class 2 contributions if you expect your trading profits to fall below a certain threshold (see Appendix 1). To apply for exception you should complete form CF10, see www.hmrc.gov.uk/forms/cf10.pdf.

If you pay Class 2 contributions when you could have been exempt you can claim a refund. Given that Class 2 contributions are only a small weekly sum most people pay them irrespective of their earnings to protect their state pension and benefit entitlement.

MULTIPLE JOBS OR SELF-EMPLOYMENTS

If you are both employed and self-employed in the same tax year, you may pay Class 1 contributions on your employed income and Class 2 and Class 4 contributions on your self-employed earnings. Depending on how much you earn it may not be necessary for you to pay all this National Insurance as there is an annual maximum limit on the total contributions that you need to make. To prevent overpayment you can apply for some of the contributions to be 'deferred' by completing form CA 72 B, see www.hmrc.gov.uk/forms/ca72b.pdf. If you have two employments or directorships you may also need to notify NICO so that you do not overpay National Insurance contributions. If you have not applied for a deferment you may be able to claim a refund if you overpay contributions.

Irrespective of the number of self-employments you have you only need to pay one lot of Class 2 contributions. Different rules apply to Class 4 National Insurance. Here the profits from all your self-employed businesses must be added together to calculate your liability.

CALCULATION

Each type of National Insurance is calculated differently:

▶ *Class 1 National Insurance is based on the employee's or director's earnings above the 'primary threshold' multiplied by the appropriate percentage. Once earnings reach the 'upper earnings limit' a reduced rate applies.*
▶ *Class 2 and 3 contributions are calculated as weekly sums set at a fixed rate for the tax year.*
▶ *Class 4 contributions are calculated at a given rate on the sole trader's or partner's profits falling between the 'lower' and 'upper' limits. Where profits exceed the 'upper' limit, contributions are charged at a reduced rate.*

The following example illustrates how Class 1, 2 and 4 contributions are calculated.

EXAMPLE

Jane is a self-employed physiotherapist who makes a profit in 2010/11 of £45,500. She pays Class 2 National Insurance of £2.40 per week (£124.80 a year) by monthly direct debit to NICO.

Jane also pays Class 4 contributions through her self-assessment return as follows:

▶ 8% of profits between £5,715 and £43,875 a year = £38,160 × 8% = £3,052.80.
▶ 1% of profits above £43,875 a year (£45,500 – £43,875 = £1,625 × 1%) = £16.25.

Her total Class 4 contributions are £3,069.05 (£3,052.80 + £16.25).

If Jane employs Harriet as a part-time receptionist paying her £150 a week, Harriet pays Class 1 employee's National Insurance contributions on the part of her salary above the weekly threshold of £110 per week. This comes to £4.40 per week (£150 – £110 × 11%). Jane deducts this sum from Harriet's wages. Jane pays Class 1 employer's contributions of £5.12 per week (£150 – £110 × 12.8%) on Harriet's salary. Jane pays both types of National Insurance contribution to HM Revenue and Customs (see Chapter 7).

Insight

If you trade as an unincorporated business, consider the National Insurance consequences of a spouse or civil partner working with you being alternatively an employee or your business partner (see Chapter 3).

10 THINGS TO REMEMBER

1 *If you run a small business as a sole trader or partner you are liable to pay income tax on your business profits plus Class 2 and Class 4 National Insurance.*

2 *You are entitled to a personal allowance unless your annual income exceeds £100,000. This means that you can earn or receive a certain amount of money before you pay tax.*

3 *If you run an unincorporated business your profits may be liable to income tax at the basic rate (20%), the higher rate (40%) or the additional rate (50%) depending on how much you make.*

4 *The higher rate of income tax applies to income over £37,400 (2009/10 and 2010/11) and the additional rate applies to income over £150,000 (2010/11).*

5 *The tax rates that apply to savings income such as dividends and bank interest differ from those used to tax your business profits or director's salary.*

6 *Tax rates, personal allowances and thresholds change each year so you will need to update the numbers in this chapter each April. See Appendix 1 for details of how to do this.*

7 *If your company profits exceed £300,000 but are less than £1.5 million you can claim marginal relief in your corporation tax return.*

8 *You may be able to claim entrepreneurs' relief against a capital gain of up to £5 million on the disposal of your business.*

9 *If you have a business you will need to make arrangements about what happens to it when you die. You will also want to plan your affairs to minimize any inheritance tax liability.*

10 *If you are self-employed or a partner and also an employee or company director you may be entitled to 'defer' payment of some National Insurance contributions. If no deferment has been made, you should check whether you are due a refund of contributions.*

2

How the tax system works

In this chapter:
- *tax returns*
- *paying tax*
- *record keeping*
- *important dates*
- *enquiries*

In the last chapter we looked at which taxes businesses pay. This chapter considers the administration of the tax system – how taxes are introduced and changed, what you must do to comply with your tax obligations and what happens if you fail to do so. A number of important dates are introduced and a full diary of these is included in Appendix 2.

Raising taxes

Raising taxes is a fundamental part of government economic policy and the extent to which tax affects small business changes according to the political agenda. For example, if the government wants to encourage new small businesses in order to create employment or generate economic growth, it will offer enterprise incentives such as reduced tax rates and increased allowances for investment in equipment.

Taxes can be levied by Parliament and local authorities. Each year the Chancellor of the Exchequer decides how much money to raise from taxing individuals and companies and how that money is to be spent. Rather like running a small business the Chancellor has to balance the books, so if less tax is collected, the amount that can be spent on health, education and welfare is accordingly reduced unless money is borrowed to cover the shortfall.

The Budget

The Chancellor sets out how much money will be raised from taxation and how it will be spent in an annual Budget. This is usually held in the spring but an interim report on the nation's finances is delivered each autumn (this is called the Pre-Budget Statement).

Insight

The Budget coverage in the media focuses on the price of alcohol and the cost of car tax. These aspects are only a small part of what the Budget is about. Major changes to all the taxes take place following the Budget in an annual Finance Act.

HM Revenue and Customs

HM Revenue and Customs (HMRC for short) are responsible for all the taxes set out in Chapter 1 except rates and council tax. HMRC also handle many other functions including administration of Child and Working Tax Credits, the national minimum wage, statutory sick pay, maternity pay, paternity and adoption pay, Child Trust funds and student loans.

If you have reason to complain to HMRC you should refer to their leaflet C/FS 'Complaints and putting things right' (see www.hmrc.gov.uk/factsheets/complaints-factsheet.pdf).

Self-assessment

Individuals are responsible for self-assessing their liability to income tax, Class 4 National Insurance, some student loan repayments and capital gains tax. Companies have to self-assess their corporation tax.

Self-assessment places the responsibility on you as an individual or company to correctly calculate how much tax you owe and report this to HM Revenue and Customs by completing an annual tax return. HMRC will neither agree nor disagree with your self-assessment unless they enquire into your return which they can do for a certain length of time after the form has been submitted (see Enquiries).

Self-assessment also requires you to pay your taxes on time. Although HMRC usually send you a reminder near the due date for payment, if they fail to do so it is still up to you to pay any tax owing at the right time otherwise you will be charged interest and may face a penalty (see Paying your tax).

Tax returns

You self-assess your tax liabilities by completing an annual tax return.

INDIVIDUALS

Individuals are sent a tax return around the end of the tax year (5 April). It must be completed with details of your income, gains and claims to allowances for the tax year concerned. It must be returned to HMRC by 31 October if you want to file a paper return by post. In this case HMRC will work out your tax bill for you. If you file your tax return electronically, you have a further three months until the 31 January which follows the end of the tax year to do so, but if you want HMRC to collect a tax underpayment of less than £2,000 through your tax code your return must be filed no later than 30 December. If you file your return electronically, the software automatically calculates your tax liability. Any return filed after the appropriate deadline is liable to a penalty.

In the unusual situation that you are not sent a tax return or a notice to complete one until after 31 October, the filing date is three months from the date that the notice or form is issued. You can file your return electronically via HMRC's website by following the links from 'Do It Online'.

If you have not been sent a tax return and think that you need to complete one, you must tell HMRC by the 5 October following the end of the relevant tax year to avoid a penalty. If you are self-employed you should be sent a return or a notice to complete a return unless you have forgotten to tell HMRC about your business or moved address and not informed them. Make sure that you notify the tax authorities within three months of starting your business otherwise you will be fined (see Chapter 3).

COMPANIES

If you trade as a limited company, the period covered by your tax return is not the tax year but your accounting period and this varies from company to company. The return must usually be filed within 12 months of the end of the company's accounting period. Different dates apply if the accounting period is longer than 12 months. If it is late the company will be charged a penalty. From 1 April 2011 all company returns have to be filed electronically (follow the links from 'Do It Online' on www.hmrc.gov.uk).

EMPLOYERS

If you have employees or trade as a limited company, you must complete and submit an employer's end-of-year return (forms P35 and P14) before 19 May. The submission date is 6 July for forms P11D and P9D. Almost all employers now file their end-of-year returns electronically.

Tax year

The tax year runs from 6 April in one year to 5 April in the next. The tax year 2010/11 means that it starts on 6 April 2010 and ends on 5 April 2011. These unusual dates are the result of an historical anachronism. Personal and employer tax returns are completed for a tax year and should include all the transactions falling between 6 April and 5 April. Company returns are completed for an accounting period not a tax year.

If you are self-employed your accounting year does not have to coincide with the tax year and you can select any date you like. Many people choose to prepare their accounts to the end of the tax year because it is simpler. You can also prepare accounts to 31 March and this is treated in the same way as if you had prepared the figures to 5 April.

Records

When you run a small business you must keep accounting records detailing all your transactions. If you are unsure how to maintain suitable records, you could refer to the Teach Yourself title *Small Business Accounting*, seek advice from an accountant or attend a bookkeeping course run by your local Business Link, see www.businesslink.gov.uk.

There are no hard and fast rules about how you should keep your accounting records because every business is different but it is a good idea to keep your business and personal records separate and to open a business bank account. The records can be hand written or computerized. You may use an accounting software package or you can record your transactions on a spreadsheet.

Your accounting records should as a minimum achieve the following:

▶ **Record your income.** *This might include a list of daily totals from your till or a running total of invoices sent to customers. You must retain your till rolls, copies of your invoices, appointment books and work diaries.*
▶ **Record sums paid into your business bank account.** *You must identify the source of all sums banked into your business bank account. You should also keep records of amounts paid into any private bank account (for example share dividends, transfers from other accounts, personal drawings or gifts). You must retain your bank statements and supporting papers such as paying-in books.*
▶ **Record all your business expenses and sums paid out of your business account.** *You need to keep records of who you have paid for business purchases and services, when and how much you paid them and the means of payment (bank transfer, cheque, cash or credit card). You must keep receipts for all business expenses unless they are for very small amounts as well as cheque books and credit card statements. You will need to find a satisfactory way of filing your receipts particularly if you have large numbers of them so that they do not get mislaid.*

In addition, to maintaining these records, at your accounting year end you will need to work out and keep records of:

▶ *The people who owe you money (debtors);*
▶ *Those who your business owes money to (creditors);*
▶ *The value of your stock, any work in hand and uncompleted contracts;*
▶ *Cash on hand including your till float and any petty cash;*

- *The equipment and assets used in your business (see Chapter 6); and*
- *Private motoring adjustments (see Chapter 4) and sums included for your home costs if you work from home (see Chapter 8).*

To complete your personal tax return, you will also need to keep records of your non-business financial transactions such as:

- *Employments, pensions received and state benefits;*
- *Rental income;*
- *Income from savings and investments;*
- *Pensions contributions paid;*
- *Gift aid payments to charity;*
- *Capital gains, for example from the sale of shares.*

Insight

Irrespective of how you maintain your accounting records, you must make sure that you do not lose them. If you keep them on a computer you should take regular printouts and back up the system. If you keep a manual book you should periodically photocopy the pages.

HOW LONG DO I NEED TO KEEP MY RECORDS FOR?

If you are self-employed you need to keep your accounting and tax records for five years ten months from the end of the tax year. This means that for the tax year which ended on 5 April 2010, you must keep the records until at least 31 January 2016 (longer if HMRC enquires into your return). If you are trading as a limited company you must maintain your accounting records for six years from the end of your accounting period (again, longer if HMRC enquires into your return). If you fail to keep records HMRC can fine you.

Although you need to keep records to support the entries in your tax return, you do not need to send them to HMRC when you submit your tax form. The only time they will want to see them is if they start a formal enquiry (see Enquiries).

Completing your tax return

This book does not explain in detail how to complete your tax return as HMRC publishes comprehensive guidance and helpsheets for individuals which can be accessed on www.hmrc.gov.uk/sa/forms/content.htm. For information about company returns refer to www.hmrc.gov.uk/ctsa/index.htm.

INDIVIDUALS

There are two versions of the paper tax return, a short tax return (SA 200) and the full version (SA 100). If HMRC has sent you the short form you should check the guidance notes to ensure that you are eligible to complete it. You must complete the full return if you are:

▶ *a company director;*
▶ *a partner;*
▶ *self-employed with sales of more than £30,000, multiple businesses, loss claims or if you want to change your accounting date.*

The full version of the return requires you to complete supplementary pages for each employment or directorship, self-employment and partnership. You do not usually need to submit accounts with the return but if your business is complex or the accounts show details not reflected on the return, you might want to send them to HMRC to ensure that you have made full disclosure. If you submit them you should highlight the reason why you are doing so. Alternatively you could use the additional information boxes on the return to provide any information which you think will help HMRC to understand the entries better. For example you might want to supply details about the private use of your car or business use of your home. Irrespective of whether you submit your accounts, you must make sure that the tax return form is fully and correctly completed.

Insight

The short tax return does not include additional information boxes to explain accounting adjustments such as the private use of your car. If HMRC need this information to appreciate that your self-assessment could be too low they could raise a 'discovery' assessment to collect any tax owing at a later date.

COMPANIES

Companies must complete a form CT600 and file it together with accounts and computations. There is a short version of the form which can be completed by most small companies. The returns require the completion of a number of supplementary pages most of which do not affect small companies. A completion guide can be accessed on www.hmrc.gov.uk/ct/managing/company-tax-return/returns/index.htm.

Inaccurate returns

If you carelessly or deliberately file an inaccurate return with HMRC to understate the tax you owe or to claim a tax refund that you are not entitled to, you will be penalized. The amount of the penalty depends on the reason why you completed the return inaccurately and the extent to which you tell HMRC about the mistake and help them to correct it. For example, if you are careless in completing your return you could be fined 30% of the tax owing but if you tell the tax authorities about the inaccuracy in the return without them asking you to do so there may be no fine to pay. If you have taken reasonable care with your return but make an honest mistake on your form which you subsequently realize needs to be amended you can correct the error by following a set procedure (see Correcting errors).

Late returns

If you are late filing a return you will be charged an automatic penalty, the extent of which depends on how late the return is. For example, if a return is a few days late the fine will usually be £100. If it is six months later the fine will be the greater of 5% of the tax due and £300, and if the form is a year late the fine may be 70–100% of the tax due.

If you fail to send in your tax return by the final filing date HMRC can raise an assessment of your tax which will be cancelled once your return is submitted.

Insight

Failing to submit a tax return on time can be an expensive mistake. Not only could you be fined but if you have not paid your tax on time because your form is outstanding you may also owe further penalties and interest (see Paying your tax late).

Paying your tax

If you file your return electronically you will know how much tax to pay, but if you file a paper form and rely on HMRC to calculate your tax the calculations may not always be correct because errors can occur when the information is transferred from your tax return to HMRC's computer system. You should therefore check any tax calculation carefully to ensure that it includes all your sources of income.

Details of how to pay your tax are given on HMRC's website, see www.hmrc.gov.uk/howtopay/menu.htm.

Insight

If HMRC ask you to pay too little tax it is up to you to have the calculation corrected otherwise you could be liable to penalties and interest if they discover the underpayment at a later date.

The dates on which you pay tax differ for individuals and companies.

SELF-EMPLOYED INDIVIDUALS AND PARTNERS

Most self-employed people pay two equal payments of tax on 31 January and 31 July. These payments are based on the amount of tax you paid in the previous tax year and are called 'payments on account'. They are eventually deducted from your total tax liability for the year. If your tax liability is more than the payments you have made on account you must make a 'balancing payment' the following 31 January. If your payments on account exceed your tax liability the excess will be refunded to you or deducted from your next tax instalment.

EXAMPLE

Magdalen's self-assessment for 2008/09 is £3,300. She has to make payments on account of her 2009/10 tax liabilities of £1,650 on 31 January 2010 and £1,650 on 31 July 2010. She works out her tax for 2009/10 when she completes her tax return in August 2010 and it totals £3,500. Magdalen has paid £3,300 as two payments on account of £1,650 but she still owes HMRC £200 which she pays on 31 January 2011.

On 31 January 2011 Magdalen owes her first payment on account for 2010/11. This is half of her total tax bill for 2009/10 so she pays £1,750 (£3,500 divided by 2) making her total tax payment on 31 January 2011 £1,950 (£1,750 + £200). On 31 July 2011 she pays a further £1,750 on account. She works out her 2010/11 tax when she completes her tax return in September 2011 and it comes to £3,000. As Magdalen has already paid two tax instalments of £1,750 i.e. a total of £3,500, she will receive a refund of the £500 she has overpaid. Her payments on account for 2011/12 will be £1,500 per instalment.

Insight

On 31 January each year you may have to pay two lots of tax – a balancing payment for the previous tax year and a payment on account for the current tax year.

NO PAYMENTS ON ACCOUNT

If your income tax for the previous tax year totalled less than £1,000 you do not have to make any payments on account. Payments on account are not required if more than 80% of your tax bill is covered by tax already deducted under PAYE or from other sources (e.g. bank interest).

If you are just starting a business you will probably make no payments on account in the first year. This means that when you prepare your first tax return you will owe tax for the whole of your first year plus you may have to make a payment on account for the next tax year. If you have not planned for these tax liabilities you could find that your business gets into financial difficulties. Chapter 3 tells you how to keep track of your tax liabilities when you start up in business. Budgeting for your tax bills once you are an established business is considered in Chapter 4.

REDUCING YOUR PAYMENTS ON ACCOUNT

If you expect your profits in the current year to be lower than those for the previous tax year so that your payments on account will exceed the tax you owe, it is possible to reduce them by completing form SA 303 (see www.hmrc.gov.uk/sa/forms/sa303.pdf). You need to be careful if you are considering this course of action because if you reduce the payments below the amount you owe you will be charged interest on the shortfall. You may also have to pay a penalty if HMRC considers that you have been negligent in your calculations.

PAYING YOUR TAX LATE

If you are experiencing financial difficulties and cannot afford to pay your tax it is important to discuss this with HMRC as soon as possible as they may be able to give you extra time to pay.

If you fail to pay your tax by the due date you will be charged interest at a set rate which changes from time to time (see Appendix 1). You may also incur surcharge penalties if you have not paid your tax within 30 days of the due date, after the end of five months and after the end of 11 months from the payment date. These penalties are based on 5% of the unpaid tax. Interest is then charged on any unpaid penalties so the costs can soon mount up.

Companies

Most companies have to pay their corporation tax nine months and one day after the end of their accounting period. Companies with annual profits above £1,500,000 have to pay their tax quarterly. If a company pays its corporation tax after the due date it will be charged interest (see Appendix 1). This can be deducted from the business profits. Penalties are also charged for late payment.

Employers

The dates by which you must pay over the PAYE and National Insurance deducted from your employees' wages to HMRC are set out in Appendix 2. Interest is charged on sums still outstanding on 19 April after the end of the tax year. Penalties are also levied at rates of between 1% and 5% of the outstanding liability depending on how many times you have defaulted in a one-year period.

Correcting errors

If you discover that an entry on your tax return is incorrect after you have submitted the form you have 12 months from the official filing date to amend it. If you have underpaid tax as a result you will have to pay interest and penalties.

The tax authorities have nine months from the date you file your return to correct any obvious errors on the form. If they do this you should check why they want to make the alteration and if you are unsure about the changes they have made you should consider taking professional advice. You will need to do this quickly as you have to reject HMRC's amendment within 30 days.

PENALTIES

HMRC have powers to charge penalties in a number of circumstances including:

- *Filing tax returns after the due date;*
- *Filing inaccurate or incorrect forms;*
- *Paying your tax late;*
- *Failing to notify a new business or activity.*

The only way that these penalties can be reduced is if you had a 'reasonable excuse' for failure. The tax authorities interpret this very narrowly. Normal domestic dramas and another person's ill-health are rarely sufficient for a successful reasonable excuse claim.

Enquiries

HMRC will never tell you that they are satisfied with your tax return and because it is up to you to self-assess your tax they have a right to check the form in detail. This process is called an enquiry, investigation or audit. HMRC handles tax enquiries in accordance with a number of Codes of Practice, see www.hmrc.gov.uk/leaflets/c11.htm.

If HMRC starts an enquiry into your return, it does not necessarily mean that you have done anything wrong. Some enquiries are selected entirely randomly to give the tax authorities information about how accurately taxpayers are completing their forms. The majority of enquiries are however chosen because HMRC considers that the form may contain one or more errors and that you may have underpaid your tax as a result. Some enquiries are into just one aspect of the return; others will scrutinize all the entries on the form.

NOTIFYING THE START OF AN ENQUIRY

A tax enquiry is a formal process and HMRC must tell you that an enquiry has started by issuing a written notice. The notice must be sent to you within a year of the date that you sent in your return. If you are a sole trader this usually means that if you filed your 2009/10 return on 31 August 2010, HMRC have until 31 August 2011 to start an enquiry into the return. If you file the return after 31 January or amend it, the period in which HMRC can enquire into the form is extended. It is worth checking that HMRC has adhered correctly to these dates because enquiry notices are sometimes issued incorrectly.

The passing of the final date for opening an enquiry into a tax return unfortunately does not give you any certainty that HMRC are satisfied with it. They can 'discover' underpaid tax for up to five years ten months following the end of the tax year (for individuals) and six years (for companies) if they can prove that your tax return contains insufficient information to enable the tax authorities to fully understand the entries you have made on the form. This period is longer if you have been fraudulent (see Discovery assessments).

WHAT DO I DO IF MY RETURN IS CHOSEN FOR AN ENQUIRY?

If you receive a notice informing you that HMRC is enquiring into your tax return, you will almost certainly require help from

an accountant who specializes in dealing with the tax authorities on these matters as HMRC have wide-ranging powers to visit your business premises and inspect your records and assets.
A tax enquiry should be taken seriously as it is likely to have financial consequences for your business. If a tax underpayment is discovered due to under-declared income or over-claimed expenses or reliefs, not only will you have to pay the tax but interest and penalties on top. A shortfall in one year may also lead to HMRC reviewing the position for previous years, so depending on the amount of unpaid tax you could end up paying the tax authorities a significant additional sum. HMRC deal with all taxes so an underpayment in one field may lead an enquiry in another, for example PAYE or VAT. You could also have to repay some of your tax credits.

WHAT HAPPENS IN AN ENQUIRY?

An enquiry will involve HMRC scrutinizing your accounting records. They may ask to see private bank statements, contracts, work diaries etc. You will have at least 30 days to comply with their request for information. You can refuse to let them see documents that you do not consider relevant to the enquiry but if you do not co-operate with HMRC any penalty charged may be higher. Ultimately HMRC can issue a notice obliging you to hand over the documents they require. To challenge this notice you would have to appeal to the First-tier Tribunal (see Can I appeal?). HMRC also have powers to search premises, seize documents and obtain information from third parties.

Once they have looked at your records, HMRC will request a meeting with you and your accountant if you have one. HMRC use these meetings to find out as much as possible about your business. They may ask to visit your business premises. Sometimes they will gather information about your business by pretending to be a customer or client. HMRC are experienced in interviewing taxpayers and you are likely to find meetings with them intimidating unless you take someone with you.

During the meeting the officer handling the enquiry will usually discuss any aspects of your return that they have problems with. Afterwards they may ask you to supply additional information, or you may wish to provide it to counter their allegations. To conclude the enquiry HMRC will either suggest you amend your self-assessment or they will amend it for you. If you disagree with HMRC's amendment you can appeal against it (see Can I appeal?). In some cases you may reach a negotiated agreement (called a settlement) with HMRC about the extent of any underpayment together with interest and penalties. When the enquiry is over HMRC should issue a closure notice informing you of the fact.

FEES AND INSURANCE

If you engage an accountant to help you with the enquiry you will not usually be able to deduct their costs as a business expense in your accounts if it turns out that you owe additional tax. It is possible to take out fee protection insurance to cover the costs of an experienced adviser to help you in the event that your tax return is chosen for an enquiry. In most circumstances these costs are also not tax-deductible.

Insight

You should note that no insurance policy will cover the cost of any additional tax you might owe as the result of HMRC investigating or enquiring into your tax affairs.

Discovery assessments

Once the final date for enquiring into your return has passed (see Notifying the start of an enquiry), HMRC can still raise a tax assessment if they 'discover' that you have underpaid tax because you provided insufficient detail on your return to make them aware that it included contentious or subjective entries. Most small business people should make written disclosure of their accounting policies, adjustments and valuations to avoid the possibility of a discovery assessment being raised. The full version of the tax return includes space for you to explain your transactions. Alternatively you can submit supplementary information with the form.

Can I appeal?

If you disagree with HM Revenue and Customs and cannot resolve the matter you can appeal to the First-tier Tribunal. If you disagree with their decision on a point of law you can appeal to the Upper Tribunal, to the Court of Appeal and ultimately to the House of Lords. The findings of the First-tier Tribunal about the facts of the case cannot usually be appealed to a higher court. The costs of dealing with an appeal can be significant and you will need to obtain information about your chance of success before undertaking this course of action.

10 THINGS TO REMEMBER

1 *HM Revenue and Customs (HMRC for short) are responsible for the administration of the tax system.*

2 *The tax year starts on 6 April and ends on the following 5 April.*

3 *Self-assessment places the onus on you to inform HMRC that you need to complete a tax return, keep records of your financial transactions, fill in forms accurately, file them on time and pay any tax due.*

4 *Failure to comply with HMRC's requirements may result in you incurring additional costs in the form of interest and penalties unless you have a 'reasonable excuse' for not doing so.*

5 *If you are self-employed you need to keep your accounting and tax records for five years ten months from the end of the tax year. If you are trading as a limited company you must maintain your accounting records for six years from the end of your accounting period.*

6 *The final deadline for filing an income tax return electronically is the 31 January after the end of the tax year if you want to avoid a penalty. If you want to file a paper return it has to be submitted three months earlier by 31 October.*

7 *If you carelessly or deliberately file an inaccurate return with HMRC to understate the tax you owe or to claim a tax refund that you are not entitled to, you may be fined.*

8 *Most sole traders pay income tax on 31 January and 31 July unless they are newly self-employed, their tax liability for the previous year was less than £1,000 or 80% or more of their tax is collected through PAYE or deducted at source.*

9   HMRC monitor the tax system by enquiring into certain taxpayers' affairs each year. Some enquiries are random but most occur because the tax authorities consider that the return does not match their expectations.

10 If HMRC enquire into your tax affairs you will almost certainly need to ask an accountant to help you as HMRC have wide-ranging powers to visit business premises and to inspect records and assets.

3

Starting a business

In this chapter:
- *choice of business medium*
- *self-employment versus limited company – a checklist*
- *am I really self-employed?*
- *notifying HM Revenue and Customs*
- *pre-trading expenditure*
- *business finance*
- *anticipating tax payments*

When you start a business, you have to decide whether to operate as a sole trader, partnership or limited company. There are many commercial and practical reasons for operating as one type of business rather than another and the choice of trading medium affects the amount and type of tax you pay.

Working on your own

If you decide to set up in business on your own you have to choose between trading as a limited company (being incorporated), or working as a sole trader (being self-employed). You may also want to review whether it is advantageous to form a limited company if you are already self-employed and your business is expanding (see Chapter 11).

Sole trader

Operating as a sole trader is the simplest trading method. No formalities are required apart from notifying HM Revenue and Customs. The disadvantage is that you are personally liable for all your business debts. This means that you could have to sell your house to pay your creditors if the business fails. There are ways to partly protect yourself such as owning your home in joint names but you should take legal advice.

Operating as a sole trader is most suitable for people who do not take many risks. They often work from home or a rented room and sell their own services rather than manufactured goods, for example therapists, consultants, artists and writers. Many trades people such as electricians and plumbers are also self-employed.

Sole traders are responsible for the following taxes:

▶ *Class 2 National Insurance paid at a weekly flat rate by monthly direct debit or quarterly payment;*
▶ *income tax and Class 4 National Insurance paid on their trading profits;*
▶ *operating PAYE on their employees' pay; and*
▶ *registering for VAT if necessary.*

Limited company

The biggest advantage of trading as a limited company is that you are not personally liable for any business debts. If your enterprise fails, whilst you may lose all the assets in the company and your shares will be worthless, your personal property is protected unless you have had to pledge the assets to the bank to secure a loan or overdraft, or you have been fraudulent.

Operating as a company is most suitable for riskier businesses which require greater capital investment (such as equipment or stock), or where a large bad debt, poor period of trading or claim could destroy the business. Trading as a company may be necessary if you want outside investors to put money into the venture. You may be surprised to discover that you cannot take any money out of the company apart from your salary, a dividend or to reimburse expenses as the company's money is separate from your own. There is also far more paperwork and bureaucracy to contend with.

Limited companies are responsible for the following taxes:

▶ *paying corporation tax on their profits;*
▶ *paying VAT if VAT registered;*
▶ *operating PAYE on employees' and directors' salaries.*

Insight

If you are considering incorporating a company you should seek professional advice. It is easy to form a company but much more complicated to close it down (see Chapter 12).

DIRECTORS' SALARIES AND PERKS

As a company director you are an employee of the company and have to pay income tax and employee's National Insurance on your salary under the PAYE system (see Chapter 7). The company has to pay employer's National Insurance on top of your salary. You will also have to pay income tax on many of the perks that the company provides you with (for example a car or private medical insurance) and once again the company has to pay employer's National Insurance on these.

DIVIDENDS

As well as being a director you will probably also own shares in the company. If the company is profitable some of the profits can be paid to you as a dividend. Dividends can also be paid to other members of your family who are shareholders. The dividend is paid with a tax credit and provided that you do not pay tax at the higher or additional rates you have no further tax to pay (see Chapter 1). Unlike a salary, no employee's or employer's National Insurance is paid on dividends. This favourable tax treatment has led to many small businesses paying their company directors small salaries and large dividends to save tax and National Insurance. HM Revenue and Customs does not like owner-managed companies saving tax in this way and they now prevent some dividend planning by tax rules known as 'IR35', the 'MSC' regime and 'the settlements legislation'. IR35 stops you saving tax and National Insurance by using an intermediary such as a company or partnership to provide personal services where you would otherwise be considered to be employed by your client (see Personal services). Rules also prohibit you saving tax by providing self-employed services through an umbrella company known as a 'Managed Service Company' or 'MSC'. The tax authorities may use the settlements legislation to stop you saving tax by paying dividends to members of your family who earn less than you do and pay tax at a lower rate as a result.

If you decide to trade as a limited company and want to take significant dividends from the company you will require professional advice otherwise you risk completing your self-assessment return incorrectly and you could have to pay extra tax, penalties and interest if HM Revenue and Customs enquires into your return (see Chapter 2).

Comparison of trading through a limited company rather than as a sole trader

Limited company	Sole trader
Directors' salaries are paid under PAYE with income tax and National Insurance deducted when the salary is paid.	Sole trader's drawings are not taxed.

(Contd)

Limited company	Sole trader
Employee's Class 1 National Insurance is paid at a higher rate than self-employed contributions.	Self-employed Class 2 National Insurance is paid at a flat weekly rate irrespective of the amount of your profits.
Employer's National Insurance is paid on directors' salaries by the company.	No employer's National Insurance is paid by a sole trader on their profits or drawings.
Company profits (after deducting directors' salaries) are liable to corporation tax. This may be charged at a higher rate than income tax.	Profits are taxed at income tax rates. Class 4 National Insurance is also due.
Many company perks are liable to income tax and National Insurance.	Perks are treated as drawings and are not liable to tax and National Insurance.
Dividends can be paid. In some circumstances these may save tax and National Insurance but HM Revenue and Customs have ways of preventing certain types of dividend planning.	Dividends only apply to companies and not sole traders or partners.
Company money is distinct and separate from your own. You can only take money from the company as a salary, dividend or to reimburse legitimate business expenses. If you take other money from the company it may be illegal and you will still be taxed on it.	There is no legal difference between the money belonging to the business and your own funds. You should however keep accounting records which accurately record all the business transactions.
Some tax reliefs for research and development, goodwill and intellectual property are only available to limited companies.	Sole traders and partners can not claim these tax reliefs.

Limited company	Sole trader
As a director and employee you will be entitled to benefits not available to sole traders and partners such as statutory maternity pay, jobseeker's allowance and the state second pension.	Sole traders are not entitled to the same state and pension benefits as employees because they pay National Insurance at a lower rate.
Tax relief is available to some private investors under the enterprise investment scheme.	No enterprise investment scheme tax relief is possible.

Should I trade as a company or sole trader?

There is no easy way to tell whether you will be financially better off trading as a company rather than a sole trader as it depends on a number of factors including:

▶ *How much profit the business makes;*
▶ *How much money you need for your personal use;*
▶ *The amount you need to leave invested in the business; and*
▶ *The scope to pay significant dividends.*

An accountant will be able to undertake calculations to help you decide whether to form a limited company; however, they can only ever be a guide as to whether using a limited company is the best option. You should bear in mind three things:

1 *Business profits, your investment requirements, tax rates and the law change continually.*
2 *Running a company is more complicated than being self-employed and your adviser may have a vested interest in recommending incorporation to increase his or her fees.*
3 *Forming a company is straightforward. Getting rid of one is not.*

Working with others

If you decide to set up in business with other people you have the
following trading options:

> ▶ *a limited company (most co-operatives are also constituted*
> *as companies);*
> ▶ *a partnership; and*
> ▶ *a limited liability partnership.*

Partnership

A partnership is similar to a sole trader but with several people
jointly running the business. There is no limit on the number of
partners you can have but where a large number of individuals
are involved it may be simpler to form a limited company.
A partnership differs from a limited company in that it is not
a separate business entity except in Scotland. Each partner is
bound by the actions of the other partners and your personal
assets may be at risk if the business fails. A partnership agreement
may be required but it is not compulsory. If you are planning
to set up a partnership you will need professional advice.

Partnership profits are shared between the individual partners
in the way that they have agreed amongst themselves. Each
partner is taxed as if they were running their own self-employed
business and pays Class 2 National Insurance, and income tax
and Class 4 National Insurance on their share of the trading
profits. A partnership is responsible for:

> ▶ *operating PAYE on its employees' pay; and*
> ▶ *VAT registration.*

Limited liability partnership (LLP)

LLPs combine some features of a limited company and some of a partnership. Like a company, the members of an LLP are not personally liable for the business debts. Provided that they are not negligent, even if the LLP becomes insolvent, the individual members only risk their partnership investment not their homes and other assets.

The income tax treatment of most LLPs is the same as an ordinary partnership. The profits are shared between the members in the way set out in the members' agreement. Each member is taxed as if they were running their own self-employed business paying Class 2 National Insurance, and income tax and Class 4 National Insurance on their share of the trading profits. The LLP is also responsible for:

▶ *operating PAYE on its employees' pay; and*
▶ *VAT registration.*

If you are planning to set up a limited liability partnership you will require professional advice as there are a number of formalities which must be complied with.

Notifying HM Revenue and Customs

Irrespective of whether you choose to operate as a sole trader, partnership, LLP or company, when you set up a business you have to notify HM Revenue and Customs about the following events:

▶ *Starting to trade;*
▶ *Taking on employees (see Chapter 7);*
▶ *Needing to register for VAT (see Chapter 9).*

Starting to trade

One of the first things to decide is the date that the business starts trading. If you fail to notify HM Revenue and Customs on time you may be penalized (see Notification process). With a limited company, LLP or partnership this is fairly straightforward. You will probably have purchased a company 'off-the-shelf', drawn up a partnership or members' agreement and opened a business bank account in readiness for your first trading transactions. With self-employment, determining a start date may be more complicated particularly if you have previously undertaken similar work as a hobby.

Insight
There are no hard and fast rules for deciding when a hobby turns into a business. It depends on the circumstances of each particular situation and factors such as profit motive, income, risk, time spent working and public perception.

Case study

Basil works full-time for the local council and is a keen gardener. He often grows more plants than he can use himself so he sells the spare ones to his friends and neighbours. He estimates that he earns about £100 a year by doing this which he reinvests in seeds and compost.

Basil is probably not self-employed. He does not grow the plants to make a profit. The money he makes is not his main source of income and he only spends his leisure time working in the garden as he has a full-time job. The people who buy from Basil would probably not consider that he was running a nursery.

Basil's circumstances change. He is made redundant and as he is not working, grows more plants. He starts selling these from his front garden and once a week sells some of them at a car boot sale.

He takes £1,000 in three months. Basil is almost certainly self-employed. He grows and sells plants to supplement his income and spends many hours a week doing so. He now takes risks and grows plants only for resale. His customers probably think that Basil is a commercial grower.

The main factors to consider when deciding when to register as self-employed are:

- *Do you aim to make a profit?*
- *Is the income significant to you?*
- *Do you spend several hours a week on the business activities?*
- *Would an impartial member of the public think that you were in business?*
- *Do you risk losing money?*

Personal services

If you provide personal services, for example you mainly sell your time and labour and not a product, HM Revenue and Customs may not always consider that you are self-employed. Instead you could be treated as an employee. There is no easy way to tell whether you are employed or self-employed for a particular contract and once again it depends on the facts.

Insight

In tax language, the main distinction between employment and self-employment depends on whether you provide a contract of service (in which case you are an employee); or whether you are fulfilling a contract for services (when you will be self-employed).

In deciding whether your are self-employed or employed for a particular contract the fact that you do not receive holiday, overtime or sick pay are not important and do not necessarily point to you being self-employed. The main factors that indicate a self-employment are:

▶ *You decide how, when and where you work rather than someone telling you what to do and giving you orders.*
▶ *You could send a substitute to do the work, for example your own employee.*
▶ *You risk making a loss, for example if you make a mistake you have to correct it in your own time.*
▶ *You provide your own equipment and not just the small tools that an employee might provide.*
▶ *You work for several people or businesses at the same time and have several different clients on your books.*

If you try to circumvent these rules by providing personal services through a company or partnership, HM Revenue and Customs can use the IR35 rules (see Limited company) to prevent you saving tax and National Insurance. They do this by pretending that the intermediary company or partnership does not exist and tax you as if you were directly employed by your client. If you work through an umbrella company or MSC they can also tax you as if you were an employee (see Limited company).

For further information see HM Revenue and Customs factsheet ES/FS1 'Employed or Self-employed for tax and National Insurance contributions' or refer to www.hmrc.gov.uk/working/intro/empstatus.htm.

Casual income

Sometimes a person will be neither self-employed nor employed but simply receiving a casual (often one-off) payment for work undertaken or services provided, for example selling a photograph to a magazine. In this case there is no need to follow the notification process below but the income will need to be declared to HM Revenue and Customs on a self-assessment tax return. If you do not usually receive a return you must tell the tax authorities that you need to complete one by 5 October following the end of the tax year in which the payment fell, otherwise you will be liable to a penalty. There is space on the tax form to enter casual income not declared elsewhere on the return. If you are unsure whether you should be registered as self-employed you may need to ask an accountant.

Notification process

HM Revenue and Customs must be notified within three months from the end of the month in which you begin to be self-employed that you are in business. If you fail to register you will be charged a penalty depending on the tax and National Insurance outstanding and the reasons why you did not register on time.

When you set up in self-employment or join a partnership you must complete HM Revenue and Customs form CWF1 'Becoming self-employed and registering for National Insurance Contributions and/or tax'. The form can be downloaded from www.hmrc.gov.uk/forms/cwf1.pdf or completed by calling the Self-Employed Registration Helpline on 0845 915 4515. The form requires the following information:

- *Name and contact details;*
- *National Insurance number;*
- *Details of previous self-employments (if any);*
- *Start date;*
- *Nature of the self-employed work;*
- *Trading name and contact details;*
- *Details of any business partners.*

If you are over state retirement age you do not need to pay Class 2 National Insurance.

Building industry sub-contractors must separately register under the Construction Industry Scheme, www.hmrc.gov.uk/cis/sub-reg-obs.htm (see Chapter 7).

If you have set up a limited company you must notify HM Revenue and Customs and complete form CT41G within three months of starting any business activity. Failure to do so can result in a fine. The form and guidance notes are available on www.hmrc/ctsa/intro-pack.htm. You should also notify your tax office that you have become a company director so that they can send you the correct tax return pages to complete in due course.

> **Insight**
>
> If you have appointed an accountant to help you, you will need to sign form 64–8 authorizing HM Revenue and Customs to deal with them on your behalf. This form can be withdrawn by you at any time by informing the tax authorities.

What does being registered with HM Revenue and Customs mean?

Once you have informed HM Revenue and Customs about your business you will start paying Class 2 National Insurance unless you are exempt (see Chapter 1). At the end of the tax year (5 April) you will be sent a tax return which must be completed with details of your business income and expenses (see Chapters 2 and 4). The form must be filed online no later than the following 31 January. Paper returns must be filed by 31 October. If you have incorporated a company, the company also has to complete an annual return.

Being registered with HM Revenue and Customs does not mean that you are automatically treated as self-employed in all circumstances (see Personal services). It is up to the person or business that you work for to determine whether you are employed or self-employed for that particular piece of work. If you want to dispute your employment status you should take professional advice before you speak to HM Revenue and Customs as in most cases they are likely to conclude that you are an employee.

Other notifications

When you start a business there are various other organizations that you should notify depending on your circumstances.

TAX CREDITS

If you receive Child Tax Credit because you have children, or Working Tax Credit because you have a low income or disability, you need to inform HM Revenue and Customs about your new business venture within one month. Failure to do so could result in a penalty. If as a result of starting your new business you expect your income to fall compared to the previous year, you may be entitled to more tax credits. If you expect your income to be more than the previous year, your tax credits may fall. For further information see www.hmrc.gov.uk/taxcredits/tell-us-changes.htm.

STATE BENEFITS

If you are in receipt of state benefits, you are required to inform the Department for Work and Pensions about the new business as it is a change in your circumstances.

BUSINESS RATES

If you are renting or purchasing business premises, or modifying your home to provide accommodation for your business you may be liable for business rates paid to the local council (see Chapter 8).

Expenditure incurred before the business starts

As we have seen in this chapter it is not always clear when a business actually starts trading. Often you will have incurred expenditure many months, or even years, before the business finally gets off the ground. Provided that you have kept a record of these 'pre-trading' expenses, any money spent up to seven years before the business starts trading is a tax-deductible expense of the first accounting period.

Equipment (including cars) purchased before trading commences can be introduced into the business valued at the asset's current market value. The item then becomes eligible for a writing down allowance. This is deducted from your taxable profit and saves you tax (see Chapter 6).

Financing the business

Raising sufficient finance to start a new business is often difficult for budding entrepreneurs. The tax consequences and implications for your choice of trading medium are considered in the following paragraphs.

BANK LOANS AND OVERDRAFTS

The interest on business loans and overdrafts is an allowable business expense and reduces your taxable profits (see Chapter 4). The loan or overdraft repayments have to be met out of the profits generated by the business and they are not deducted from your taxable income.

PARTNERSHIP LOANS

A partner can obtain tax relief on the interest on a loan taken out to invest in a partnership. No relief is available for investment in some types of LLP.

LOANS TO INVEST IN A COMPANY OR CO-OPERATIVE

Individuals (provided that the investor and company meet various conditions) can obtain tax relief on the interest on a loan taken out to invest in a small company or co-operative.

PRIVATE INVESTORS

You may find that friends, family and other private investors want to invest in your business. If so you will probably need to trade through a limited company. Where a company qualifies for the Enterprise Investment Scheme, an investor can obtain tax relief on their investment provided they hold onto the shares for a set period of time (see Appendix 1). When the shares are sold they are also exempt from capital gains tax provided that the investment and the company satisfy detailed rules. You will require professional advice if you want to raise funds for your business in this way.

Anticipating tax payments

As described in Chapter 2, there is often a significant time delay between earning the profits and paying the tax on them particularly in the early days of a new business. If you forget this, you may have an unpleasant surprise when you calculate your first tax bill. Sole traders and partners pay income tax and Class 4 National Insurance on 31 January and 31 July each year but not during the first year of a new business. This can cause financial difficulties if the tax liability is not anticipated well in advance.

There are two ways to plan for potential tax bills. The first is to do nothing and if necessary to borrow the money when the liability falls due. The second approach is to put money aside on a regular basis to meet the liability.

Insight

Banks do not always like lending money to pay tax bills. If you have to borrow funds to pay your tax the interest is not tax-deductible as personal tax payments are private expenditure and part of your drawings (see Chapter 4).

HOW MUCH MONEY SHOULD I ALLOCATE FOR MY TAX PAYMENTS?

It can be difficult to know how much to allocate for your tax bills particularly in the first year of trading, as you will probably not know how much your profits will amount to. As a very general rule, if your profits are between £15,000 and £30,000 and you provide services rather than manufacturing a product or running a shop, your tax bill will usually be 15–25% of your takings or sales. If you run a shop or manufacturing business the percentage will usually be lower than this.

The following table shows the approximate amount of tax and National Insurance that you will owe on annual profits between £10,000 and £35,000 based on the rates for 2010/11.

Annual profits	Tax and Class 4 National Insurance	Tax as a percentage of annual profits
£	£	%
10,000	1,047	10
15,000	2,447	16
20,000	3,847	19
25,000	5,247	21
30,000	6,647	22
35,000	8,047	23

Case study

Jasmine leaves her job in a city hairdressing salon to set up in business as a mobile hairdresser. She reviews the advantages and disadvantages of trading as a sole trader or a company and decides that because the business is not particularly risky that she will operate as a sole trader under the name 'Jasmine Hair'. She takes out a business bank loan and acquires a small van along with the necessary scissors, appliances and products. Jasmine starts visiting customers on 1 May.

On 1 June Jasmine notifies HM Revenue and Customs that 'Jasmine Hair' started trading on 1 May. She completes form CWF1 and starts paying Class 2 National Insurance contributions by monthly direct debit backdated to 1 May. She expects to take £1,500 a month from customers in her first year of trading and does not need to register for VAT. She decides not to do so voluntarily.

Jasmine starts to keep records of her business income and expenses. She is concerned about how much tax she will have to pay so she puts 20% of her takings away at the end of each month in a separate deposit account.

The following April Jasmine receives her self-assessment tax return. She remembers to claim tax relief on the business loan interest and some towels and gowns that she purchased before she started trading. She also makes a note to claim annual investment allowances on the van and hairdressing equipment she purchased (see Chapter 6).

When Jasmine comes to pay her income tax the following 31 January plus a payment of half as much tax again as a payment on account for the current year, she is pleased to find that she has more than enough put away in her tax account to meet the bill.

10 THINGS TO REMEMBER

1 Operating as a sole trader is the simplest trading method and no formalities are required apart from notifying HM Revenue and Customs within three months of starting the business on form CWF1.

2 It is not always clear when a person starts trading, particularly if they have done similar work in the past as a hobby or on a casual basis. The commencement date of the business will merit careful consideration.

3 Trading as a limited company is more suitable for riskier businesses that require greater capital investment or outside investors.

4 If you trade through a limited company and you are employed by the company as a director you have to pay employer's National Insurance on top of your salary and perks. This can add considerably to the cost of trading through a company.

5 One advantage of trading through a company is the potential to pay dividends. You need to be aware of various anti-avoidance rules such as 'IR35' and the settlements legislation which may cause you difficulties and negate any benefit obtained from paying a dividend rather than a salary.

6 If you provide personal services rather than selling a product, HM Revenue and Customs can treat you as an employee rather than self-employed if the facts of your self-employment point to you really being an employee rather than being self-employed.

7 If you claim Child or Working Tax Credits or state benefits you must remember to inform the relevant departments about your new business as it will probably affect your entitlement.

8 *You can obtain tax relief for expenditure incurred in the seven years prior to starting your business in certain circumstances.*

9 *There are various tax reliefs available to help you raise business finance.*

10 *Failing to plan in advance for your tax payments is one reason why businesses fail. Budgeting for your tax bills is considered in this chapter and in Chapter 4.*

4

Profits

In this chapter:
- *choice of accounting year end*
- *calculating your business profits*
- *which expenses are tax-deductible?*
- *special situations*
- *how much tax do I owe on my profits?*

By now you will probably have decided whether you are going to operate as a sole trader, partnership or limited company and you may have started trading. This chapter helps you with the next stage – choosing a suitable accounting year end, understanding how your taxable profits are calculated and learning which expenses are tax-deductible. This information will enable you to keep accurate accounting records from which you will prepare your tax return in due course.

Choice of year end

Within the first few months of starting your business you should choose a suitable accounting year end date to prepare your first accounts to. After it has passed, you will need to draw up accounts or make entries on your tax return to reflect all the trading transactions for your first accounting period. This period is unlikely to be for exactly 12 months and will probably be between six and 18 months long. In subsequent years you will usually prepare a statement of your income and expenses on an annual basis unless you change your accounting date or cease trading.

SOLE TRADERS

If you are a sole trader or a partner, there are basically two choices of year end date:

▶ *A year end which coincides with the end of the tax year (5 April or 31 March); or*
▶ *Another date (usually the last day of the month for convenience). This date may be the anniversary of your starting the business or another suitable date, for example a date occurring during a quiet period if the business is seasonal or to coincide with one of your VAT returns if you are VAT registered.*

Insight
Using an accounting date other than 5 April or 31 March will make your tax affairs more complicated particularly in the first two years. You may need to take advice so that you calculate your profits correctly.

You will not save tax by your choice of year end date because the income tax system is designed to tax all your profits over the lifetime of your business but there are good reasons for selecting one year end over another. If your profits are on a rising trend you may defer a higher tax bill for a year by using a year end other than 5 April or 31 March (see the Example of Linda). The disadvantage is that you may owe more tax than you expect in a subsequent tax year or when you cease the business.

You also need to use a year end which gives you enough time to prepare your accounts so that you can submit your tax return on time. If you started trading early in the year, say on 1 February 2010, you may be tempted to use 31 January 2011 as your accounting year end. In the first tax year you will either have to submit your tax return with provisional entries or send in the form late – not an auspicious start to your self-employment. This is because your 2009/10 tax return which has to be submitted by 31 January 2011 requires you to include two months' worth of the profits from your accounts to cover the period 1 February 2010 to 5 April 2010. As your year end is not until 31 January 2011 it is impossible to file an accurate return on the due date. If you submit your tax return with provisional entries you will pay tax based on estimated figures and if you pay too little tax as a result, you will be charged interest.

USING A YEAR END OF 5 APRIL OR 31 MARCH

Many sole traders select 5 April as their accounting date. As it is the end of the tax year it makes completing the tax return as straightforward as possible. You can also use a date of 31 March and the tax authorities treat it as if it is 5 April. This means that:

▶ *If you choose 31 March as your year end, your tax return for the year to 5 April 2010 will show your income and expenditure for the period 1 April 2009–31 March 2010.*
▶ *If you use a 5 April date, your return for the year to 5 April 2010 will include your accounting transactions for the period 6 April 2009–5 April 2010.*

If you use either a 5 April or 31 March date, it is unlikely that you will have traded for a full year by the time you come to draw up your first set of accounts. In this case your return will show your profits or losses from the date you started to trade to either 5 April or 31 March even if this period is only a few months long.

Example
Anil starts his business on 1 November 2010. He wants to make completing his tax return as straightforward as possible and chooses an accounting date of 31 March. His tax return to 5 April 2011 shows his transactions from 1 November 2010 to 31 March 2011.

PREPARING ACCOUNTS TO ANOTHER DATE

If you decide to use an accounting date other than 5 April or 31 March it may be for commercial reasons to fit in with your trading cycle. For example, a nursery school might adopt 31 July to coincide with the end of the school year.

A date which is not either 5 April or 31 March will result in profits being taxed more than once in the early years. This is not necessarily as bad as it sounds, particularly if your profits are increasing. Tax relief is given for these 'overlap' profits when you cease trading, or in some cases if you change your accounting date. You will need to calculate your overlap profits and enter them on your tax form each year.

Example

Linda starts up a business as sole trader on 1 July 2010. She decides to prepare her first accounts for a year to 30 June 2011. She calculates her profit as £16,000.

▶ *Her tax return to 5 April 2011 will tax profits of £12,000 covering the period from when she starts the business to the end of the tax year. This is the period 1 July 2010–5 April 2011. She calculates her profits by taking nine months out of the 12-month accounting period. That is £16,000 × 9 months divided by 12 months = £12,000.*

▶ *Linda will also use the accounts for the year to 30 June 2011 to complete her tax return for the tax year to 5 April 2012 because this is a set of accounts which ends in the tax year covered by the return (6 April 2011–5 April 2012). Her taxable profits for 2011/12 are therefore £16,000.*

▶ *You may have noticed that Linda has already paid tax on nine months' worth of these profits (£12,000) in the previous tax year to 5 April 2011. These profits which are taxed twice become Linda's 'overlap' profits. Linda can claim relief for these if she ceases to be self-employed or she changes her accounting date to a date nearer to 31 March within the tax year (see Chapter 12).*

- ▸ *Linda's second set of accounts for the year to 30 June 2012 show a profit of £20,000. The profits will be taxed in the tax year to 5 April 2013.*
- ▸ *From then on Linda will always use the accounts to the accounting date falling in the tax year until she ceases her business. This is known as the current year basis of assessment.*

You might find it easier to understand this in table form.

Tax year	Accounting period	Months taxed	Taxable profit	Overlap profits
2010/11	1 July 2010–30 June 2011 (12 months)	1 July 2010–5 April 2011 (9 months)	£16,000 × 9/12 = £12,000	
2011/12	1 July 2010–30 June 2011 (12 months)	1 July 2010–30 June 2011 (12 months)	£16,000	£12,000 (1 July 2010–5 April 2011)
2012/13	1 July 2011–30 June 2012 (12 months)	1 July 2011–30 June 2012 (12 months)	£20,000	

If Linda had used a year end of 31 March, making profits for the nine months 1 July 2010–31 March 2011 of £12,000; year to 31 March 2012 of £20,000 and year to 31 March 2013 of £22,000, her taxable profits would be as follows:

Tax year	Accounting period	Months taxed	Taxable profit	Overlap profits
2010/11	1 July 2010–31 March 2011 (9 months)	1 July 2010–31 March 2011 (9 months)	£12,000	
2011/12	1 April 2011–31 March 2012 (12 months)	1 April 2011–31 March 2012 (12 months)	£20,000	
2012/13	1 April 2012–31 March 2013 (12 months)	1 April 2012–31 March 2013 (12 months)	£22,000	

Using a 31 March year end increases Linda's profits in 2011/12 and 2012/13 because her profits are on a rising trend. She may therefore prefer to use 30 June as a year end because it gives her a cash-flow advantage by deferring some of the profits (and tax) to a later tax year. The only disadvantage is that she is not up to date with her tax liabilities.

Insight

If you use an accounting year end other than 31 March or 5 April for your business it is important to keep track of your tax liabilities on a regular basis; see 'How much tax do I owe on my profits?' later in this chapter.

In the example of Linda you can see that she has apportioned her accounting profits by reference to whole months. It is also possible to divide them on a daily basis which will give a slightly different result. Whichever method you adopt, you should be consistent and use it in subsequent years.

CHANGING YOUR YEAR END

It sometimes turns out that the year end date you have chosen is inconvenient. You can change it in the second or third tax year without complication but after that you have to meet various conditions for the change to be effective. You are likely to need an accountant to help you make the calculations and comply with the requirements laid down by HM Revenue and Customs.

PARTNERS

Partnerships are taxed in a similar way to sole traders and the choice of a partnership year end is governed by the same factors.

Each partner is taxed on his or her share of the partnership profits as if they were a sole trader carrying on an independent business. This means that if partners join or leave the partnership, the new or retiring partners will be taxed differently from the others. You may need professional help with these calculations.

If you trade as a limited company your choice of accounting period is not related to the tax year. Instead you should select any date (usually a month end) that suits the business' trading pattern. You can make up accounts for longer or shorter than 12 months but a longer period is split into two periods, one for 12 months and one for a shorter period. This will require the completion of two tax returns.

Example

Turtle Ltd starts operating on 1 October 2010 and prepares its accounts to 30 September 2011. Its corporation tax liability is based on the profits for the 12-month period. There is no need to apportion the profits and there are no overlap profits as these do not apply to companies.

If Turtle Ltd had decided to prepare its accounts for the 16 months to 31 January 2012, it would have two accounting periods:

▶ *1 October 2010–30 September 2011 (12 months); and*
▶ *1 October 2011–31 January 2012 (four months).*

The next accounting period would be for the year to 31 January 2013.

Accounts

Having selected a suitable accounting year end date, we now look at how you prepare accounts from your books and records for tax purposes. In order to calculate your tax bill you need to draw up a trading and profit and loss account which summarizes your income and expenditure for the accounting period. Most businesses apart from those which are very small, also prepare a balance sheet setting out the business' assets, liabilities and capital at the selected accounting date. The accounts are then used to complete your tax return.

This chapter does not tell you how to maintain accounting records (see Chapter 2) or how to prepare 'double-entry' accounts from those records; instead it looks at how to present your accounting records for tax purposes and considers which expenses are tax-deductible. For information on bookkeeping and accounting you should refer to the Teach Yourself title *Small Business Accounting*.

Accounts are prepared according to specific rules known as generally accepted accounting principles (GAAP). This means that they have to include at the accounting year end:

▶ *Outstanding debtors (people who owe you money) and creditors (people to whom you owe money). The only exception to this rule are barristers and advocates who can work out their profits for the first seven years based on the income they have received or the fees that they have delivered;*
▶ *Stocks of materials and goods, and work-in-progress valued according to set criteria (see Problem areas – Stock and work-in-progress);*
▶ *All your income, even on contracts which you have not completed at the year end; and*
▶ *Liabilities only when they become due.*

Insight

An accountant can help you prepare accounts that comply with accounting principles. If your business has complex transactions or you are unfamiliar with bookkeeping and accounting, using a professional will minimize the risk of making a mistake on your tax return.

Tax return

If you run a small unincorporated business it is not necessary to prepare formal accounts for HM Revenue and Customs. Instead details of your income, expenditure and balance sheet (if you prepare one) can be entered directly onto your tax return.

You may however need to give accounts to your bank manager, other financiers and mortgage lenders.

If you trade as a limited company you will require accounts for shareholders and Companies House as well as the tax authorities.

Income

The first stage to working out your accounting profit is to calculate your income. Income is also called turnover or sales revenue. It represents the money you have earned in your accounting period from selling goods or services. If you run a shop or other business where you do not make sales on credit, working out your income is relatively straightforward. If you sell goods, or supply services on credit (i.e. your customers do not pay you straight away), then you must adjust your sales receipts for opening and closing debtors (that is for the amount that customers owed you for goods or services supplied before your accounting date). You add your closing debtors to your sales figure and deduct your opening debtors from it. If you are paid in advance you will need to consider whether you should adjust your income figure for this receipt. The more adjustments you have to make to your sales income or turnover, the greater the chance that you could make a mistake in calculating the figure so you may need help from an accountant.

If you supply services over a period of time you must include a proportion of this income (including any profit that you will eventually make on the contract) even if you do not invoice your client for the work until after your accounting year end. You may need professional help to make this calculation. For further information see Helpsheet 238 'Revenue Recognition in Service Contracts'.

Turnover includes not just sales of goods or services but commission received, tips and gratuities, payments in kind, recharged items and disbursements. It is usually expressed excluding (net of) VAT (see Problem areas – VAT). If you receive income from which tax has been deducted you should include the total payment before tax on your return and make a separate entry for the tax.

Turnover excludes interest received on a business bank account, rental income and profits from selling assets all of which must be shown separately on your tax return form.

Insight

You need to be able to calculate turnover accurately in order to work out whether you need to VAT register. If you are approaching the VAT registration limit take extra care when calculating your sales to make sure that you register on time and avoid a penalty.

EXAMPLES

Maggie runs a newsagents. Her taxable sales turnover for the year to 31 March is calculated as follows:

▶ *Total of her daily till takings excluding VAT*; plus
▶ *Customers yet to pay their accounts for papers delivered before 31 March*; less
▶ *Amounts owed by customers calculated the previous 31 March.*

Desmond is a self-employed plasterer. He sometimes works for private clients but he usually sub-contracts for a large building company who deduct tax from his payments. He charges his time by the day and adds the cost of materials on top. His sales turnover for the year to 5 April is calculated as follows:

▶ *Total value of invoices raised for the tax year, including recharged materials, tax and invoices which have not yet been paid*; plus
▶ *Any work undertaken up to 5 April but invoiced in the following year*; less

- *Sums owed by clients and work-in-hand calculated the previous 5 April.*

Desmond will claim a deduction for the tax he has already paid and for the cost of his materials on his tax form.

Spencer is a freelance author. His only income in the tax year is an advance for a book he is writing. At 5 April he calculates that he completed 75% of the work on the title, with 25% left to complete in the next tax year. His sales turnover for the year is calculated as follows:

- *Advance from publisher;* less
- *25% carried forward to the next tax year to represent the uncompleted work.*

Julie is a beautician. She receives payments from clients and tips. She lets the flat above her shop to a friend. Her sales income is calculated as follows:

- *Payments from customers including all her tips but excluding VAT.*

The rental income is shown separately on her tax form.

Expenses

After calculating your income you need to work out all the deductions you can claim. There are two main types of expense:

- *Direct expenses or cost of sales; and*
- *Overheads.*

In addition you can claim a deduction for capital allowances on your equipment (see Chapter 6).

DIRECT COSTS

The direct costs are those that you have to incur in order to be able to sell your products or services and they vary according to the business you run. For example:

▶ A *plumber's direct costs will be pipes, fittings, materials and loose tools.*
▶ A *builder's direct costs will include materials, equipment hire and payments to sub-contractors and employees.*
▶ A *taxi driver's direct costs will include fuel.*
▶ A *hairdresser's direct costs will be hair products, gowns and towels.*
▶ A *gift shop's cost of sales may be purchases of goods for resale, carriage and commission.*
▶ A *manufacturer of sunglasses will have a more complex cost of sales that includes components, materials, fixings, discounts given to customers and the wages and associated costs of employees directly concerned with the manufacturing process.*
▶ A *PR agency's direct costs include recharged expenses and sums spent on behalf of its clients (disbursements).*

Direct costs are always tax-deductible but they must be adjusted for opening and closing stock and work-in-progress and items bought for personal use (see Problem areas – Stock and work-in-progress and Goods taken for personal use). Depreciation of plant and equipment is not tax allowable but you can claim capital allowances instead (see Chapter 6).

OVERHEADS

Overhead expenses are common to many businesses and consist of administrative costs and the costs incurred in selling its goods and services. They are usually tax-deductible provided that they are incurred 'wholly and exclusively' for business purposes.

The following table sets out the overhead expenses in the order that they appear on the full self-employment pages of the income tax return together with a note of the type of expense which falls into each category, details of whether they are tax allowable and any restrictions on the claim. If you trade as a limited company expenses are deductible on the same basis but with some differences (see Problem areas – Companies).

Tax return entry	Comments
Wages, salaries and other staff costs	Salaries, wages, bonuses (paid within nine months of the accounting date), pensions, benefits and employer's National Insurance for all non-direct labour employees (permanent, temporary and casual) are tax-deductible. Wages paid to a spouse or civil partner must be justified by the work that they do for the business. Staff welfare costs such as canteen expenses and counselling for redundant employees are tax-deductible, as are recruitment agency fees and sub-contractor costs not included as a direct cost. Payments to yourself such as your own wages, drawings, pension payments or National Insurance must be excluded (see Drawings).
Car, van and travel expenses	The business proportion of costs such as insurance, servicing, repairs, MOT, fuel, hire and leasing charges, parking and breakdown cover are tax-deductible but fines and penalties are not. The costs must exclude travel between home and work and the cost of buying a vehicle, although capital allowances may be due (see Chapter 6). Rail, air and taxi fares are deductible as are hotels, accommodation costs, reasonable subsistence and similar costs when staying away from home overnight for work purposes (see Subsistence and entertaining).

Tax return entry	Comments
Rent, rates, power and insurance costs	Rent, business and water rates, power, insurances, security and similar expenses are tax-deductible. Use of home expenses (business proportion only) should be included here but not the cost of buying business premises (see Chapter 8).
Repairs and renewals of property and equipment	Repairs, renewals and maintenance of business premises, machinery and tools are tax-deductible but not the cost of their alteration, renovation or improvement (see Capital or revenue expense?). Distinguishing between a 'repair' and a 'renovation' can be difficult and many cases end up in the courts. You may require professional help if the costs are significant.
Telephone, fax, stationery and other office costs	Telecoms, Internet, postage, stationery, printing, computer software, printing and small items of office equipment.
Advertising and business entertainment costs	Advertising and promotion of the business through various media including newspapers, mail-shots, trade directories, websites, free samples and loyalty cards are tax-deductible. Entertainment and hospitality costs (clients, prospective customers and suppliers) are not tax-deductible. Staff entertaining up to £150 per head per year is allowed. Expenditure on gifts is disallowed except promotional items with a conspicuous advert which cost less than £50 each (excluding food, drink, tobacco and vouchers).
Interest on bank and other loans	Interest on business loans and overdrafts and alternative finance payments are allowable but not the capital repayments (see Chapter 3: Financing the business).

(Contd)

Tax return entry	Comments
Bank, credit card and other finance charges	Bank charges, business credit card charges, hire purchase interest, leasing payments and similar costs including the cost of obtaining the finance and alternative finance payments are deductible but not the capital repayments.
Irrecoverable debts written off	Amounts owed to you at your accounting date but which you consider you will never be able to recover and will have to write-off are bad debts and tax-deductible. The sums must be specific. A lump sum provision created just in case a portion of your debtors do not pay is not deductible, nor are debts relating to fixed assets. Amounts recovered against a previous bad debt should be shown as 'other income'.
Accountancy, legal and other professional costs	Accountancy and bookkeeping fees, legal costs for business, trade and employee matters, surveyors, architects, stock takers and similar professional fees are all tax allowable. Professional indemnity insurance premiums can also be claimed (see Chapter 10). Fines and penalties are not tax-deductible nor is the cost of settling a tax dispute (see Chapter 2: Enquiries). The legal costs of buying property and plant or machinery are not tax-deductible as the expenditure is treated as part of the cost of the asset.
Depreciation and loss/profit on sale of assets	Depreciation is calculated to write-off your equipment over its useful life. Losses (or profits) may occur when you sell equipment and other assets. Depreciation and a loss on sale are not tax-deductible expenses but you may be able to claim capital allowances (see Depreciation and capital allowances). A profit on sale does not have to be included as income but you may have a capital gains tax liability (see Chapter 1).

Tax return entry	Comments
Other business expenses	Trade or professional press, subscriptions expenses (excluding personal clubs and associations), and other similar costs are tax-deductible. Necessary protective clothing is usually allowable but not ordinary clothing for everyday use. Personal expenditure is not tax-deductible. Contributions to local enterprise agencies, training and enterprise councils and urban regeneration companies can be claimed but donations to charity are not usually allowed, nor are donations to political parties. Illegal payments such as bribes and protection money are not tax-deductible.

Problem areas

As you have just seen, deciding whether an expense is tax allowable is not always as straightforward. There are a number of further difficulties which bear consideration.

DUAL EXPENSES

To be tax-deductible an expense must be incurred 'wholly and necessarily' for business purposes. This would on the face of it appear to deny a tax deduction for many everyday expenses which businesses incur. For example a car will often be used for work and privately and a telephone line may serve for both home and business use. Provided that the expense can be divided into a part relating to the business and a part that is private (for example by reference to miles driven or phone calls made), the business element is tax-deductible. HM Revenue and Customs usually take a pragmatic view of telephone calls and in practice a proportion of both calls and line rental should be tax-deductible. The rules for companies differ (see Companies).

Where a sole trader incurs expenses which have a dual purpose a means has to be found to divide the costs between business and private use. You could keep a record of your business or domestic car mileage, or a log of business telephone calls. There are no hard and fast rules for doing this but some records should be kept even if only for a representative sample period.

Example

Chris is a freelance landscape designer. He has an office but sometimes uses his home phone to make business calls in the evening. He uses his car for both work and private travel and is unsure how to calculate his motor and telephone expenditure.

Telephone: When he receives his phone bill, Chris notes from the itemized call list that he spends about £2 per night for four nights a week making calls to clients. He claims a deduction of £8 per week for each week he is working and reviews this claim twice a year to make sure it is still reasonable. He keeps copies of his itemized calls and the phone bills in case HM Revenue and Customs ask to see them.

Car: As his motor expenses are quite considerable, Chris attaches a notepad to his dashboard. When he has finished a business journey he notes the business mileage and the name of the client. Once a week he transfers his business mileage to a spreadsheet and files his back-up notes in an envelope. He uses this information to bill his clients.

At the end of his accounting period Chris checks his milometer and compares it with his mileage reading at the end of the previous year. He finds that he has driven a total of 14,000 miles. His business mileage spreadsheet totals 10,500 miles. Chris therefore claims a tax deduction for 75% (10,500 divided by 14,000) of his total expenditure on fuel, insurance, road tax and servicing.

He claims a deduction for all his business parking but he does not claim for a parking fine as this is not tax allowable.

If Chris makes a journey which is partly for business and partly for private purposes, the cost is not strictly deductible but providing that the private part is purely incidental, he can treat the journey as wholly business.

CARS – AN ALTERNATIVE

Many sole traders find it burdensome to keep detailed records of their motor expenses. If your business has sales turnover below the VAT registration threshold at the time when you first use the vehicle, you can calculate your motor expenses based on the authorized mileage rate (see Appendix 1) multiplied by your business mileage. The authorized mileage rate includes all your vehicle expenses except tolls, parking and the congestion charge.

Insight
Although claiming a tax deduction based on the authorized mileage rate can simplify your record keeping, it may not be the most tax effective thing to do if you have a large car or one which is expensive to run.

CAPITAL OR REVENUE EXPENSE?

Capital expenditure is not tax-deductible but you may be able to claim capital allowances (see Chapter 6). Most revenue expenses on the other hand are tax-deductible. Distinguishing between capital and revenue expenses takes a bit of practice. One way to differentiate them is to think of capital expenditure as an apple tree (it is fixed and permanent) and the revenue costs as the apples (these come each year). This can be applied to many situations:

▶ *Interest (including arrangement fees) is a revenue cost and tax-deductible; the loan, overdraft or hire purchase agreement is capital and the repayments are not deductible.*

- ▶ *Repairs to a building or machine are revenue costs and tax-deductible but the property or asset being repaired is capital. The cost of improving or altering the asset is capital and not deductible.*
- ▶ *Depreciation of equipment, cars, etc. is a revenue cost and although it is not tax-deductible, capital allowances are (see Chapter 6). The cost of buying the equipment or car is capital expenditure and not tax-deductible.*

DRAWINGS

Sums that a sole trader or partner takes from the business for their personal expenditure are called drawings. These 'wages' are not a tax-deductible expense of the business rather they are the withdrawal of the business profits.

Payments which are drawings include:

- ▶ *Regular payments to yourself by cash, cheque, transfer, direct debit or standing order;*
- ▶ *Payment of personal bills from the business bank account;*
- ▶ *Tax and Class 4 National Insurance payments;*
- ▶ *Class 2 National Insurance;*
- ▶ *Pension contributions.*

Example

Helen who has been self-employed for many years made self-employed profits for the year to 31 May 2010 of £25,000. Each month she withdraws £1,200 from the business bank account for her personal living expenses and in the accounting period paid £6,000 to HM Revenue and Customs for tax and National Insurance. Her drawings total £20,400 (£1,200 × 12 = £14,400 + £6,000). Helen has not withdrawn all her business profits. She has left £4,600 (£25,000 – £20,400) invested in the business to meet future expenses. Helen is taxed on the £25,000 profit not her drawings of £20,400. Subject to her having the available funds she could increase her monthly drawings or withdraw a lump sum instead of leaving her excess profits invested in the business and still pay the same tax.

GOODS TAKEN FOR PERSONAL USE

If you take goods from the business for your personal use you must increase your taxable profit to take into account the market value (not the cost) of these items. For example if you run a fruit and vegetable market stall you must include an adjustment in your tax return for the produce taken to feed your family valued at its market value. If you only eat the items left over at the end of the day with little or no commercial value, then this adjustment may be small but it should still be made.

If your business provides services, your accounts must be adjusted for the cost (not the selling price) of providing free services to yourself or your family and friends. If you are a sole trader with no staff, the cost of providing the service is probably nothing or minimal, because as we have just seen proprietors' drawings are not a cost to the business.

STOCK AND WORK-IN-PROGRESS

Your accounts must include an adjustment for opening and closing stock and work-in-progress valued according to set rules. At your accounting year end, stocks of unsold goods, parts and components must be valued at the lower of:

▶ *their cost; or*
▶ *their selling price.*

For example a business selling specialist pens would value any unsold pens at its accounting year end at the amount they cost to buy.

If the items were damaged or only saleable for less than their cost they would be valued at their selling price. In most situations, stock will be valued at cost, since this is usually less than the selling price of the items. A manufacturer or similar business that has work on hand at the end of the accounting period, must also value any work-in-progress at the lower of its cost or selling price.

Service businesses must include the value of any uncompleted contracts at the end of the accounting period in their accounts. You do this by including the portion of the contract that has been completed during the year. For example, a designer is half-way through a design concept for a new product at their year end. The contract when completed will be worth £20,000. The designer must include £10,000 in their accounts to reflect the value of the uncompleted work. If the work is contingent on a future event, for example 'no win, no fee' the accounts do not have to be adjusted.

VAT

If you are not VAT registered, your expenses include VAT and the total cost is tax-deductible.

If you are VAT registered you will reclaim the VAT on most of your expenses through your VAT returns (see Chapter 9). As a result you cannot claim a tax deduction for the VAT unless you incur irrecoverable VAT on otherwise allowable expenses. In this case it can be deducted or included in a claim for capital allowances.

Most VAT registered businesses draw up their accounts excluding VAT from their income and expenses, i.e. using the net of VAT amounts. You can use the VAT-inclusive figures (this is usual if you use the flat-rate scheme) but you must then make an adjustment to your return for the VAT paid to or reclaimed from HM Revenue and Customs. The adjustment should be entered under 'Other business expenses' if it is a net payment or under 'Other business income' if it is a net repayment. If either of these figures includes

VAT on machinery, equipment or vehicles, details should be provided in the 'Any other information' box.

If you registered for VAT during the tax year you should provide details of the date of registration and confirm whether you have included VAT in recording income and expenses from the date of your registration in the 'Any other information' box. If your registration was cancelled during the course of the year, you should enter details in the 'Any other information' box of the date of deregistration and confirm whether your income and expenses before that date included VAT.

COMPANIES

Expenses incurred by companies are tax-deductible in a similar way to sole traders and partnerships but with some important differences:

▶ *Expenses cannot be incurred for both business and private purposes (dual expenditure).*
▶ *Interest and bad debts which do not relate to the trade have to be accounted for under what is known as the 'loan-relationship rules'.*
▶ *Companies can claim tax relief on goodwill and tax credits on research and development and to clean up contaminated land.*

Profits

You pay tax on your profits calculated as follows:

▶ *Income;* less
▶ *Deductible expenses;* less
▶ *Capital allowances.*

If this calculation gives a positive number, the business has made a taxable profit. If it is negative the business has made a loss (see Chapter 5 for the tax treatment of losses). If the calculation gives a positive figure before capital allowances but a negative one after deducting them, it may be tax effective not to claim the capital allowances (see Chapter 6: Increasing your claim).

The profits generated by your business may have to be adjusted further as follows:

▶ *Apportioned between tax years depending on your choice of year end date (see Choice of year end);*
▶ *Averaged over more than one tax year – creative artists and authors and farmers (see Profit averaging);*
▶ *Subject to special treatment – (see Foster and adult carers).*

PROFIT AVERAGING

Artists, authors and farmers often experience fluctuating profits. In some years they earn little or no income whilst in others they make a considerable profit. This means that they can waste their personal allowances in a lean year whilst paying tax at a higher rate during a good one. To minimize this disadvantage, artists and authors wholly or mainly creating artistic works or designs, and farmers, are allowed to average their profits over consecutive tax years. Profits for these purposes are calculated after deducting capital allowances but before loss relief (see Chapter 5). Averaging relief can be claimed by sole traders and partners but not if you operate through a limited company. It cannot be claimed in the year in which a trade commences or ceases.

Profit averaging applies if:

▶ *the profits of the lower year are less than 75% of the profits of the higher year; or*
▶ *the profits for one (but not both) tax years are nil (this would be the case if you made a loss).*

If the profits for one of the years are more than 70% but less than 75% of the profits for the other year, the profit in each year is calculated according to a set formula. The result of the calculation is added to the profit of the lower year and deducted from the profit of the higher year.

Example

Dorinda is a well-known sculptor. Her profits are £3,000 in 2009/10 and £50,000 in 2010/11. She elects to average her profits to £26,500 (£3,000 + £50,000 divided by 2) for both 2009/10 and 2010/11. In doing so she avoids wasting some of her personal allowance in 2009/10 and does not pay tax at a higher tax rate in 2010/11 (see Appendix 1).

The averaging relief is given in Dorinda's 2010/11 tax return, the second of the two years involved and requires two entries to be made on the form. No adjustment is made to the earlier year's return.

> ▶ *The profit on the self-employed or partnership pages is adjusted to the averaged profit by means of an addition or deduction in Box 71 (self-employed) or Box 10 (partners).*
> ▶ *A separate entry is required in either Box 13 of the Tax calculation summary (if it is an increase) or Box 14 (if it is a reduction), to reflect the adjustment to the first year's profits.*

The claim must be made by the second 31 January falling after the end of the later tax year, so Dorinda must claim for 2009/10 and 2010/11 by 31 January 2013. If her profits for either year are adjusted for any reason (for example during an enquiry) the averaging claim is treated as if it had never been made, although she could make a new claim if it is still within the above time limit.

If Dorinda did not average her profits for 2008/09 and 2009/10, she cannot go back and average 2008/09 with the now averaged 2009/10. If Dorinda can also average her 2011/12 profit with that for 2010/11, she must make sure that she uses the average profit for 2010/11 in her calculations and not the actual profit.

Making the correct entries on your tax return for averaging relief is quite complicated and you may require professional help to make sure that you receive all the tax relief that you are entitled to. Further information is available in Help Sheets 224 and 234.

Insight

Averaging relief may affect the capital allowances you wish to claim and the way in which you want to use any losses. It may also affect the amount of pension contributions that it is tax effective to pay.

FOSTER AND OTHER CARERS

Foster carers looking after children under a foster care agreement are taxed on their profits using special rules. If you have foster care receipts below a set threshold you are exempt from income tax and any profit or loss is treated as nil. If your receipts are above the threshold you can choose to deduct an amount equal to the threshold if you make an election in writing by the second 31 January falling after the end of the tax year. If no election is made you must calculate your profits using the rules outlined earlier in this chapter for working out trading profits.

The threshold and set amount is made up of two parts:

▶ *A fixed amount of £10,000 per residence (this can be a caravan or houseboat) per year. Where more than one person at the same address fosters children, the fixed amount is divided equally between them. If the income period is other than an exact year the fixed amount is apportioned pro rata.*
▶ *A weekly amount for each child being fostered depending on their age – £200 a week (or part week) for a child under 11, £250 a week (or part week) for a child aged 11 or over.*

Example

Mavis fostered two children aged 8 and 10 for the whole of the tax year to 5 April 2010. Under an agreement with her local authority she is paid £225 per week for the younger child and £285 per week for the 10-year-old. Her total foster care receipts are £26,520. No tax liability arises on Mavis's income because the receipts fall below the relevant threshold. In Mavis's case this is:

▶ *£30,800 (£10,000 plus £200 for two children per week).*

If Mavis was paid a further £450 per week by the local authority to foster a baby with special needs her total foster care receipts would be £49,920 and her relevant threshold would rise to:

▶ *£41,200 (£10,000 plus £200 for three children per week).*

Mavis can choose between paying tax on £8,720 (receipts of £49,920 less the set amount of £41,200) or she can keep records of all the expenditure she incurs to look after the children as if it were a small business. If she thought that the costs would exceed £41,200 she would be better off being taxed on her 'true' profit. It is however more likely that deducting the set amount will not only save Mavis tax but the inconvenience and difficulty of keeping records. If Mavis chooses this latter option she must elect for it to apply for 2010/11 by 31 January 2013.

Similar tax arrangements apply to Shared-lives Carers providing supported living for elderly or vulnerable adults and children in their home.

_____

How much tax do I owe on my profits?

In Chapter 3 we looked at the pattern for income tax payments in the early years of a new business (see Anticipating tax payments). This trend will continue throughout the lifecycle of your enterprise.

Ignoring your tax obligations is one of the principal reasons why businesses fail so for your venture to be successful you need to adopt a system to keep track of your tax liabilities as your profits rise and fall over the years. One way to do this is to estimate your tax bill on a regular basis.

MONITORING YOUR TAX

Now that you have read this chapter you have the skills to calculate your profits. Using the information in Chapter 1, you should be able to work out the income tax and Class 4 National Insurance charged on those profits if you are a sole trader or partner, or your corporation tax liability if you trade as a limited company. Knowing the amount of your profits and your tax liability will enable you to calculate your tax as a percentage of your profits. You do this by taking your total tax liability for the year and dividing it by your profits. This will give you a percentage that you can apply to future profits to estimate your future tax bills. You could check this figure by reviewing the amount of tax you have paid and profits for the last two years. If the percentage varies, you should consider which figure is more representative of your business for the future. It is important to be realistic. Deluding yourself that your tax bill will be smaller than it actually will be will only cause you problems in the future.

There are disadvantages to estimating your tax in this way because most small businesses only calculate their profits once or twice a year. Estimating your tax bills based on a percentage of sales turnover is more flexible as most businesses review their sales monthly. So to calculate a suitable percentage:

▶ *Review your last tax return and find the figures for your sales and total tax.*
▶ *Divide the tax by the sales income to come to a percentage.*
▶ *Make similar calculations for two previous years and see if they are consistent. If not which percentage seems most realistic to use?*

▶ *Apply the percentage to your current sales to provide an estimate of your likely tax bill.*

Example

Wendy runs a clothing shop. Her profits, turnover and tax bills for the last three years were as follows:

Year	Sales	Profit	Tax	Tax:sales	Tax:profit
	£	£	£	%	%
2010/11	200,000	40,000	10,000	5	25
2009/10	160,000	25,000	6,000	4	24
2008/09	155,000	24,000	5,700	4	24

Although Wendy's turnover and profits have increased significantly in the last year as a result of renovating the shop and stocking new ranges of garments, the percentage of tax to sales and profits have remained quite consistent. As she expects her profits to remain at the 2010/11 level she should allocate at least 5% of her sales to tax.

During the accounting year to 31 March 2012, Wendy records her sales on a spreadsheet and keeps a running total of her estimated tax liability. This is shown in the following table.

Month	Sales (£)	Tax estimate 5% (£)
January	18,000	900
February	10,000	500
March	15,000	750
April	20,000	1,000
May	22,000	1,100
June	16,000	800
July	17,000	850
August	11,000	550
September	19,000	950
October	21,000	1,050

(Contd)

Month	Sales (£)	Tax estimate 5% (£)
November	16,000	800
December	20,000	1,000
Total	**205,000**	**10,250**

Provided that Wendy allocates at least 5% of her sales turnover each month for income tax, she should always have sufficient funds to pay her tax bills when they fall due on 31 January and 31 July each year.

It is not necessary that she opens a separate bank account as a tax reserve (although some businesses do) because she operates her shop with loans and overdrafts. Wendy should however keep in mind the amount of tax she owes when budgeting for her business expenditure.

Case study

Matthew is a sole trader manufacturing blinds and awnings. He employs three people and operates from a rented workshop. He has been trading for five years and prepares his accounts to 31 October each year. He keeps his accounting records on a computer package which produces the balances listed below at the end of the year. Matthew is keen to work out his taxable profit for the year to 31 October 2010 so that he knows how much income tax he owes and to enable him to complete his tax return to 5 April 2011.

Year to 31 October 2010	Figures from accounts package £
Sales	125,000
Purchases of materials	−40,000
Rent and rates	−10,000
Power and insurance	−3,000
Telephone	−1,800
Staff costs and National Insurance	−40,000
Motor expenses	−1,500

Year to 31 October 2010	Figures from accounts package £
Office and administration costs	−5,000
Bank charges	−500
Advertising	−1,200
Loan interest	−2,500
Drawings	−20,000
Tax payments for self	−7,100
Pension payments for self	−2,500

At 31 October 2010 Matthew works out that three customers owe him a total of £25,000. Last year he was owed £10,000. During the year one client refused to pay for a blind and Matthew does not believe that he will ever recover the £900 he is owed.

Matthew counts his stock of materials on hand at 31 October which comes to £5,000. The previous year it was only £2,000. At the year end he is half-way through making blinds for one customer who will eventually pay him £1,600. He had no partly finished work at 1 November 2009.

Matthew pays most of his bills by monthly standing order or direct debit but he owes a supplier £200 for fixings. Nothing was outstanding at the beginning of the year.

When Matthew goes through his accounting records he finds out that his office administration costs include £150 for a meal for a valued customer. This is entertaining expenditure which is not tax-deductible. Matthew must exclude the cost from his administration expenses because it has been wrongly categorized in his accounting records. It should be included in 'advertising and business entertainment costs' and then shown on his tax return as disallowable expense. Matthew also remembers that he has forgotten to include a subscription to a trade magazine (total annual cost £50) and the cost of meter parking (averaging £5 per week).

(Contd)

Matthew owns a number of machines which he uses in his business, a computer, office furniture and a car. He calculates that he is entitled to claim capital allowances on these of £2,800 (see Chapter 6).

Matthew should adjust his records as set out in the following table. The layout follows the income tax return self-employment pages.

Tax return 2010/11	£	Comments
Income	140,000	Sales £125,000 + Closing debtors £25,000 – Opening debtors £10,000 debtors
Cost of goods bought for re-sale or goods used	–36,400	Purchase of materials £40,000 + Owed to supplier £200 + Opening stock £2,000 – Closing stock £5,000 – Closing work-in-progress £800
Wages, salaries and other staff costs	–40,000	
Car, van and travel expenses	–1,760	Motor expenses £1,500 + Parking £260 (£5 × 52 weeks)
Rent, rates, power and insurance costs	–13,000	Rent and rates £10,000 + Power and insurance £3,000
Telephone, fax, stationery and other office costs	–6,650	Telephone £1,800 + Office and administration costs £5,000 – Entertaining £150
Advertising and business entertainment costs	–1,200	Advertising £1,200 (Entertaining £150 is added but then must be excluded as it is not tax deductible)
Interest on bank and other loans	–2,500	
Bank, credit card finance charges	–500	
Irrecoverable debts written off	–900	Owed by customer but not paid
Other business expenses	–50	Subscription

Tax return 2010/11	£	Comments
Capital allowances	−2,800	
Taxable profit	34,240	Amount on which Matthew pays income tax

Matthew does not deduct the drawings, tax payments or pension contributions when working out his taxable profits (see Drawings).

Matthew could complete the balance sheet pages of the return with details of his equipment, debtors, stock, work-in-progress, creditors, loans and capital but as he is inexperienced in double-entry bookkeeping he chooses not to do so. There is no obligation on him to complete these boxes on the return but HM Revenue and Customs could ask Matthew to prepare a balance sheet if they were to enquire into his return.

Using the information on income tax and Class 4 National Insurance in Chapter 1 and Appendix 1, Matthew now works out the income tax and Class 4 National Insurance that he owes on his taxable profit for 2010/11.

Income tax liability 2010/11	£
Profits	34,240
Personal allowance	−6,475
Income subject to income tax	**27,765**
Basic rate: 20%	5,553.00
Class 4 National Insurance: (£34,240 − £5,715 = £28,525) × 8%	2,282.00
Total income tax and Class 4 National Insurance	**7,835.00**

Matthew's tax liability is 6% of his sales turnover (£7,835 divided by £140,000) and 23% of his profit (£7,835 divided by £34,240). If he has allocated tax on a regular basis he will have sufficient to pay his tax bills when they are due.

(Contd)

Matthew's income tax liability for 2009/10 was £7,100. He will therefore pay the following tax bills for 2010/11 (see Appendix 2):

31 January 2011	£3,550 – Payment on account 2010/11 based on 50% of his 2009/10 tax bill (£7,100 divided by 2).
31 July 2011	£3,550 – Payment on account 2010/11 based on 50% of his 2009/10 tax bill (£7,100 divided by 2).
31 January 2012	£735 – Balancing payment 2010/11. Matthew owes £7,835 in total less the £7,100 he has paid on account in two installments of £3,550.

On 31 January 2012 Matthew will also pay £3,917.50 on account of his tax for 2011/12 – 50% of his 2010/11 tax bill of £7,835. He will pay a further £3,917.50 on 31 July 2012.

10 THINGS TO REMEMBER

1 *Each business needs to select an accounting date. The tax system is designed so that you cannot save tax by choosing one date over another but depending on your profit trend you could obtain a cash flow benefit by choosing an appropriate date.*

2 *Many sole traders select 5 April or 31 March as their accounting date. As these dates coincide with the end of the tax year they make completing your tax return more straightforward.*

3 *You will need to prepare business accounts from your accounting records in order to work out your tax bill.*

4 *Tax is paid on business profits which are calculated as income less deductible expenses less capital allowances.*

5 *Business expenses are tax deductible provided that they are incurred 'wholly and necessarily' for the purposes of the business.*

6 *If you operate an unincorporated business some expenses such as motor expenses and home telephone costs that have both business and personal elements can still be tax deductible provided that the costs can be divided into a business portion and a private portion.*

7 *Entertaining clients, prospective customers or suppliers is not a tax deductible business expense but staff entertaining of up to £150 per head per tax year is allowable.*

8 *In your first and last accounting period you may have to apportion your accounting profits between different tax years in order to calculate your tax liability.*

9 *If you are a creative artist, designer, author or farmer you may be entitled to average your profits between years to save tax. If you are a foster or other carer calculating your profits according to a set formula may simplify your tax affairs.*

10 *It is important to calculate how much tax you owe on your business profits on a regular basis so that you do not receive any unpleasant surprises at the end of the tax year. It may be simpler to estimate your tax bills based on a percentage of your sales turnover.*

5

Losses

In this chapter:
- *calculating income tax losses*
- *company losses*
- *capital losses*
- *tax relief for business investments that go wrong*

In Chapter 4 we looked at how profits are taxed. The reality of the business world is that instead of making profits small ventures often make losses particularly in the first few years. This chapter looks at how you can save tax by claiming loss relief.

Losses are calculated in the same way as profits and arise when business expenses exceed income leaving a negative profit. Losses also occur in other situations and these are examined later in the chapter.

Claiming income tax losses

When a sole trader or partnership makes a trading loss they are treated as if they had made neither a profit nor a loss for the accounting period. Tax relief is then claimed for the loss in a variety of ways depending on whether it occurs in the early years of a business, when the business ceases to trade or somewhere in between. Claiming losses reduces your tax bill for the year of the claim and you either receive a tax refund or pay less tax.

Table of possible income tax loss claims

The following table summarizes the possible income tax loss claims you could make.

Loss...	Use...	Claim reference
Claimed against your other sources of income	In the year of the loss or the previous year	Section 64
Claimed against any capital gains	In the tax year of the loss or the previous year	Section 71
Carried forward against your future profits	Against the first profits the business makes after the loss-making period	Section 83
Occurring in the first four tax years of a new business	Against your other income of the previous three tax years	Section 72
Occurring in the 12 months to the date your business ceases	In the tax year when the business stops and the three previous tax years	Section 89

We now consider each of the possible loss claims in turn.

USING LOSSES AGAINST OTHER INCOME

If you make a loss on your trading activities you can deduct it from any other income you receive in the same tax year. Alternatively you can claim it against your income for the previous tax year. You can claim some of the loss in one year and some in the other if it is a large loss and you have insufficient income in just one year to set it against. Relief for the loss must be claimed by the second 31 January following the end of the tax year in which the loss arose.

Example

Denis, a sole trader, prepares accounts to 31 March. He makes losses in two tax years during which he also receives income from renting a property.

	Loss	Other income
	£	£
31 March 2010 (2009/10 tax year)	5,000	13,000
31 March 2011 (2010/11 tax year)	10,000	9,500

Denis's taxable business profits in 2009/10 and 2010/11 are £0 because he made losses. He makes the following loss claims:

▶ *He uses the £5,000 loss from 2009/10 against his other income for the same tax year. This reduces his rental income to £8,000 (£13,000 – £5,000). His tax bill will be reduced by £1,000 (the £5,000 loss multiplied by tax at 20%) (see Appendix 1).*
▶ *He uses £9,500 of the 2010/11 loss against his other income for the same tax year. This reduces his rental income to £0 (£9,500 – £9,500). As Denis has only used £9,500 of his £10,000 loss the remaining £500 can be deducted from his rental income for the previous year. This claim reduces Denis' 2009/10 rental income to £7,500 (£13,000 – £5,000 (2009/10) – £500 (2010/11)).*

The example illustrates some of the complexities of loss claims:

▶ *The losses must be used until either the loss or the income against which the loss is claimed has gone. In 2010/11 this wastes Denis' personal allowance. Although his income has been reduced to £0 so he owes no tax, he does not benefit from his personal allowance. Denis cannot claim just a part of the loss so that he does not waste his personal allowance and then use the balance of the loss in a different way, for example by carrying it forward against his future profits.*

▶ *Section 64 loss claims can be split between different years. Denis uses £9,500 of his 2010/11 loss against his other income in 2010/11 and the remaining £500 against his other income for the previous year. In 2009/10 this means that Denis can deduct losses from two different tax years.*

▶ *Instead of using the £500 loss from 2010/11 against his income in 2009/10, Denis could have chosen to carry it forward against any future profits by making a Section 83 claim. If Denis anticipated that he would owe tax at a higher rate in 2011/12 than 2009/10, this would prove a good decision.*

Insight

In order to make the loss claim, Denis must be carrying on his business on a commercial basis with an expectation of making a profit in the near future. If he continues to make losses HM Revenue and Customs could enquire into his affairs and deny him loss relief.

PROBLEMS FOR SPECIFIC BUSINESSES

There are special rules which restrict the loss claims of some businesses in certain circumstances. If you are a partner in a partnership where you spend less than ten hours a week working personally in the trade, or your business is involved with farming and market gardening, leasing equipment or film production you should seek help from an accountant if you want to claim loss relief.

CLAIMING RELIEF AGAINST CAPITAL GAINS

If a Section 64 loss claim does not work for you because you have insufficient income, any unused losses can be deducted from your capital gains in either the year of the loss or the previous year. Calculating this loss relief can be complicated and you may require professional help.

CARRIED FORWARD LOSSES

If you do not have any other source of income or gains to set your trading losses against in the current or previous tax year, you can carry them forward to a year in the future when you make a profit. To claim this relief you must meet three conditions:

▶ *You must use the loss against your first available profits. This may mean that you waste your personal allowance in that year.*
▶ *There must have been no changes in ownership of your business.*
▶ *You must officially claim the loss within five years of the 31 January after the end of the tax year in which the loss arose. When you want to use the loss you then receive the tax relief automatically and you do not need to make a further claim.*

Example

Christine made a trading loss in 2010/11 of £25,000. She makes a further loss in 2011/12 of £5,000 but a profit in 2012/13 of £40,000. If Christine has no other income against which to relieve her losses she will carry them forward. She will not use the 2010/11 loss in 2011/12 because she makes a further loss in that year. Instead she will use the £30,000 of losses (£25,000 + £5,000) against her 2012/13 profit leaving her with taxable profits of £10,000 (£40,000 – £30,000).

If Christine had made a profit in 2012/13 of £28,000 (instead of £40,000) she could use all of the £25,000 loss from 2010/11 against the profit plus £3,000 of the loss from 2011/12 leaving her with taxable profits of £0. Christine cannot decide to carry the whole of the £5,000 loss from 2011/12 forward to another tax year. She has to use as much of it as possible in the first tax year in which she makes a profit even if it means wasting her personal allowance. Christine will carry forward the remaining £2,000 loss (£5,000 – £3,000) to a later tax year.

FORMING A LIMITED COMPANY

If you transfer your unincorporated business to a limited company in return for shares but have unused losses, you may be able to claim loss relief against director's fees and dividends paid to you by the new limited company (see Chapter 11).

LOSSES IN THE EARLY YEARS OF A BUSINESS

Many unincorporated businesses make losses when they first start trading. Fortunately there are tax provisions to help you to make the most of them. If you make a loss in any of your first four tax years you can carry the loss back and deduct it from any other source of income you had in the previous three tax years. This enables you to use the loss against income you earned or received before you started the business. There are three conditions you must comply with to claim loss relief in this way:

▶ *You must deduct the loss from the income of the earliest year first. So if the loss occurred in 2010/11 you must use it against the income of 2007/08 in preference to 2008/09 and against 2008/09 in preference to 2009/10.*
▶ *Your business must be carried on commercially with a reasonable expectation that it will make a profit in the near future.*
▶ *You must claim the loss by the second 31 January following the end of the tax year in which the loss arose.*

Case study

Antonia was a student in 2008/09 and 2009/10 with no taxable income and she was then employed by a nursery school in 2010/11. On 6 April 2011 she starts a business as a children's party entertainer. She prepares her first accounts to 5 April 2012 and they show a trading loss of £10,000. In each subsequent tax year she makes profits. As Antonia had no taxable income in either 2008/09 or 2009/10 she must use the £10,000 loss against her 2010/11 salary. Her tax calculation for 2010/11 is as follows:

2010/11	Income £	Tax £
Salary and tax deducted under PAYE (see Chapter 7)	20,000	2,705.00
Less: Loss claimed under Section 72	−10,000	
Less: Personal allowance	−6,475	
Taxable income	**3,525**	
£3,525 at 20%		705.00
Tax refund due as a result of the loss (£2,705−£705)		**2,000.00**

Antonia's tax rebate of £2,000 is equal to 20% tax on a £10,000 loss (£10,000 × 20%). Originally she paid tax on her salary of £2,705. As a result of the loss her tax liability falls to £705 giving her a tax overpayment of £2,000. Antonia must claim the loss by 31 January 2014.

You may have noticed that Antonia's claim is the same as it would have been if she had claimed tax relief for the loss under Section 64 (see Using losses against other income). If Antonia had earnings in 2008/09 or 2009/10 she would have used the loss against the earliest year's income first.

It is easy to confuse tax years and accounting periods when dealing with loss claims in the early years of a new business.

Example

John starts a small business as a sole trader on 1 November 2006. He prepares his first accounts to 31 October 2007 and these show a loss of £15,000. He makes further losses of £12,500 in the year to 31 October 2008, £2,500 to 31 October 2009 and £1,500 to 31 October 2010. The losses are allocated to tax years as follows:

Losses	£
2006/07 (accounts 1.11.06–5.4.07) loss £15,000 x 5 months/12 months	6,250
2007/08 (accounts 1.11.06–31.10.07) loss £15,000 less portion already allocated to 2006/07 – £6,250	8,750
2008/09 (accounts 1.11.07–31.10.08)	12,500
2009/10 (accounts 1.11.08–31.10.09)	2,500
2010/11 (accounts 1.11.09–31.10.10)	1,500

John cannot use the 2010/11 losses under Section 72 because it is the business' fifth tax year even though the profits only cover four accounting periods: 31.10.07, 31.10.08, 31.10.09 and 31.10.10. The 2010/11 loss can be used against John's other income in 2010/11 or 2009/10 under Section 64. Alternatively it can be carried forward against his future profits under Section 83.

LOSSES WHEN A BUSINESS CEASES

If you make a trading loss in the 12 months to the date that you cease running your business and you have not used the losses in a different claim, relief may be due under the 'terminal' loss provisions. This means that you can use the loss against your trading profits (if you have any) of the tax year when the business stops and the three previous tax years. You must set the loss against the profits of the later years before the earlier years.

Insight

When you cease in business remember to claim overlap relief if you make up your accounts to a date other than 5 April or 31 March. It will increase or even create a terminal loss (see Chapter 12, Overlap relief).

Terminal loss relief must be claimed within five years of the 31 January after the tax year in which the business stopped trading. For example if a business closes down in 2009/10 the loss claim must be made by 31 January 2015.

Calculating a terminal loss is not straightforward and you may need to ask an accountant to help you with the claim.

Example

Kerry ceased her business on 30 June 2010. She made a profit of £30,000 in her accounting period for the year to 30 September 2009. In the nine months to 30 June 2010 she made a loss of £10,000. Kerry has overlap relief of £5,000. Her terminal loss for her last 12 months of trading is calculated as follows:

Tax year	Accounting period	£	Terminal loss £
2010/11	6.4.10–30.6.10: loss £10,000 × 3 months/ 9 months		3,333
	Overlap relief		5,000
			8,333
2009/10	1.10.09–5.4.10: loss £10,000 x 6 months/ 9 months	6,667	
	1.7.09–30.9.09: profit £30,000 x 3 months/ 12 months	–7,500	
			0
	Terminal loss		**8,333**

In 2009/10 the profit of £7,500 (apportioned from the £30,000 profit for the year to 30 September 2009) cancels out the £6,667 loss which is allocated to the same tax year. As a result nothing further is added to Kerry's terminal loss claim for this period. Her claim for the last 12 months she was in business consists of £3,333 of the £10,000 loss plus overlap relief of £5,000. Kerry can claim the remaining £6,667 (£10,000 – £3,333) of losses under Section 64 if she has any other income to use them against.

Company losses

A company may make a number of different losses depending on its sources of income (for example trading, property, overseas or capital losses). This section is concerned only with trading and capital losses.

TRADING LOSSES

Trading losses are calculated in the same way as profits. Sometimes a company will deliberately create a loss by paying money into its pension scheme or as directors' bonuses.

Companies claim tax relief for their losses in a similar way to individuals so they can be:

▶ *Deducted from the company's other profits and gains of the same accounting period. Any remaining balance can be carried back and off-set against the profits or gains of the previous year.*
▶ *Carried forward to be used against future profits.*
▶ *Used when a company ceases to trade. A loss arising in the last 12 months can be carried back against the company's profits for the previous three years, using the later years first.*

If the company changes hands, alters the nature of its business or the way it operates within a three-year period HMRC may refuse the loss relief claim.

Insight
If the company is a member of a group, its losses can also be relieved against the profits of other members of the group in certain circumstances (and vice versa).

Capital losses

Capital losses can be deducted from a company's capital gains for the same accounting period or carried forward. They cannot be carried back against previous years except in some limited circumstances. Capital losses generated as part of a tax-avoidance scheme will be refused.

CLAIMS

Losses which are to be off-set against the same or previous year must be claimed within two years. No specific claim is required if the losses are carried forward although an entry must be made on the company's corporation tax return. The claim will usually give rise to a tax repayment.

Insight

When deciding the best way to use company losses you should consider the corporation tax rate for each year affected by the claim. Claiming loss relief against an accounting period liable to corporation tax at a higher rate will give you a bigger tax saving (see Appendix 1).

CAPITAL LOSSES

Capital losses arise if you sell capital assets (for example shares) for less than you bought them for. Both individuals and companies may make capital losses but company losses are dealt with as part of the corporation tax return (see Company losses). This section looks at the position of individuals who make capital losses.

Capital losses are calculated in the same way as capital gains (see Chapter 1). If you make a capital gain and a loss in the same tax year you deduct the loss from the gain before deducting the annual exemption. In some circumstances this may mean that some or all of your annual exemption is wasted. If you make multiple gains and losses in the same tax year, they are aggregated to give you a net gain or a net loss.

CARRYING BACK LOSSES

Unlike income tax losses, capital losses cannot be carried back against the gains of an earlier year. One notable exception is if the loss arises in the year when a sole trader or partner dies when it can be carried back for three tax years.

CARRYING FORWARD LOSSES

Any loss you make in excess of your gains for a tax year can be carried forward to be used in a future tax year. When you come to use the loss, if you have losses arising in that tax year and losses brought forward from an earlier year, the losses of the year in question are used before the earlier year's losses.

You must tell HM Revenue and Customs about your capital losses by completing the capital gains tax pages of your tax return, or notifying them separately in writing within five years of the 31 January following the end of the tax year.

MAINTAINING THE ANNUAL EXEMPTION

When a capital loss is carried forward to a future tax year you only need to deduct as much of it as you require to reduce your gain to the level of the annual exemption (see Appendix 1). This prevents some of the carried forward loss from being wasted and any balance can then be carried forward to a subsequent year.

Example
Colin is a self-employed plumber. He bought a freehold yard and storage unit for use in his business on 1 June 2006 for £50,000. On 1 August 2009 he sells it for £90,000. He is not entitled to entrepreneurs' relief. On 6 April 2009 Colin has capital losses totalling £4,000 carried forward from a previous tax year from the sale of an inherited shareholding.

Colin's capital gains tax calculation for 2009/10 is as follows:

	£	£
1.8.09 Sale of yard	90,000	
1.6.06 Purchase of yard	−50,000	
Gain		40,000
Less: Capital losses brought forward		−4,000
Gain after off-setting losses		36,000
Annual exemption (see Appendix 1)		−10,100
Chargeable gain		**25,900**

If Colin's losses carried forward were £34,000 instead of £4,000, he would choose to use just £29,900 of them to reduce his gain to £10,100 (the level of the annual exemption in 2009/10). He can carry forward the remaining £4,100 (£34,000 − £29,900) of losses and use them against any capital gains he makes in the future. In this situation Colin's capital gains tax calculation would then be as follows:

	£	£
1.8.09 Sale of yard	90,000	
1.6.06 Purchase of yard	−50,000	
Gain		40,000
Less: Capital losses carried forward		−29,900
Gain after deducting losses		10,100
Annual exemption (see Appendix 1)		10,100
Chargeable gain		0

CAN CAPITAL LOSSES BE CLAIMED AGAINST INCOME?

Capital losses cannot usually be claimed against your business income but if certain business investments fail you can claim income tax relief instead of deducting the loss from a capital gain (see Loss claims for business investments that go wrong). You will want to choose this option if you do not have any chargeable capital gains to use the loss against.

CAN INCOME TAX LOSSES BE DEDUCTED FROM CAPITAL GAINS?

As we saw earlier in this chapter you can use certain income tax losses against your capital gains (see Claiming income tax losses: Claiming relief against capital gains).

When a business ceases to trade any expenditure incurred in the seven years after cessation can be deducted from your capital gains if your income is insufficient (see Chapter 12: Income and expenses incurred after the final accounting period).

Loss claims for business investments that go wrong

An individual (but not a company) can claim income tax relief if they invest in shares in an unlisted trading company that fails. If the shares become worthless you calculate a capital gains tax loss in the usual way but instead of deducting it from a capital gain you deduct it from your income.

In order to make this loss claim it is not necessary for you to sell your shares. Instead, under what are known as the 'negligible value' rules, the shares are treated as if you sold them to yourself at their current market value (i.e. for nothing). You must make the claim for the year in which you incurred the loss or the previous year and it takes priority over a Section 64 or 72 loss claim (see Claiming income tax losses). It must be claimed in writing on or before the second 31 January occurring after the tax year in which the loss arose.

> **Insight**
>
> Making a loss claim for a business investment that has gone wrong is likely to require professional advice because the shares must be held in 'a qualifying trading company' and you have to meet many detailed conditions.

10 THINGS TO REMEMBER

1 If you make a loss you will be keen to recoup some of the money. You can do this by claiming tax relief for the loss. This may result in you receiving a tax refund from HMRC or in you paying less tax.

2 Tax relief is available for most losses provided that you make the claim in accordance with strict time limits.

3 Losses are calculated in the same way as profits (see Chapter 4).

4 There are often a number of different loss relief options and you may want to seek professional advice about the best way to use your losses to maximise your tax savings.

5 Special rules apply to loss relief in the early years of a new unincorporated business and when a business is closed down.

6 Losses can always be carried forward and used against future profits but this may not always be the most advantageous thing to do and alternative claims should be considered.

7 Rules apply to restrict the losses of some businesses including those involved with farming and market gardening, equipment leasing and film production. Partners working in a partnership for less than ten hours a week may also have their losses restricted.

8 In order to claim loss relief a business must be being run commercially with a view to making a future profit. If a business changes hands entitlement to loss relief may be lost.

9 *Capital losses are offset against the capital gains of the same year and then carried forward to be used against future gains. They cannot be carried back like income tax losses. Company capital losses are dealt with as part of the corporation tax return.*

10 *In some situations income tax losses can be off set against capital gains, but capital losses can only be deducted from income in certain circumstances when a business fails.*

6

Equipment

In this chapter:
- *types of capital allowances*
- *calculating capital allowances*
- *increasing your capital allowance claims*

To operate efficiently most small businesses require tools, equipment and vehicles. As you saw in Chapter 4 you cannot deduct the cost of these items from your income as an expense when calculating your business profits. Instead you must claim capital allowances. This is one of the more tricky aspects of completing your tax return and amongst taxpayers without an accountant one of the main reasons for errors. Failing to recognize that equipment must be treated differently from other business expenses and completing the capital allowance boxes on the tax return incorrectly could result in HM Revenue and Customs enquiring into your affairs.

On which items can you claim capital allowances?

Equipment (or plant and machinery as it is known in the tax legislation) seems an obvious expression but some items of equipment are not eligible for allowances. Different rates of allowances may apply, depending on the nature and cost of the assets acquired (see Appendix 1).

For most small businesses the equipment on which capital allowances can most commonly be claimed are:

- ▶ *Tools (needed to do your work);*
- ▶ *Machinery (including computers and items in a building such as lifts and escalators);*
- ▶ *Furniture (for your workplace); and*
- ▶ *Vehicles (such as cars and vans but note that there are special rules for cars).*

There are no hard and fast rules that define plant and machinery. Machinery is usually fairly easy to identify but 'plant' is not and many cases end up in dispute ultimately to be considered by the courts. To be eligible for capital allowances the asset must be necessary to the functioning of your business not just to create a pleasant setting in which it is conducted. There is a fine (and not always obvious) distinction between the two. When it comes to plant and machinery incorporated in a building (an 'integral feature'), allowances can usually be claimed but if you have purchased a significant number of assets or they are expensive, you will benefit from professional advice to maximize your claim particularly if you are acquiring fixtures with a property (see Chapter 8).

Capital or revenue expenditure?

Capital allowances are claimed on capital items. Broadly this is something that is going to benefit the business over a period of more than 12 months. For example a computer is a capital asset (you expect it to last for more than a year) whereas your monthly broadband connection is a revenue expense, after one month's subscription has expired you will not remain connected to the Internet unless you pay the charges for a further month (see Chapter 4).

COST

There is no monetary limit that defines capital expenditure.
A builder may purchase a £10 hammer that lasts for ten years
or a hairdresser may buy scissors costing £20 that last for
three years. Whilst both items could be defined as capital
equipment since they are of continuing use to the business,
it is more usual to treat them as revenue expenditure on the
basis that:

▶ *both items cost less than £100 (this is a commonly adopted*
  limit); and
▶ *small items are usually replaced regularly because they*
  frequently get lost or break.

Loose tools costing less than £100 such as the hammer or
scissors are therefore usually written off as a revenue expense
(see Chapter 4). Equipment purchases that cost more than
£100 are usually capital expenditure and you will need to claim
capital allowances on them. The £100 limit is not however a
hard and fast rule. The size of your business and the frequency
with which you replace items may make a £200 limit for
example more appropriate.

LENGTH OF LIFE

There are special rules relating to assets which have a long life and
those with a short life. Those that will last for more than 25 years
(for example ships and aeroplanes) are known as 'long-life assets'.
You will probably require professional help if you are thinking
of buying these assets for your business. Items you expect to last
for less than five years are called 'short-life assets'. Your capital
allowance claim may be increased by identifying such assets
separately if you have spent more than the annual investment
allowance limit (see Appendix 1) on plant and machinery in a
12-month accounting period (see Increasing your claim).

FINANCING THE PURCHASE

You can claim capital allowances on equipment irrespective of whether you buy the item outright, you finance the purchase with a bank loan or buy the item on hire purchase. If you enter into a leasing agreement, it is the leasing company who gets the allowances not you (see Leasing businesses, at the end of the chapter). If part of the purchase cost is paid for by an insurance company their contribution must be deducted from the cost of the asset (see Chapter 10). This also applies to some (but not all) grants and subsidies.

Types of capital allowance

There are three main types of capital allowances for investment in equipment:

- ▶ *annual investment allowances;*
- ▶ *first year allowances; and*
- ▶ *writing down allowances.*

ANNUAL INVESTMENT ALLOWANCES

Most small businesses can claim annual investment allowances on their equipment. Provided that your annual expenditure on plant and machinery is less than the annual investment allowance limit (£100,000 until April 2012), you are entitled to a tax deduction of 100% of the cost. This means that you can write-off the whole cost of the item in the year when you first buy it and this is the end of the story. If you spend more than the annual investment allowance limit on equipment in a year you can claim annual investment allowances up to the limit and then writing down allowances or first year allowances on the excess expenditure depending on what you buy.

The annual investment allowance can be claimed on expenditure on plant and machinery, features integral to a building and long life assets. It cannot be claimed on cars so if you buy a car your claim will be limited to a writing down allowance unless it is an electric car or van, or a very low emissions car, when you can claim a first year allowance. If you claim the annual investment allowance, you cannot claim a first year allowance or writing down allowance on the same assets.

Annual investment allowances are calculated for an accounting period and not the tax year (although the rates are set for a tax year), so if your accounting period runs for more or less than a year (see Chapter 4: Choice of year end) the annual investment limit is proportionately increased or decreased.

Case study

Max starts up a self-employed printing business on 1 October 2010. In his first accounting period to 31 March 2011 he spends £55,000 on computer equipment and £4,000 on a car emitting 140 g/km of CO_2 which he uses only for work. The annual investment allowance is reduced from £100,000 to £50,000 to reflect the fact that the accounting period is only six months long. Max can claim the following capital allowances:

▶ *Annual investment allowance on the computer equipment of £50,000 (£50,000 × 100%);*
▶ *Writing down allowance on the excess expenditure on the equipment of £1,000 (£55,000 − £50,000 = £5,000 × 20%);*
▶ *Writing down allowance on the car of £800 (£4,000 × 20%).*

Max completes his tax return with details of the £51,800 (£50,000 + £1,000 + £800) of allowances claimed. They are deducted from his profit and save him income tax and Class 4 National Insurance.

The unclaimed expenditure on the equipment and car is carried forward to the next accounting period.

If Max could have deferred £5,000 of his expenditure on computer equipment until his accounting period ending 31 March 2012 he would have obtained 100% annual investment allowances

(Contd)

providing that his total expenditure on qualifying assets was less than £100,000 (the limit for that year).

Other areas of potential difficulty include:

▶ *If you have any related businesses such as another company, you may only be entitled to one annual investment allowance depending on whether the businesses operate from the same premises or undertake similar activities.*
▶ *If you use the asset privately as well as for business purposes, the allowance must be restricted to the business percentage.*
▶ *In the year that you cease your business you cannot claim annual investment allowances (see Chapter 12).*

Insight

Although annual investment allowances seem simple enough there are several difficult aspects to watch out for. You may need to ask an accountant for help with these more complex calculations.

FIRST YEAR ALLOWANCES

100% first year allowances are given to encourage businesses to buy certain approved plant and equipment and energy efficient vehicles. You will only be concerned with first year allowances if your expenditure on equipment exceeds the annual investment allowance threshold.

There are two main schemes in operation for the purchase of:

▶ *Energy-efficient equipment; and*
▶ *Water-conservation plant and machinery.*

For a full list of qualifying technologies see www.eca.gov.uk.

New electric cars and those with CO_2 emissions no greater than 110 g/km are eligible for 100% first year allowances until 31 March 2013. Refuelling equipment for natural gas, hydrogen and biogas also qualifies if the expenditure is incurred before that date. For expenditure incurred on or after 1 April 2010, 100% first year allowances can be claimed on new, unused electric vans.

Periodically temporary first year allowances are introduced to help businesses. For example between 1 April 2009 and 31 March 2010 a 40% first year allowance was available on plant and equipment excluding cars, integral features, long life assets and assets used for leasing.

Special rules enable loss-making companies to obtain cash payments in respect of their first year allowances from the Government in certain circumstances. You are likely to need help with making such a claim.

Example

Carlos who has already used up his annual investment allowance, invests £40,000 in water-saving equipment for his sports and leisure club which meet the necessary standards to qualify for 100% first year allowances. Carlos claims 100% first year allowances on the expenditure and deducts £40,000 (£40,000 × 100%) from his profit in the year in which he incurs the expenditure.

Insight

If you invest in plant and machinery which has not qualified for either the annual investment allowance or a first year allowance you can probably claim writing down allowances.

WRITING DOWN ALLOWANCES

Writing down allowances are given at the rate of 20% on the cost of:

▶ *Some cars (these are subject to further rules, see Cars); and*
▶ *Plant and machinery exceeding the limit for the annual investment allowance and ineligible for first year allowances.*

In the first year, the writing down allowance is deducted from the initial cost of the asset. In the second and subsequent years, the allowance is 20% of the balance remaining in the 'pool'. This reduces annually by the amount of the previous year's allowance. Once the balance in the equipment pool reaches £1,000 or less the whole amount can be written off (see Increasing your claim).

Disposals

If you sell or otherwise dispose of an asset in the pool, the way in which you calculate the disposal depends on whether you are claiming allowances on only one asset or whether the pool has a balance that represents the purchase of many assets acquired over a period of time.

Case study

Eleanor is a film maker. She spends £60,000 on camera equipment on 10 May 2009 when the annual investment allowance was £50,000 (see Appendix 1). She claims the maximum annual investment allowance of £50,000 leaving her with a balance of £10,000 (£60,000 – £50,000). She is entitled to claim a 20% writing down allowance on this expenditure giving her total allowances of £52,000 (£50,000 × 100% + £10,000 × 20%).

What happens to the £8,000 (£10,000 – £2,000) that Eleanor has not been able to claim allowances on in this year? This sum is carried forward to the following year when she will be able to claim further writing down allowances on the unused balance. In order that you do not inadvertently forget to claim these allowances in the following year it is a good idea to keep a note of the unclaimed balance. You could note the number in the 'Any other information' box on the tax return or keep a running total of your claims in a 'pool' (see opposite).

Eleanor will continue claiming a writing down allowance each accounting period until there is no balance left, or as is more likely, she stops using the equipment and either sells it or scraps it.

Capital allowance computation	Cost	Allowances
Year to 31 March 2010	£	£
10.5.09 bought camera equipment	60,000	
Annual investment allowance (£50,000 × 100%)	−50,000	50,000
	10,000	
Writing down allowance (£10,000 × 20%)	−2,000	2,000
Carried forward to next accounting period	**8,000**	
Total allowances claimed		**52,000**
Year to 31 March 2011		
Brought forward balance from previous period	8,000	
Writing down allowance (£8,000 × 20%)	−1,600	1,600
Carried forward to next accounting period	**6,400**	
Total allowances claimed		**1,600**
Year to 31 March 2012		
Brought forward balance from previous period	6,400	
Writing down allowance (£6,400 × 20%)	−1,280	1,280
Carried forward to next accounting period	**5,120**	
Total allowances claimed		**1,280**

Disposals

If Eleanor buys new camera equipment on 1 June 2012 for £30,000 and on the same day scraps her old equipment because it no longer works and has no commercial resale value, her capital

(Contd)

allowances for the year to 31 March 2013 would be calculated as follows:

Capital allowance computation	Cost	Allowances
Year to 31 March 2013	£	£
Brought forward balance from previous period	5,120	
1.6.12 equipment scrapped	0	
Balancing allowance	–5,120	5,120
1.6.12 bought new equipment	30,000	
Annual investment allowance (£25,000 × 100%)	–25,000	25,000
	5,000	
Writing down allowance (£5,000 × 18%)	–900	900
Carried forward to next accounting period	**4,100**	
Total allowances claimed		**31,020**

Eleanor has only claimed capital allowances on one item of camera equipment so when she disposes of it she can claim a balancing allowance. This is equal to the difference between the pool balance brought forward from the previous tax year and the sales proceeds. In this case as Eleanor has scrapped the equipment there is no sales income and a balancing allowance arises. A balancing allowance is an additional capital allowance to ensure that Eleanor has received tax relief on the total cost of the equipment spread over her period of ownership. You should note that in the calculation, the disposal of the old camera is dealt with before the acquisition of the new one.

If instead of scrapping the equipment Eleanor sells it to another film maker for £8,000, a balancing charge of £2,880 would arise (£8,000 – £5,120). This reduces her capital allowance claim for the year. A balancing charge is a negative capital allowance and is necessary to limit Eleanor's capital allowance claim to the cost of the asset less any income she receives from its sale. Eleanor must show the balancing charge separately from her capital allowances when completing her tax return.

Capital allowance computation	Cost	Allowances
Year to 31 March 2013	£	£
Brought forward balance from previous period	5,120	
1.6.12 equipment sold	−8,000	
Balancing charge	2,880	−2,880
1.6.12 bought new equipment	30,000	
Annual investment allowance (£25,000 × 100%)	−25,000	25,000
	5,000	
Writing down allowance (£5,000 × 18%)	−900	900
Carried forward to next accounting period	**4,100**	
Total allowances claimed		**23,020**

The calculation would be different again if Eleanor had more than one asset in her pool. In this case the sale proceeds would reduce the value of the pool rather than giving rise to a balancing allowance or charge. Eleanor would have to be making a significant investment in film making equipment for this situation to arise as the following calculation illustrates:

Capital allowance computation	Cost	Allowances
Year to 31 March 2013	£	£
Brought forward balance from previous period	5,120	
1.6.12 equipment sold	−8,000	
Balancing charge	**2,880**	−2,880
1.6.12 bought new equipment	30,000	
1.8.12 bought new equipment	20,000	
1.1.13 bought new equipment	5,000	
	55,000	

(Contd)

Capital allowance computation	Cost	Allowances
Annual investment allowance (£25,000 × 100%)	−25,000	25,000
	30,000	
Writing down allowance (£30,000 × 18%)	−5,400	5,400
Carried forward to next accounting period	**24,600**	
Total allowances claimed		**27,520**
Year to 31 March 2014	**£**	**£**
Brought forward balance from previous period	24,600	
30.7.13 equipment sold	−10,000	
	14,600	
Writing down allowance (£14,600 × 18%)	−2,628	2,628
Carried forward to next accounting period	**11,972**	
Total allowances claimed		**2,628**

Note that there is no balancing allowance or charge on disposal in this situation. The brought forward balance of £24,600 represents several items of camera equipment so when one is sold for £10,000 on 30 July 2013 the pool is reduced and no balancing allowance or charge arises.

Cars

There are special rules which apply to cars. They do not apply to vans or motorcycles and these are dealt with in the same way as equipment. In most cases you can only claim writing down allowances on cars. You cannot claim the annual investment allowance and only electric and very low emissions cars are eligible for first year allowances. The writing down allowance is based on a car's carbon dioxide (CO_2) emissions. Expenditure on cars with CO_2 emissions of less than 160 g/km qualifies for the full 20% writing down allowance. Expenditure on cars with CO_2 emissions over 160 g/km is only eligible for a writing down allowance of 10%. These cars are allocated to a 'special rate pool'.

If you operate as a sole trader or partner you have to reduce your writing down allowance by the percentage that you use the car for private as opposed to business purposes. These cars are allocated to a 'single asset pool'.

Insight

The best way to calculate the percentage of time that you use your car privately as opposed to for business purposes is to keep a log of your business and/or private mileage even if it is only for a sample period of time, for example three months.

EXAMPLE

Rashid and his two brothers are directors of Petromax Ltd which operates three fuel stations. In its 12-month accounting period to 31 March 2011, the company provides each brother with a company car. Rashid's car costs £18,000 and emits 180 g/km of CO_2. His brothers drive cars that cost £10,000 each and these cars emit only 140 g/km of CO_2. The company's capital allowance computation is as follows assuming that there were no balances brought forward on 1 April 2010:

Capital allowance computation	20% pool for cars emitting less than 160 g/km CO_2 and equipment	10% special rate pool for cars emitting more than 160 g/km CO_2	Allowances
Accounting period to 31 March 2011	£	£	£
New cars	20,000	18,000	
Writing down allowance (£20,000 x 20%)	−4,000		4,000
Writing down allowance (£18,000 x 10%)		−1,800	1,800
Total allowances			**5,800**
Carried forward to the next accounting period	**16,000**	**16,200**	

As the cars are owned by a company the allowances do not have to be reduced for the private use of the vehicles. Instead each director incurs a benefit in kind charge on the perk of having a company car (see Chapter 7).

Insight

Claims for writing down allowances on cars are completely different from the calculation of an employee's company car benefit in kind charge although both are based on a car's CO_2 emissions.

Capital allowance claims

Capital allowances must be claimed on your income tax or corporation tax return in the year when you incur the expenditure. If you do not make a claim you may lose entitlement to first year allowances, although you will still be able to claim writing down allowances in future years. The following paragraphs illustrate various ways of increasing the value of your claim.

Insight

If you are a partner you must claim capital allowances on all your assets on the partnership return. You cannot make a separate claim on your own tax return for items such as your car or other personally owned assets.

DISCLAIMING ALLOWANCES

Sometimes you will be better off not claiming all the capital allowances that you are entitled to. This is most likely to occur if your profits are low or you have losses.

You can claim capital allowances on some assets but not others, claim a fixed sum, or disclaim all the allowances for the year. It doesn't matter whether the capital allowance concerned is an annual investment allowance, first year allowance, writing down allowance or an equipment pool balance of less than £1,000. Disclaiming the allowances results in you carrying forward a higher balance to a year when you are a taxpayer and you will save tax then.

Insight

If you have made a loss and have other income to set the loss against it may be better to claim all the capital allowances that you are entitled to as they will increase the loss and any tax rebate which you can claim.

Example

Martin's profits as a piano tuner are £5,000 in his accounting period to 5 April 2009. He is entitled to claim annual investment allowances on his tools of £200 and writing down allowances on his car of £500 but he decides not to as his profits are below his personal allowance (see Appendix 1). As he has no other taxable income that year, to claim the allowances would waste them. If his profits are £10,000 in the year to 5 April 2010, the unclaimed

allowances will save him tax and Class 4 National Insurance of
£196 in that year.

WRITING-OFF SMALL BALANCES

Once the balance in your equipment pool reaches £1,000 or less
you can write off the whole balance in one go if you want to
(see Putting it all together). This rule applies to all equipment
eligible for writing down allowances but not to items in single
asset pools, for example cars subject to a private use restriction.

SUBSTANTIAL INVESTMENT IN COMPUTERS AND OTHER SHORT-LIFE ASSETS

Another way to increase your capital allowance claim where your
expenditure exceeds the limit for the annual investment allowance
is to elect for assets other than cars (usually computers and other
technological equipment) with a limited life-span to be treated as
'short-life' assets. This means that these items are not included in the
'pool' with other equipment and when they are sold or scrapped a
balancing allowance arises. The assets are treated separately until four
years from the end of the accounting period when they were acquired.
At this point any remaining balance is transferred to the 'pool'.

In order to qualify for short-life asset treatment you must elect for
it to apply. This is done by including separate calculations for each
item of equipment with your tax return. Once the election is made
you cannot change your mind. If you purchase several assets that
you want short-life asset treatment to apply to, the tax authorities
will accept that items bought in the same year and qualifying for
the same allowances can be combined together in a single claim.

> ## Insight
> If you are an individual you must elect for short-life asset
> treatment to apply within one year of the 31 January
> following the end of the period of account concerned. If you
> trade as a company the time limit is two years after the end
> of the relevant accounting period.

INTRODUCED ASSETS

When you commence in self-employment you may own various items that you subsequently start using in your business such as a car, computer, tools and office furniture. You can introduce these into the business at an appropriate value and claim writing down allowances on them. This is best done by making a list of the items at their market value.

Insight

You should keep details showing how you arrived at the value of any introduced assets (such as reference to a published car price guide or auction sale) in case HMRC asks to see it during an enquiry or investigation.

BUY EQUIPMENT BEFORE THE END OF YOUR ACCOUNTING PERIOD

You can accelerate your capital allowance claim by buying any equipment you need before the end of your accounting period rather than shortly afterwards. This means that you can claim a deduction for capital allowances a whole year earlier. You must start using the asset in order to qualify for the allowance so it is no use ordering it before your year end for delivery afterwards. You should also only buy equipment you actually need and bear in mind how much tax it will actually save.

Insight

Be aware that buying a £1,000 machine will not save you £1,000 in tax. Assuming entitlement to annual investment allowances of 100% and a combined tax and Class 4 National Insurance rate of 28%, spending £1,000 on equipment will save you just £280 of tax in the year of purchase.

DEFER PURCHASES TO THE NEXT ACCOUNTING PERIOD

You may benefit by deferring the purchase of equipment until the next accounting period if your asset purchases exceed the limit for the annual investment allowance. For example if you have already spent more than the limit on equipment in a 12-month period and a few weeks before the period end are considering whether it is advantageous to spend another £5,000 on equipment, it is worth bearing in mind that unless you qualify for first year allowances, you will only be entitled to a writing down allowance on the £5,000 excess expenditure. If however you wait until the new accounting period you will obtain 100% relief. The disadvantage is that you will have to wait for another year to obtain the benefit. You should only defer a purchase if it will not harm your business to do so.

Research and development

If your business carries out research and development (R&D) you may be entitled to special capital allowances and tax reliefs. You should seek professional help if you incur such costs.

Leasing businesses

Leasing businesses are subject to special rules which restrict their capital allowance claims in some cases. If your business is involved in asset leasing you will require specialist advice.

Putting it all together

So far the capital allowance calculations we have seen have been relatively straightforward. In practice they can become much more complex as assets are purchased and sold. In some years the accounting period may not be exactly 12 months long and in others it may not be advantageous to claim capital allowances at all (see Increasing your claim).

Case study

Joanne operates a mobile coffee bar. She starts her business on 1 October 2009 and prepares her first accounts for the six months to 31 March 2010. In October she buys a diesel van at a cost of £16,000 fitted with equipment costing £8,000. She also acquires a computer and office furniture costing £3,000. The following year she acquires the right to stock and maintain various coffee machines in offices throughout the city. She buys a car costing £5,000 in November 2010 which she estimates that she uses 70% of the time for this work. The car emits 150 g/km of CO_2. She invests a further £2,000 in equipment for her mobile coffee bar in March 2011. Joanne continues to claim writing down allowances. In the year to 31 March 2014 the value of the assets in the equipment pool is less than £1,000 so Joanne writes off the whole balance. The capital allowances are calculated as follows:

Capital allowance computation	Equipment pool	Single asset (car) pool (70% business use)	Allowances
Accounting period to 31 March 2010	£	£	£
1.10.09 equipment bought (£16,000 + £8,000 + £3,000) (Note 1)	27,000		
Annual investment allowance (£50,000 × 6/12 = £25,000 × 100%) (Note 2)	−25,000		25,000
	2,000		
Writing down allowance (£2,000 × 20%)	−400		400
Total allowances claimed			**25,400**

(Contd)

Capital allowance computation	Equipment pool	Single asset (car) pool (70% business use)	Allowances
Carried forward to the next accounting period	**1,600**		
Accounting period to 31 March 2011	£	£	£
Brought forward from previous period	1,600		
1.11.10 car bought (Note 3)		5,000	
1.3.11 equipment bought	2,000		
Annual investment allowance (£2,000 × 100%)	−2,000		2,000
Writing down allowance (£1,600 × 20%)	−320		320
Writing down allowance (£5,000 × 20% × 70%) (Note 3)		−1,000	700
Total allowances claimed			**3,020**
Carried forward to the next accounting period	**1,280**	**4,000**	
Accounting period to 31 March 2012	£	£	£
Brought forward from previous period	1,280	4,000	

Capital allowance computation	Equipment pool	Single asset (car) pool (70% business use)	Allowances
Writing down allowance (£1,280 × 20%)	−256		256
Writing down allowance (£4,000 × 20% × 70%) (Note 3)		−800	560
Total allowances claimed			**816**
Carried forward to the next accounting period	**1,024**	**3,200**	
Accounting period to 31 March 2013	£	£	£
Brought forward from previous period	1,024	3,200	
Writing down allowance (£1,024 × 18%)	−184		184
Writing down allowance (£3,200 × 18% x 70%) (Note 3)		−576	403
Total allowances claimed			**587**
Carried forward to the next accounting period	**840**	**2,624**	
Accounting period to 31 March 2014	£	£	£

(Contd)

Capital allowance computation	Equipment pool	Single asset (car) pool (70% business use)	Allowances
Brought forward from previous period	840	2,624	
Writing down allowance (whole balance as less than £1,000)	–840		840
Writing down allowance (£2,624 × 18% × 70%) (Note 3)		–472	330
Total allowances claimed			**1,170**
Carried forward to the next accounting period	**0**	**2,152**	

Notes:

1 *The van is treated as an item of equipment rather than a car.*
2 *The annual investment allowance is restricted as the accounting period is only six months long. As Joanne spends more than £25,000 she claims the annual investment allowance up to the maximum available for the year (£25,000 in her case) and writing down allowances on the balance (£2,000)*
3 *The car has to go into a separate column or 'single asset pool' as it is used privately as well as for business. When Joanne sells the car a balancing allowance or charge will arise (see Disposals). Joanne claims a writing down allowance of 20% of the total cost of the vehicle (£1,000) because the carbon dioxide emissions are less than 160 g/km. This is then restricted by the amount she uses the car privately (30%).*

10 THINGS TO REMEMBER

1 *When calculating your tax bill, capital allowances take the place of commercial depreciation. Rather than claiming a tax deduction for depreciation you claim capital allowances instead.*

2 *Capital allowances are claimed on capital items. This is usually something that is going to last for more than a year.*

3 *If you buy equipment (other than cars) costing less than £100,000 (April 2010/11 rate) in a 12-month accounting period you can usually claim a 100% deduction in the form of an annual investment allowance.*

4 *If you spend more than £100,000 (April 2010/11 rate) on equipment during a 12-month accounting period you may be entitled to a writing down allowance or first year allowance depending on what you buy.*

5 *The £100,000 (April 2010/11 rate) annual investment allowance limit will vary according to whether your accounting period is longer or shorter than a year.*

6 *Cars are subject to special rules and you can only claim writing down allowances on them. Cars with over 160 g/km of CO_2 emissions are liable to a lower rate of writing down allowances.*

7 *First year allowances are available on a limited range of energy efficient and water-saving plant and machinery, electric vans, and electric and very low emission cars.*

8 *If you dispose of equipment you will need to make special calculations if you have 'pooled' assets.*

9 Once the balance in your capital allowances pool reaches £1,000 or less you can write off the whole balance in one go if it is advantageous to do so.

10 You can increase the tax value of your capital allowance claim in certain circumstances by alternatively buying equipment before the end of your accounting period or deferring a purchase. You may need professional advice to avoid the many pitfalls.

7

Employees

In this chapter:
- **who is an employee?**
- **operating a PAYE scheme**
- **taxing perks**
- **tax-efficient staff benefits**
- **the construction industry**

Taking on staff is a significant event. Few small businesses can function without them and employees' wages will be one of the first major expenses that you will incur. If you have only just taken on staff, how have you been managing until now? Have you been the only person working in the business? In addition to understanding the numerous tax consequences associated with paying your staff, you also need to learn who is and who is not an employee if you are to avoid the additional cost of penalties. Furthermore if you fail to ensure that all your employees are permitted to work in the UK you could be committing a criminal offence.

In Chapter 3 you saw how difficult it can be to decide when you are self-employed. It can be equally problematic to know whether someone you engage to help you with your business is an employee. Falling foul of the PAYE rules can be expensive and taking on staff is an occasion when consulting an accountant is advisable. There are also numerous dates to bear in mind when dealing with PAYE. These are set out in a diary in Appendix 2.

Employer's responsibilities

As an employer you are responsible for the following taxes and related functions:

- *Ensuring that all employees are paid at a rate equivalent to at least the National Minimum Wage;*
- *Deducting income tax and Class 1 National Insurance from their wages through the Pay As You Earn (PAYE) system;*
- *Paying employer's Class 1 National Insurance contributions;*
- *Operating statutory payments – statutory sick pay (SSP), statutory maternity pay (SMP), statutory paternity pay (SPP) and statutory adoption pay (SAP);*
- *Administering and deducting student loan repayments;*
- *Notifying HM Revenue and Customs about perks and benefits so that your employees can be correctly taxed on them via their tax code;*
- *Paying Class 1A or Class 1B National Insurance on certain employee perks;*
- *Monthly (or quarterly) paying over to HM Revenue and Customs the tax, National Insurance and student loan repayments deducted from your staff less any statutory payments.*

You probably feel exhausted already! Dealing with this long list of requirements can be extremely burdensome for new employers and you probably have many other priorities that you would prefer to deal with including getting the business off the ground.

> **Insight**
> Complying with the PAYE rules and regulations is compulsory. It is also essential for good employee relations. No member of staff will be pleased to find that they have been taxed incorrectly so you need to find ways to meet your obligations cost-effectively.

Who is an employee?

There is no hard and fast definition of 'employee' but most people who work for you are likely to be employees.

EMPLOYED OR SELF-EMPLOYED?

Having read the list of employer's responsibilities you may think that it would be more cost-effective and less onerous to use people who are self-employed to provide you with services rather than take on employees. In some cases outsourcing work to other small businesses in this way can benefit your business but most people who work for you on your premises are likely to be employed by you. This is the case even if they do not work for you full-time and they do not have a written employment contract. Mistakenly or deliberately failing to operate PAYE on an employee's pay is a serious matter. You may have to pay the tax and National Insurance on the amounts you erroneously paid them at a later date and you will be unlikely to recover this tax from your worker. You will probably incur a penalty as well.

In deciding whether someone who works for you is an employee, HM Revenue and Customs look at the facts of the case and your relationship with that person. The factors they consider are shown in the table on pages 142–143. For further information see www.hmrc.gov.uk/employment-status/index.htm and HMRC's Employment Status Indicator (ESI) Tool on www.hmrc.gov.uk/calcs/esi.htm.

Even if the worker has their own self-employed business HMRC can still decide that in the particular circumstances of the work that they perform for you they are your employee (see Chapter 3). Resolving whether someone is an employee or self-employed is called an 'employment status dispute'. Should this situation arise, using the services of an accountant or tax adviser will help you to obtain the best outcome.

Table of factors relevant to deciding whether a person is an employee or self-employed

HM Revenue and Customs will examine the following issues to create a complete picture of the relationship between you and the person working for you:

▶ *Control over the worker is a strong pointer to employment. This includes control of what work is done, how, when and where.*

▶ *Personal service by the worker indicates employment. Few employment contracts permit a substitute or replacement to be used.*

▶ *Provision of major equipment such as a commercial vehicle may indicate self-employment but supplying tools of the trade is not usually persuasive either way. If you provide all the equipment the worker is more likely to be employed.*

▶ *Financial risk borne by the worker may indicate self-employment. For example if they make a mistake do they have to correct it in their own time, pay any additional costs or work without pay? Could the worker make a loss undertaking their duties, for example because of the way you pay them?*

▶ *Basis of payment – employees are usually paid a fixed monthly or weekly wage or salary and work under a service contract, although some employees are paid by 'the piece'. People who are self-employed supply their services under a contract for services and are paid a fee for a particular piece of work agreed to be undertaken in a specified time.*

▶ *Mutuality of obligation – for there to be an employer–employee relationship there must be an obligation by the employer to pay the employee a salary or wage for their work in return for which the employee provides services using their labour or skill.*

> ▶ *Holiday pay, sick pay, maternity or paternity pay and the ability to join the employer's pension scheme usually indicate an employer–employee relationship although the absence of these rights if the employment is short-term does not create a self-employed relationship.*
> ▶ *Being part and parcel of the organization – is the worker an integral part of the organization such that they appear to an outsider to be an employee, for example do they wear a uniform or a badge?*
> ▶ *The length of engagement does not usually determine whether the contract is one of employment or self-employment. An employee may work for an employer for a day, a week or 20 years; a person who is self-employed may also work for an organization for a day, several months or periodically for many years.*
> ▶ *The intention of the parties if genuinely held may be relevant in some borderline cases.*

DIRECTORS

Company directors are almost always employees and their salaries are taxed under PAYE. There are special rules relating to their National Insurance treatment; see www.hmrc.gov.uk/nitables/ca44.pdf and www.hmrc.gov.uk/calcs/nicd.htm.

In a few limited circumstances a professional person such as a lawyer or accountant who is also a company director may be able to be treated as self-employed with regard to a modest director's salary.

FAMILY MEMBERS

Many small businesses rely on help from family members. You will need to decide whether a family member working in your business is your employee, partner or co-director. You may need to seek professional advice to determine the most tax-efficient structure.

Family members living in the same household do not need to be paid the National Minimum Wage.

YOURSELF

If you are self-employed or a partner any amounts that you pay to yourself or take from the partnership are your drawings. They are not a salary or wages and you are not an employee (see Chapter 4). If you are a director of a limited company the rules are different and sums you take from the company must be either taxed under PAYE or paid to you as dividends (see Chapter 3).

Paying employees

NATIONAL MINIMUM WAGE

You must pay your employees at a pay rate at least equivalent to the National Minimum Wage (see Appendix 1) and keep records to prove that you have done so. The applicable rate which is enforced by HM Revenue and Customs varies according to whether the worker is an adult, trainee apprentice or young person. The National Minimum Wage legislation applies to all employees including agency staff, piece workers, employees with disabilities and those paid by commission. It does not however apply to the following people:

- ▶ *Those who are self-employed;*
- ▶ *Company directors unless they have an employment contract; and*
- ▶ *Family members who live in the same household and work in a business together.*

Calculating whether an employee's gross pay (before deducting tax and National Insurance) meets the National Minimum Wage is not always straightforward particularly if the employee is paid bonuses, commission, tips, overtime and perks. For

further information about the National Minimum Wage refer to
www.hmrc.gov.uk/nmw/.

WHAT IS AN EMPLOYEE'S PAY?

Employees' pay consists of their salary or wages plus overtime,
holiday pay, commission and bonuses. This pay before deductions
are taken off is known as 'gross pay' and is the sum used to
calculate PAYE and National Insurance. Tips and other amounts
paid through the payroll are also treated as gross pay and so are
statutory sick pay and statutory maternity, paternity and adoption
pay. If you reward staff with assets such as commodities and shares
these also count as taxable income unless the shares are part of an
approved share scheme (see Chapter 11). Most perks and benefits
are taxed (see Taxing perks). Sometimes they are treated as gross
pay but in most cases the employee's tax code is altered to take the
benefit into account (see Understanding tax codes).

Insight

It may be tempting to pay staff a set amount of net pay rather
than gross pay. Such arrangements should be avoided as
employees' tax codes change for reasons beyond your control
which could leave either you or your member of staff out of
pocket (see Understanding tax codes).

NATIONAL INSURANCE NUMBERS

All your employees must provide you with a National Insurance
(NI) number. A valid NI number consist of two letters, followed
by six numbers, followed by one letter either A, B, C or D.
Temporary NI numbers with the pre-fix TN and based on the
employee's date of birth and gender (F for female and M for
male) are not acceptable. If an employee does not have a National
Insurance number, they should apply to their local Jobcentre
Plus office for one. If a NI number has been lost, HMRC will
be able to trace it upon submission of form CA 6855; see
www.hmrc.gov.uk/forms/ca6855.pdf.

Taxing employees

If you have employees you must operate a PAYE scheme so that you can deduct income tax, National Insurance and student loan repayments correctly and pay them statutory sick pay and statutory maternity, paternity and adoption pay when appropriate.

OBTAINING A PAYE SCHEME

PAYE schemes are obtained from HM Revenue and Customs either online on www.hmrc.gov.uk/employers/new-emp-email.htm or by contacting the New Employers' Helpline on 0845 60 70 143. They will send you a starter pack, may suggest that you attend a workshop or offer you a face-to-face meeting with a business support adviser. There are many payroll packages available but you should choose one which is approved by HMRC. Almost all employers must now file their returns online.

For further details see 'Do it online: Small employers guide to filing PAYE returns' www.hmrc.gov.uk/employers/onlineguide_ smallemp.htm, 'Understanding and using PAYE online for employers' www.hmrc.gov.uk/paye/onlinefiling-understanding.htm and 'Register for PAYE Online' www.hmrc.gov.uk/paye/ file-or-pay/fileonline/register.htm.

Insight

In spite of the help available from the tax authorities many small businesses decide that it is more time-saving and cost-effective to use an agency to run their payroll for them.

RUNNING A PAYE SCHEME

Once you have set up your PAYE scheme you need to learn how to pay and tax your employees. The basic steps are set out in the following Guide to operating a PAYE scheme.

Guide to operating a PAYE scheme

▶ *Each time you pay an employee, the payment falls into a designated month (for monthly-paid staff) or week (for weekly-paid employees).*

▶ *Every employee has a tax code (see Understanding tax codes). The code is used in conjunction with PAYE tables (which form part of your computer software) to calculate their income tax deduction (or refund) for the month or week in question.*

▶ *National Insurance tables (again part of your payroll software) are used to calculate the Class 1 employee's deduction and your employer's contribution monthly or weekly.*

▶ *Additional tables (incorporated in the computer software) are used to calculate statutory additions such as SSP, SMP, SPP and SAP (see Statutory pay) plus student loan repayments.*

▶ *Each employee's gross pay, statutory additions, deductions for PAYE, National Insurance and student loans are recorded on an individual form P11 (usually computer-generated). The cumulative pay and PAYE are shown along with the employee's tax coding and National Insurance number.*

▶ *Every time that an employee is paid, he or she is given a payslip summarizing the details on the form P11, their net pay and any other employer-specific adjustments such as season-ticket loan repayments and pensions.*

▶ *At the end of the month you have to pay HMRC the amounts deducted from your employees' wages plus your employer's National Insurance contributions less any sums paid out for statutory sick pay, maternity pay etc. Employers whose average monthly payments are less than £1,500 have the option of paying over their PAYE and National Insurance quarterly. The payment dates for both monthly and quarterly options are set out in Appendix 2.*

▶ *After the end of the tax year you must give your employees a form P60 summarizing their pay and tax. Staff receiving perks must receive a form P11D (sometimes a form P9D). You also have to complete an end of year return (form P35) reconciling the amounts that you have paid to HMRC with the details entered on the forms P60 (HMRC's copies of these forms are called P14s). The dates for completion and delivery of these forms are provided in Appendix 2.*

Further information: HMRC's 'Paying someone for the first time', www.hmrc.gov.uk/forms/p49.pdf.

Taking on a member of staff

When a new member of staff joins your business in addition to complying with employment law matters such as checking that they are legally entitled to work in the UK, you need to process their form P45 or issue them with a form P46.

FORMS P45 AND P46

▶ *First you should ask them for parts 2 and 3 of the form P45. This will have been given to them by their previous employer.*

▶ *Next you should check the P45 (see 'Taking on a new employee' on www.hmrc.gov.uk/paye/employees/start-leave/ new-employee.htm). If the P45 was issued in the current tax year and the details are correct use them (including the tax code) to complete a deductions working sheet (form P11) for the employee.*

▶ *Then send part 3 of the P45 to HMRC to notify them that the person is now employed by you. If the appropriate box on the form is marked you should continue to deduct student loan repayments.*

▶ *If the employee does not have a form P45, ask them to complete a form P46 and send it to HMRC. The employee will be taxed according to which statement they have ticked on the form (see Understanding tax codes) until such time as HMRC advises you to use a new tax code.*

▶ *In all cases you must check that the employee's National Insurance number appears to be valid (see National Insurance numbers).*

▶ *If the employee is entitled to a company car notify HMRC using form P46 (Car).*

If you take on an employee for less than one week special rules apply.

FORMS

In addition to handling forms P45 and P46 there are various other payroll forms that you may will across. These may be generated by your payroll software, downloaded from HMRC's website or sent to you by HMRC. They are summarized in the following table.

Form	Description
P9	Notification of an employee's new tax code sent to you by HMRC. Individual changes are notified on form P9T. Those for all other employees on form P9X.
P9D	Summarizes perks and benefits received by employees earning less than £8,500 a year. You complete it after the end of the tax year.
P11	Deductions working sheet for an employee recording their details for the tax year (including pay, PAYE and National Insurance).
P11D	Summarizes an employee's perks and benefits in kind. You complete it after the end of the tax year.
P11D(b)	Return of employer's Class 1A National Insurance contributions due on benefits in kind completed after the year end.
P14	End of year summary of an employee's pay and deductions for the tax year. It is sent to HMRC with the end of year return (see also P60).
P32	Employer's payment record, recording sums paid over each month to HMRC.
P35	Employer's end of year return.
P38A	Supplementary form to the P35 for employees paid without the deduction of tax and National Insurance.
P38(S)	Supplementary form to the P35 recording students' income where the student only works for you in vacations and where earnings are less than the personal allowance.

(Contd)

Form	Description
P45	Certificate given to an employee when they leave employment. Parts 2 and 3 of the form are given to you when a new employee starts work.
P46	Completed by a new employee who does not have a form P45 (for example because they were previously self-employed).
P46 (Car)	Form to notify HMRC that an employee or director has a company car.
P60	End of year summary of pay and deductions for the tax year given to an employee (see also P14).

Deductions

Having looked in outline at the operation of a PAYE scheme, we now consider each of the deductions you have to make from gross pay. These are:

- ▶ *PAYE;*
- ▶ *National Insurance; and*
- ▶ *Student loan repayments.*

All sums that you deduct are paid over to HM Revenue and Customs monthly (occasionally quarterly) together with employer's National Insurance (see Employer's National Insurance). Any statutory payments you have to make can be deducted in full or part from your payment (see Statutory pay).

PAYE

PAYE is the means of deducting income tax from an employee's gross pay by using a combination of a tax code, free pay and taxable pay tables (incorporated into payroll software). The taxable pay tables apply the various income tax rates (see Appendix 1) to the employee's pay after adjusting it for his or her personal allowance and all the other items included in their tax code (free pay).

Understanding tax codes

An employee's tax code is an integral part of the PAYE system. Many employees will have the same tax code but you will find that some employees have different tax codes. You will only be told the number you must use and not the composition of coding because this is confidential to the employee.

Tax codes may include the following items:

▶ *The employee's personal allowance (see Appendix 1);* plus
▶ *Any tax-deductible expenses;* plus
▶ *Higher or additional rate tax relief for gift aid payments and pensions;* less
▶ *Tax owed for a previous tax year (as long as it is less than £2,000);* less
▶ *Sums to tax perks;* less
▶ *Adjustments to collect tax on other sources of income such as investment and property income.*

A typical tax code for 2010/11 is 647L. This is also known as the 'emergency tax code' if it is applied on a 'week 1' or 'month 1' basis ignoring all previous pay and tax in the year.

▶ *647 stands for the basic personal allowance (tax-free pay) of £6,475.*
▶ *L refers to the fact that the code contains the basic personal allowance. The letter is for administration purposes and does not affect the calculation of the coding.*

You may notice that some tax codes include other letters. This is what they mean:

▶ **K** *at the start – is used to add an amount to an employee's pay because their deductions are more than their allowances. This would be the case where the employee has significant benefits* *in kind such as a company car or a tax underpayment from an earlier year. The tax deducted under a K code is restricted to no more than 50% of the employee's pay.*

▶ **P** *or* **Y** *at the end – shows full personal allowances for those aged over 65 (see Appendix 1).*

▶ **T** *at the end – is used if there are any items HMRC needs to review. It does not mean 'temporary code'.*

BR and Do codes are usually used where the employee has a second source of income and all their tax allowances have been included in a notice of coding applied to the first source of income. BR means basic rate tax; Do means higher rate tax (see Appendix 1). NT means that no tax is to be deducted.

Tax codes can be cumulative or they can be calculated by reference to the week or month for which pay is operated. This is denoted by the P45 being marked 'week 1' or 'month 1' or you being instructed by HMRC to apply the tax code in this way.

HMRC's website includes an online pay adjustment calculator at www.hmrc.gov.uk/employers/calc_pay_adjust.htm which provides an indication of an employee's tax-free pay, or the addition to it if a K code applies.

Operating tax codes
You will obtain information about an employee's tax codes from the following sources:

▶ *Form P45 – for new employees. Provided that the form is for the same tax year you should use the same tax code as the previous employer taking care to operate the coding either cumulatively or on a week 1 or month 1 basis.*

▶ *Form P46 – for new employees without a form P45. Depending on which statement your employee ticks, you must choose which tax code to operate, see www.hmrc.gov.uk/paye/employees/ start-leave/new-employee.htm.*

▶ *P9 – sent by HMRC notifying you of a new tax code for your employee.*

> ▶ *Annual increase – most tax codes apart from BR and D0*
> *change in May each year to reflect the annual increase in*
> *personal allowances. You will be sent a notice on form P9X*
> *instructing you to increase all employees' codes of a certain*
> *type to a new figure.*

EMPLOYEE'S NATIONAL INSURANCE

An employee's National Insurance contributions are calculated by
reference to two main factors:

- ▶ *Whether they are contracted into or out of the state second*
  pension (S2P); and
- ▶ *The level of their earnings.*

For the applicable rates see Appendix 1. National Insurance tables
to work out the appropriate contributions are incorporated in your
payroll software and are available from HMRC.

When an employee's income exceeds the employee's threshold
(ET, see Appendix 1), most employees have to pay National
Insurance contributions (see Chapter 1 for details of those who
do not). Where an employee's earnings exceed the upper earnings
limit (UEL) they pay additional contributions at the rate set out in
Appendix 1 on those earnings above the UEL. The lower earnings
limit (LEL) is the minimum level of earnings that an employee
needs to qualify for state benefits such as retirement pension and
jobseeker's allowance. If an employee's earnings reach or exceed
the LEL, but do not exceed the employee's threshold (ET), they will
not pay any National Insurance contributions. They will however
be treated as having paid them when claiming state benefits.

....
Insight
Understanding how employee's National Insurance works
may help small family businesses to set appropriate pay rates
for family members working in the business. This will enable
them to qualify for benefits without incurring the cost of
employee's (or employer's) contributions.
....

When setting pay rates for other workers the National Minimum Wage will apply (see Paying employees – National Minimum Wage).

Case study

Ray is 19, lives at home with his family and works in his father's import/export business. In 2010/11 he earns £109 per week. This is above the lower earnings limit of £97 per week but below the earnings threshold of £110 per week. As a result he pays no employee's National Insurance but still qualifies for state retirement pension and jobseeker's allowance should he need to claim it. Furthermore his father as his employer does not have to pay employer's contributions. He must however keep records of the sums paid to his son as he would do for any other employee. If this is Ray's only source of income he will not pay any income tax under PAYE as it falls below his personal allowance. As he lives at home with his family and works in a family business the National Minimum Wage rules do not apply to him.

STUDENT LOAN REPAYMENTS

HM Revenue and Customs is responsible for collecting repayments of loans made to students by the Student Loans Company. You must deduct repayments from employees earning in excess of the repayment figure set out in Appendix 1 each pay day using the loan deduction tables (usually incorporated into your payroll software). The sums deducted will be paid over to HMRC once a month along with your PAYE and National Insurance.

Further information: Employer's Help Book, E17, 'Collection of Student Loans', www.hmrc.gov.uk/helpsheets/e17.pdf.

Statutory pay

Employers are not just responsible for deducting sums from their employees. There are four occasions when they must give them statutory payments. These are:

- *Statutory Sick Pay (SSP);*
- *Statutory Maternity Pay (SMP);*
- *Statutory Paternity Pay (SPP); and*
- *Statutory Adoption Pay (SAP).*

Any statutory payments you make are deducted (in full or part) from the amounts you have to pay over to HM Revenue and Customs for PAYE, National Insurance and student loan repayments. If you pay employees additional sums over the statutory minimum these amounts cannot be recovered from HMRC.

STATUTORY SICK PAY (SSP)

SSP is paid to employees who are unable to attend work because they are sick or incapacitated and who have average weekly earnings above a certain threshold (see Appendix 1). It is paid for up to a maximum of 28 weeks.

You must pay a sick employee SSP if they are sick for at least four or more days in a row including weekends and bank holidays (this is known as a period of incapacity for work) as long as they have provided you with appropriate evidence of their indisposition. Employees can self-certify periods of sickness of up to seven days.

Calculating SSP can be complicated and you will need to complete additional forms to record the sums paid. The calculations and forms are usually produced by your payroll software. Alternatively, HMRC have an SSP calculator on their website; see www.hmrc.gov.uk/calcs/ssp.htm.

You can claim back any SSP you have paid over and above a certain percentage of your National Insurance liability for the same tax month in which you pay SSP (see Appendix 1).

Example
Amy pays Class 1 National Insurance before deductions of £1,310.35 in November 2010. She pays total SSP paid in that month to two sick employees of £237.45.

Her recovery percentage is 13% of £1,310.35 = £170.34.

As the total SSP paid (£237.45) is more than the 13% recovery percentage (£170.34) by £67.11 Amy can deduct £67.11 from her National Insurance. Amy should now pay Class 1 National Insurance of £1,243.24 (£1,310.35 – £67.11) to HMRC for November 2010. She has to bear £170.34 of the cost of the SSP herself (£237.45 – £67.11) plus the cost of any sums she pays her staff over and above the statutory minimum.

Insight

Small employers may experience financial difficulties if employees are off work sick as the business may owe no PAYE, National Insurance or student loan repayments against which to off-set the SSP. In such situations you can ask HMRC to repay the SSP you have incurred.

Further information: See 'Employer Helpbook for Statutory Sick Pay' E14 on www.hmrc.gov.uk/helpsheets/e14.pdf.

STATUTORY MATERNITY PAY (SMP)

SMP is paid to pregnant female employees who have average weekly earnings above a certain threshold (see Appendix 1). It is paid for up to a maximum of 39 weeks. Most mothers are also entitled to a further 13 weeks of unpaid leave making a year in total.

You must pay an employee SMP if she has been employed by you without a break for at least 26 weeks into the 15th week before the week in which the baby is due. She must give you written evidence of her pregnancy on certificate MAT B1. The earliest that SMP can start is the 11th week before the week in which the baby is due.

There are many detailed rules concerning the payment of SMP and you will need to complete forms to record the sums paid. Once again these will usually be produced by your payroll software. HMRC also have an SMP calculator on their website; see www.hmrc.gov.uk/calcs/smp.htm.

The amount of SMP that you can recover from HM Revenue and Customs depends on how much National Insurance you pay them. If your National Insurance bill before deductions for the last complete tax year ending immediately before the 15th week before the baby is due was £45,000 or less you are entitled to claim 100% of the SMP you pay plus compensation at the rate of 4.5%. If your annual National Insurance is more than £45,000 you can only claim back 92% of the SMP and you receive no compensation (see Appendix 1). If your contributions are around the £45,000 threshold, HMRC will assist you to calculate your recovery rate. If you pay your employees on maternity leave more than the statutory minimum you cannot recover the excess.

If you only have a small workforce and have insufficient PAYE, National Insurance and student loan repayments to off-set your SMP payments against, HMRC will refund you the payments at the end of each month if you apply to them in writing.

Further information: See 'Employer Helpbook for Statutory Maternity Pay' E15 on www.hmrc.gov.uk/helpsheets/e15.pdf.

STATUTORY PATERNITY PAY (SPP)

SPP is paid to employees of either sex whose spouse or partner gives birth to or adopts a child, provided that they have earnings above a certain threshold (see Appendix 1). It is paid for up to two weeks which must be taken either as one week or one two-week period. It cannot be taken for two separate weeks or as odd days and it must be taken within 56 days of the date of the baby's birth or the date an adopted child is placed with the adopter (unless the baby is premature). You must pay an employee SPP if the employee has been employed by you without a break for at least 26 weeks into the 15th week before the week in which the baby is due or placed. The earliest that SPP can start is the date of the birth.

The parents of children born on or after 3 April 2011 and the adoptive parents of children matched after that date are entitled to up to six months additional paternity leave (some of it paid) if the child's mother (or in the case of adoptions the primary adopter) returns to work without exercising their full entitlement to maternity leave and the child is over 20 weeks old (or an adopted child has been with its adoptive parents for 20 weeks).

There are detailed rules regarding the operation of SPP and once again you will need to complete forms recording the payments. The procedures for recovering SPP are the same as SMP (see Statutory Maternity Pay).

Further information: See 'Employer Helpbook for Statutory Paternity Pay' E19 on www.hmrc.gov.uk/helpsheets/e19.pdf.

STATUTORY ADOPTION PAY (SAP)

SAP is paid to employees (female or male) who are adopting a child (from the UK or abroad) provided that they have earnings above a certain threshold (see Appendix 1). It is paid for up to 39 weeks but the employee may be entitled to a further 13 weeks unpaid leave. The male or female partner of such an employee eligible for SAP may be entitled to Statutory Paternity Pay.

You must pay an employee SAP if they have been employed by you without a break for at least 26 weeks into the week in which the adopter found out from the adoption agency that they had been matched with a child. The earliest that SAP can start is 14 days before the placement. In the event that the employee adopts more than one child only one period of SAP is permitted. Entitlement remains if the placement is disrupted after it has started, or if the child dies after placement with the family.

There are detailed rules regarding the operation of SAP and again forms recording the payments must be completed. The procedures for recovering SAP are the same as SMP (see Statutory Maternity Pay).

Further information: See Employer Helpbook for Statutory Adoption Pay E16 on www.hmrc.gov.uk/helpsheets/e16.pdf.

Employer's National Insurance

In addition to making deductions from their employee's wages and paying them any statutory entitlements, you also have to pay employer's Class 1 National Insurance (see Appendix 1). This adds significantly to the cost of employing staff and when budgeting for employment costs it must not be overlooked.

Example

Mona runs a delivery business. She employs two members of staff (Jeff and Ken). Jeff earns £1,000 per month and Ken £800 per month. Assuming that their personal allowances are used elsewhere, the income tax rate is 20% and the employee's National Insurance rate is 11%, she makes the following deductions from their wages paying them net pay of £690 and £552 respectively. If the employer's National Insurance rate is 12.8%, Mona's total employment costs are £2,030 not £1,800 per month – £2,760 a year more than she may have been expecting.

Per month	Jeff	Ken	Total
Staff receive:	£	£	£
Wages	1,000	800	1,800
Less: PAYE	−200	−160	−360
Less: Employee's National Insurance	−110	−88	−198
Net pay	**690**	**552**	**1,242**
Mona's costs:			
Net pay	690	552	1,242
Employee's deductions paid to HMRC (PAYE + Employee's National Insurance)	310	248	558
	1,000	**800**	**1,800**
Employer's Class 1 paid to HMRC	128	102	230
Total cost of employing staff	**1,128**	**902**	**2,030**

(Contd)

Per month	Jeff	Ken	Total
Mona pays each month:			
Net pay to Jeff and Ken	690	552	1,242
PAYE and National Insurance to HMRC	438	350	788
Total monthly payments	**1,128**	**902**	**2,030**

Insight

New businesses in certain deprived areas of the country do not have to pay:

▶ *the first £5,000 of employer's Class 1 National Insurance;*
▶ *in respect of the first ten employees;*
▶ *hired in the first year of the business;*
▶ *during the first twelve weeks of their employment.*

In addition to paying Class 1 National Insurance employers also have to pay Class 1A and Class 1B contributions on most perks, benefits in kind and miscellaneous staff payments (see Taxing perks).

Taxing perks

Employers sometimes provide members of staff with perks or benefits in kind instead of pay. If you are a company director you may also be interested in rewarding yourself with a few perks and be wondering how they are taxed. Any reference to 'employee' includes directors. Although perks are more common in larger businesses, many small employers provide their staff with company cars, vans and private medical insurance (see Chapter 10). Others may inadvertently stray into the benefits in kind regime when reimbursing employees' expenses or providing them with a credit card.

Most employees (unless they earn less than £8,500 a year including the value of the perk) are liable to pay income tax on any benefits in kind you provide them with, although some perks are tax-free (see Tax-efficient perks).

Before providing any employee with remuneration other than
their salary you should consider the tax, National Insurance
and administrative implications. It may be simpler and more
cost-effective to give your employee a pay rise.

Tax on benefits in kind is usually collected by adjusting an
employee's tax code. At the end of each tax year you have to report
all benefits in kind (including reimbursed expenses unless there is a
dispensation in force) to HM Revenue and Customs on form P11D
(occasionally P9D). Copies of these forms must be provided to
your employees.

One of the most important things to remember is that if an employee
perk is taxed, you usually have to pay Class 1A National Insurance
on top which adds significantly to the cost. As this is collected as a
lump sum after the end of the tax year, it is easy to overlook when
calculating the cost of providing your employees with a benefit in kind.

If you provide employees with perks that cannot easily be divided
between them (such as free on-site chiropody) or provide occasional
gifts (for example flowers for a sick employee), the tax and Class 1B
National Insurance can be paid by you under a PAYE Settlement
Agreement (PSA) without involving the employees concerned.

If you reimburse staff expenses, give them credit cards or provide
minor items such as uniforms you should negotiate a 'dispensation'
with HM Revenue and Customs to cover these costs. Once
negotiated not only do you no longer have to report the details
on form P11D but no Class 1A National Insurance is due (see
Applying for a dispensation).

Each different kind of perk that you provide to your employees
has its own tax rules. The following sections outline the principal
benefits in kind that a small business might be interested in
providing to its staff. As there are many detailed rules which affect
each benefit in kind, if you want to provide a perk to a member
of staff you should read more widely on the subject or seek
professional advice. HMRC's website contains an alphabetized

guide to the tax and National Insurance treatment of each
benefit in kind and the entries to be made on the form P11D;
see www.hmrc.gov.uk/paye/exb/a-z/a/index.htm.

CARS

Cars are the most popular perk but many are highly taxed. Income
tax is calculated on the vehicle as a percentage of the car's original
list price even if you acquire it second-hand. The relevant percentage
is assessed according to the level of its carbon dioxide (CO_2)
emissions, with cleaner cars taxed more favourably (see Appendix 1).
No charge applies to electric cars for a five-year period from
6 April 2010. Classic cars and those registered before 1 January
1998 are subject to special provisions. There are many detailed rules
which govern the operation of the car benefits regime and you may
need to take advice. You must inform HMRC about any employee
who has a new company car by completing form P46 (Car).

Example
Liam provides his employee Melanie with a company car costing
£15,000. It has CO_2 emissions of 150 grams per kilometre, so in
2011/12 the relevant percentage is 20%. Her scale charge is calculated
as £15,000 × 20% = £3,000 (see Appendix 1). If Melanie is a basic
rate taxpayer the company car will cost her £600 (£3,000 × 20%)
in tax each year. Her tax code will be adjusted to include the scale
charge so she pays the tax on it in monthly instalments through the
PAYE system. If Melanie is provided with additional accessories
for her car she will pay extra tax. Liam will pay Class 1A National
Insurance on the car of £414 (£3,000 × 13.8%) in a lump sum after
the end of the tax year (see Appendix 2).

HM Revenue and Customs website contains a company car and
car fuel calculator on www.hmrc.gov.uk/calcs/cars.htm.

Insight
In some cases it may be more tax-effective for your employee
to buy their own car and for you to reimburse them tax-free
business mileage at the authorized rate (see Appendix 1).

Free fuel

Providing your employees with free fuel for private journeys attracts a further benefit in kind charge. This is based on a sum set each year by HMRC multiplied by the car's CO_2 percentage (see Appendix 1). In many cases this perk is not worthwhile providing; it depends on how many private miles your employee drives.

Authorized mileage

It is more usual for employers to reimburse their employees for their business journeys. Provided that the payment does not exceed the authorized rate (see Appendix 1), the payment is free of income tax and National Insurance. Your employee should compile a record of their business mileage to justify the claim which you should keep with your payroll records.

VANS

If your employee is a van driver and you let them use the vehicle privately they will pay income tax and you will pay Class 1A National Insurance. The annual tax charge could amount to £710 (£3,000 + £550 = £3,550 × 20%) for a basic rate tax payer in 2011/12 and employer's National Insurance to £489.90 (£3,550 × 13.8%) if fuel for private journeys is also provided (see Appendix 1). No charge applies to electric vans for a five-year period from 6 April 2010. Pool vans are also tax free. If two employees share a van the tax charge is reduced.

Another way round this tax charge is to restrict your employee's private use of the van to travel between home and work and vice versa (ordinary commuting). This means that there are then no tax implications if your employee takes the van home overnight. Insignificant private use is permitted without triggering a charge (for example using the van in an emergency or for an occasional short journey). HM Revenue and Customs will look closely at the arrangements you have with staff that drive vans and they may question their private use unless your paperwork is in good order. Two further points to note are firstly that the ordinary commuting rule does not apply to cars and secondly that defining a van is not always straightforward. Some vans are cars and some are heavy goods vehicles and in each case different rules apply.

Insight

You should make it an employment condition that your employees cannot drive non-electric vans on private journeys unless they reimburse you for the full cost – and you must enforce this policy. This should result in there being no income tax or National Insurance liability.

TRAVEL AND SUBSISTENCE

Reimbursing your employees for necessary business travel does not attract a tax charge provided that the journey is not home to work travel (ordinary commuting). The definition of ordinary commuting is complex particularly if your employee works somewhere else temporarily or is site-based. In this case you may need to consult an accountant to ensure that you complete your end of year returns correctly. For further information see 'Employee travel: A tax and NIC's guide for employers', on www.hmrc.gov.uk/helpsheets/490.pdf.

If an employee needs to stay away from home for business reasons reimbursing their hotel bills and the cost of modest meals should not attract a tax charge in most cases. In addition you can pay employees who stay away from home overnight for work reasons up to £5 per night tax-free for personal incidental expenses (£10 if they are working abroad). Payments above this amount are fully taxable. It is usual to agree a dispensation with HM Revenue and Customs for such payments for staff that travel regularly (see Applying for a dispensation). Your business records should distinguish between subsistence payments and entertaining because subsistence expenditure is tax-deductible whereas entertaining expenditure is not (see Chapter 4: Expenses).

EXPENSE CLAIMS

Reimbursing business expenses incurred by your staff (and yourself if you are a company director) is another area where it is possible to inadvertently get into difficulties. You should only reimburse legitimate business expenses for which you have receipts. Round sums, floats or advances could be subject to tax and National Insurance. The best way to avoid problems with your employee's expense claims is to apply for a dispensation.

Applying for a dispensation

A dispensation is a written agreement from HM Revenue and Customs that relieves you from reporting expenses payments and benefits in kind on form P11D where the tax authorities are satisfied that no tax is payable on them. If you have a dispensation a further benefit is that the payments do not count as earnings for National Insurance purposes which may save you a considerable sum.

Expenses typically included in a dispensation are travel, hotel and subsistence expenses (but not business mileage payments) and amounts incurred 'wholly, exclusively and necessarily' in the performance of the duties of the employment such as business entertaining and reimbursements for buying stationery and other sundry items. The dispensation can cover reimbursement made by any means including business expenses paid for by a company credit card. If an employee or director uses a company credit card to buy personal items, this expenditure is either a taxable perk or is treated as income.

Any employer can apply for a dispensation using the form P11DX at www.hmrc.gov.uk/forms/p11dx.pdf or the online version provided that:

▶ *the expenses are not taxable; and*
▶ *the expense claims are independently checked and authorized within the firm and where possible supported by receipts.*

Insight

If you trade as a one-person company you can usually obtain a dispensation provided that the expenses are supported by adequate documentation. HMRC will review your dispensation periodically usually as part of a PAYE inspection.

Tax-efficient perks

There are a number of benefits that you can provide to your staff (including directors and family members) that do not attract a tax or National Insurance charge. These are set out in the table below. Even though the perk listed is not taxable, you should still keep records of the payments to demonstrate to HM Revenue and Customs that any conditions applicable to the provision of the benefit are met.

Table of tax-efficient perks

Perk	Comments
Private use of office equipment including computers and personal digital assistants such as a 'Blackberry'. Facilities for employees with special needs.	The equipment must be primarily provided for work purposes and the private use must be 'insignificant'.
Provision of one mobile phone.	A second phone is taxable. The tax treatment of landline phones depends on the nature of the contract with the supplier.
Contribution towards the extra costs of working from home.	Up to £3 per week if the employee works at home under a home-working agreement.
Office parties.	Not exceeding £150 per head per tax year.
Canteen meals.	In a canteen open to all your staff as long as the arrangements are not part of a salary sacrifice scheme.
Electric cars and vans	For five years from 6 April 2010.

Perk	Comments
Authorized mileage payment for business journeys by car, motorbike and bike and for extra passengers.	Not exceeding the rates in Appendix 1.
Bikes, related safety equipment and cyclists breakfasts on cycle to work days.	Provided primarily for work journeys.
Some works bus services.	Mainly for journeys between home and work.
Travel facilities for employees with disabilities.	Between home and work.
Parking spaces at or near work.	For all vehicles including bikes.
One medical check-up or health screening per year, eye tests for employees using computers, insurance for overseas travel and medical costs incurred whilst travelling abroad.	Medical insurance or treatment in the UK is taxable.
Welfare counselling, for example on redundancy.	Excluding legal and financial advice (but see Pensions).
Pensions and pension advice.	Worth up to £150 per year (see Chapter 10).
Work-related training.	Including retraining if made redundant.
University scholarships.	A set sum per academic year.
Childcare.	See Childcare (below).
Sporting and recreational facilities.	In facilities not available to the general public.
Personal gifts – for example if an employee gets married.	Where the employee is an individual.

(Contd)

Perk	Comments
Long service awards.	For those with 20 years of service or more, up to £50 per year worked.
Cheap or interest-free loans.	Up to £5,000.
Relocation costs.	Up to £8,000.
Security facilities.	Where there is a threat to the employee's physical security or safety because of the job.
Directors' and employees' liability insurance.	See Chapter 10.

Insight

Even though a particular perk is tax efficient, as a small employer you may decide that the administrative effort involved in providing the benefit in kind does not make it commercial for your business to do so.

CHILDCARE

If an employer provides a workplace nursery for the children of its employees the places are tax-free. Whilst not many small employers are likely to set up their own childcare facility, you can provide your employees with up to £55 per week in tax-free childcare payments or vouchers. From 6 April 2011 the tax relief on childcare vouchers will be restricted to the basic rate of tax. Whilst providing childcare vouchers seems on the face of it to be a good perk for certain employees they can reduce the value of your Child and Working Tax Credits so may not be suitable for all members of staff with children. To check the suitability of this perk use the online calculator on www.hmrc.gov.uk/calcs/ccin.htm.

Construction industry

If you are a contractor or sub-contractor in the construction industry you are affected by special tax rules known as the Construction Industry Scheme (CIS). Even if your business is not in the construction industry you may be affected by CIS because a 'contractor' includes any business undertaking construction work of more than £1 million per year.

CONTRACTORS

Contractors must register with HM Revenue and Customs and ensure that any sub-contractor working for them is not really an employee by following the guidance set out www.hmrc.gov.uk/cis/contract-or-sub.htm. The contractor's monthly return (CIS 300) requires a signed declaration confirming that none of your workers is an employee. You can be charged a penalty for making a false declaration, so it is important to determine the employment status of your workers correctly. If you are unsure about whether someone working for you is yo ur employee or a subcontractor you may need help from an accountant. You could also use HMRC's employment status indicator tool on www.hmrc.gov.uk/calcs/esi.htm or read the guidance at www.hmrc.gov.uk/employment-status/index.htm. If your worker is an employee, they should be taxed under PAYE. For details of your obligations in this circumstance see 'Paying employees'.

If your worker is a sub-contractor who has not worked for you in the current tax year or either of the two previous tax years, you need to confirm with HMRC that they are registered with the tax authorities. HMRC will tell you whether you must pay the sub-contractor after making a tax deduction from the payment (see Appendix 1 for the rates) or whether you can pay them gross (this means that you do not have to deduct any tax). You can 'verify' a subcontractor's status online or by calling the CIS Helpline on 0845 366 7899.

Monthly, you must give your sub-contractors a written statement showing your contractor details, the amount of the payment and the amount of tax deducted by the 19th of the following month. You must also complete form CIS 300 detailing the payments made to all your sub-contractors and tax deducted from them and send it to HMRC. The tax deducted must be paid over to the tax authorities and reconciled at the end of the tax year. HMRC prefer contractors to use the online filing service. Contractors are obliged to keep sub-contractor payment records for at least three years. For further details see www.hmrc.gov.uk/cis/con-reg-obs.htm.

SUB-CONTRACTORS

If you are a sub-contractor in the construction industry you should register with the tax authorities by calling the CIS Helpline on 0845 366 7899. If you do not register, your contractor will deduct tax at a higher rate from your payments (see Appendix 1).

Once you are registered you will receive payments with tax deducted at source at the standard rate but no deduction should be made from amounts shown on your invoice for materials, supplies, plant hire, VAT or levies.

At the end of the tax year the tax deducted at source will be set against the tax you owe on the profit made by your self-employment, partnership or limited company. If the tax deducted at source is more than your tax liability you will receive a tax refund. If the tax deducted at source is less than the tax you owe on your profits, you will settle the balance in the usual way under self-assessment.

Example
Sam works as a sub-contract carpenter. He invoices contractors £22,000 in 2010/11. Materials make up £2,000 of the total so no tax is deducted from this amount. Tax of £4,000 is therefore deducted at source. Sam prepares accounts to 5 April 2011. His allowable expenses including materials come to £3,500. He calculates his tax refund as follows:

Tax calculation 2010/11	£
Profits (£22,000 –£3,500)	18,500
Less: personal allowance	–6,475
	12,025
Tax at 20% (£12,025 × 20%)	2,405.00
Class 4 National Insurance (£18,500 – £5,715 = £12,785 × 8%)	1,022.80
Total tax and Class 4 National Insurance	**3,427.80**
Tax deducted by contractors	4,000.00
Tax refund due	**–572.20**

In some circumstances you can apply to the tax authorities to be paid gross (with no tax deductions). To qualify for gross payments you have to pass three strict tests.

▶ Business: *Your business must carry out construction work (or provide construction labour) in the UK and operate mainly through a bank account.*
▶ Turnover: *For the 12 months before you apply for gross payments your construction turnover (ignoring VAT and the cost of materials), must be at least £30,000 if you are a sole-trader, £30,000 per partner or director (for a partnership or limited company), or at least £200,000 for the whole partnership or company.*
▶ Compliance: *You and any directors or partners must have submitted your tax returns, supplied any information requested by the tax authorities and paid all your taxes on time in the year before your application. HMRC permits a few lapses, see www.hmrc.gov.uk/cis/advice-sub-pay.htm.*

10 THINGS TO REMEMBER

1 *If you have employees you must operate a PAYE scheme. You can do this yourself but there is a considerable amount of work involved in administering employees' salaries. You may find it more efficient to use a payroll agency.*

2 *Deciding whether a worker is your employee is not always straightforward. You may require expert advice particularly if you work in the construction industry.*

3 *If you are self-employed or a partner you are not employed by your business but if you are a company director you are taxed as an employee.*

4 *HM Revenue and Customs provide a wealth of information on their website to help employers; see www.hmrc.gov.uk/ employers/index.shtml.*

5 *All your employees must provide you with a valid National Insurance number. Remember that it is a criminal offence to employ workers that do not have the required permissions to work in the UK.*

6 *You must deduct PAYE, Employee's Class 1 National Insurance and in some cases student loan repayments from your employees' salaries and wages. You pay these sums over to HMRC along with Employer's Class 1 National Insurance. If you have made any statutory payments such as statutory sick pay, or statutory maternity, paternity and adoption pay, you are permitted to deduct these from your payment in certain circumstances.*

7 *Employer's Class 1 contributions have to be paid on top of each employee's pay unless you are entitled to relief because you are a new business in a deprived area. When budgeting for new staff, do not forget to take this cost into account and* *from 6 April 2011 note that the cost of employer's National Insurance rises from 12.8% to 13.8%.*

8 *Perks are taxed in a variety of ways depending on the nature of the benefit in kind. Most are liable to income tax and Class 1A National Insurance but some perks are tax-free.*

9 *Apply for a dispensation for staff expenses – it will make your paperwork easier and may save you Class 1A National Insurance.*

10 *HM Revenue and Customs visit all employers periodically to check that they are operating their PAYE schemes correctly so make sure that you keep your records in good order otherwise you may face a financial penalty.*

8

Premises

In this chapter:
- **working from home**
- **renting premises**
- **business rates and council tax**
- **buying and selling business property**

All small businesses need to operate from some form of premises. Many ventures progress from a spare room in the house (or even the garden shed) and move on to rented premises as the business expands. At some stage you may decide to purchase your own leasehold or freehold business premises and in turn these may be rented to a tenant or eventually sold. Each option has tax implications for your business. If you are thinking about investing substantial sums in property you should always take expert advice about the tax consequences.

Working from home

Increasing numbers of self-employed people work from home. Being home-based covers a wide range of possibilities from working on a corner of the dining room table to having a self-contained office. You can claim a tax deduction for some of your home costs but in doing so you must exercise care. There are many grey areas, little Revenue guidance and overlapping tax implications.

Before you claim any expenses you need to:

▶ *Note how much space your business occupies. You could calculate this based on the number of rooms in your home or in square metres.*
▶ *Ascertain whether the space your business takes up is used exclusively for work purposes (as might be the case with a purpose built garden office) or whether the room has mixed business and domestic use (such as a study which also doubles as a guest bedroom).*

Insight

If you operate your business through a limited company claiming a tax deduction for your home costs is difficult. You should seek professional advice before making a claim to avoid potentially costly errors.

RUNNING COSTS

In order to claim a tax deduction for home running costs that relate to the whole property you need to apportion the costs between those that relate to the business and those that are for your domestic use.

Costs relating to the building such as heat and light, council tax, water rates and rent can be apportioned based on the area used for business purposes. Landline telephone costs are better allocated using a call log and Internet connections can be based on your business as opposed to private use of the service. If you have a separate business phone line all the costs are tax-deductible (see Chapter 4). Home insurance covering your office or other business equipment could be allocated according to the value of the items insured.

Other home costs which may be tax-deductible include a proportion of security costs (such as alarm maintenance), cleaning (but be aware that a cleaner may be your employee – see Chapter 7) and repairs and renewals (such as redecorating).

Example

Jenny is a full-time freelance illustrator who has a home studio. She rents a two-bedroom flat with three other rooms so that she can work from home. Her rent is £650 per month (£7,800 a year) and her other home bills (utilities, council tax etc.) total £2,000 a year. Based on room numbers her studio represents one-fifth of rooms in the flat. Jenny works full-time so she claims one-fifth (or 20%) of her total domestic costs (£9,800). Her tax deduction is £1,960 (£9,800 × 20%).

As Jenny rents her flat she will have no problems with capital gains tax.

MORGAGE INTEREST

If you use part of your home exclusively for an unincorporated business a proportion of any mortgage interest may be tax-deductible. You cannot however claim a deduction for the capital repayments or payments into an endowment policy (see Chapter 10).

Insight

If you use a room in your home exclusively for business purposes and you claim a tax deduction for part of your mortgage interest you could incur a capital gains tax charge when you come to sell the property. You may also have to pay business rates.

USE OF HOME ALLOWANCE

If you are a self-employed homeowner one way to avoid the issue of capital gains tax is not to claim a tax deduction for a proportion of your mortgage interest and any domestic expenses but rather to claim a 'use of home allowance' instead. Deducting a set amount per week or month has no legal basis but a modest claim (a few pounds per week) should be acceptable. You should provide details of the amount deducted in the 'Any other information' box on your tax form. You may need to take advice from an accountant as to a suitable sum to claim.

BUSINESS RATES

If you use a room in your home exclusively for business purposes you may be liable to pay business rates in some situations. If you do you can deduct the whole cost as a business expense.

You are most likely to be liable to business rates if you have modified your home to accommodate your business. For example:

- ▶ *Converting a garage into an office;*
- ▶ *Turning a downstairs room into a surgery, practice room or office where members of the public come to see you;*
- ▶ *Modifying a driveway to accommodate clients' cars.*

Further information about business rates can be obtained from your local authority.

CAPITAL COSTS

The costs of altering, improving or expanding your home to enable you to work there is capital expenditure so no income tax deduction is permitted. Repairs are tax-deductible but as it can be difficult to distinguish 'repairs' from 'improvements' you may require advice if you are making a substantial claim for repairs in your accounts.

Insight

Even though capital expenditure is not deductible for income tax purposes, it can be deducted from a future capital gain, so you should keep a note of any conversion costs in case you make a capital gain when selling your home in the future.

SELLING A HOME YOU HAVE WORKED FROM

When you sell your home there is usually no capital gains tax to pay but if you have used any part of it exclusively for business purposes a capital gains tax charge could arise. You will be able to reduce the gain by deducting any capital costs relating to your business use. In the unlikely event that the sale is part of the disposal of your business as a going concern you may be entitled to entrepreneurs' relief (see Chapter 1). You may also be entitled to claim rollover relief (see Selling business property). Calculating the gain and any tax liability will probably necessitate professional help.

Renting premises

Renting business premises is the simplest option as far as tax consequences are concerned. You will be entitled to a tax deduction for all the premises costs you incur including:

- *Rent;*
- *Business rates;*
- *Water rates;*
- *Heat and power;*
- *Insurance;*
- *Security costs;*
- *Repairs;*
- *Legal and professional fees.*

If you rent business premises with a residential flat attached, for example if you live in a flat above a shop or a pub, you will need to apportion the expenses between the business premises on a sensible basis (such as floor area). You should provide details of how you have divided the expenses between business and private use in the 'Any other information' box on your tax return.

Buying business property

At some stage if your business expands you may decide to purchase freehold or leasehold premises (feu in Scotland). As purchasing property is an expensive decision, you will need expert advice to make sure that you understand all the tax consequences of the transaction.

STAMP DUTY LAND TAX

All purchases of commercial land and buildings costing more than £150,000 incur a stamp duty land tax (SDLT) charge at one of three rates depending on the purchase price (see Appendix 1). SDLT is charged on the whole purchase cost including VAT if it is charged.

Example

> Dave buys a freehold workshop for use in his joinery business which costs £200,000. He pays stamp duty land tax of £2,000 (£200,000 × 1%) (see Appendix 1). This cost is deductible from any capital gain arising when the premises are sold.

FINANCING THE PURCHASE

Most business people require a mortgage or loan, or the Islamic equivalent (known in the legislation as 'alternative finance') to purchase business premises as few can afford to buy it outright. There are two aspects to a mortgage and each is treated differently for tax purposes:

▶ Interest charged on the sum advanced. *The interest on the mortgage or loan is fully tax-deductible against your accounting profits. If you have taken an interest-only loan there is nothing further to consider.*
▶ Funding the mortgage repayment. *Many lending institutions require you to repay the sum you have borrowed over a set period of years through a repayment mortgage, endowment policy, pension or other means of saving such as an Individual Savings Account (ISA). Repaying the sum borrowed or saving to repay the mortgage is not a tax-deductible business expense as it is the repayment of a capital sum. Funding the repayments with a pension mortgage can be tax-effective for some people as the premiums attract tax relief (see Chapter 10).*

CAN I CLAIM TAX RELIEF ON MY PROPERTY PURCHASE?

As we have seen, you receive no tax relief when you repay money borrowed to finance the purchase of business premises as it is a capital transaction. The same rules apply to the purchase price of the property or a building's construction costs. In many cases there is no tax relief you can claim against your business profits for these costs (but see Allowances). You do however receive tax relief when you come to sell the property. At this time the amount you paid for the property reduces your capital gain (see Selling business premises).

Example
Shadi buys the freehold of a café for £230,000. She finances the purchase with a repayment mortgage and spends £30,000 having the building improved and converted to suit her business.

Shadi can deduct the interest on the repayment mortgage from her trading profits. She will not obtain any income tax relief for the mortgage repayments, the £230,000 purchase price or the £30,000 spent on alterations unless part of the expenditure qualities as an 'integral feature' (see Fixtures).

When Shadi comes to sell the property she will owe capital gains tax if she sells the café for more than she paid for it. She should keep records of the purchase price, the building work and the date of acquisition so that she can deduct these costs from the eventual sale proceeds, thereby reducing her capital gains tax liability (see Selling business property).

Capital allowances
Income tax and corporation tax relief is available on the purchase of property in the form of capital allowances in two circumstances:

▶ *The renovation of vacant owned or leased commercial premises in a disadvantaged area which has been empty for at least a year; and*
▶ *The conversion of unused space above a shop into a residential flat or flats.*

Business premises renovation allowances and flat conversion allowances reduce trading profits in a similar way to capital allowances on equipment (see Chapter 6). Both allowances are subject to many detailed conditions but should the project qualify, an initial allowance of up to 100% of the cost is given with a 25% writing down allowance if the initial allowance is not claimed in full.

Prior to 6 April 2008 there was a more extensive capital allowance regime for expenditure on certain industrial and agricultural buildings and hotels via industrial buildings allowances and agricultural buildings allowances. These reliefs are progressively phased out between 6 April 2008 and 5 April 2011. Buildings in designated enterprise zones could qualify for industrial buildings allowance but this relief is also withdrawn on 6 April 2011.

Fixtures
Expenditure on a feature integral to an industrial building used for a qualifying activity is eligible for an annual investment allowance (see Chapter 6). Where the expenditure exceeds the annual investment allowance threshold (see Appendix 1), it qualifies for a 10% writing down allowance. Integral features are systems for electricity, lighting, water, heating, ventilation, air cooling and purification and any related floor or ceiling, lifts, escalators and moving walkways, external solar shading and facades. When you buy an existing property the purchase price may need to be apportioned between the building and its fixtures so that you can make an appropriate claim.

LEASES

If you purchase leasehold business premises you are sometimes asked to pay an extra up-front payment known as a lease premium to the landlord or outgoing tenant. If the lease is for less than 50 years you may be able to claim a deduction against your trading profits for part of the premium each year.

Sometimes a landlord will persuade you to take a lease of business premises by paying you a lump sum. This is known as a reverse premium and is usually treated as your taxable income. As the terms of each lease are different you should seek professional advice to confirm the tax treatment.

VAT

VAT on the purchase of land and buildings is complicated and different rates of VAT apply to different types of property. New freehold commercial and industrial buildings and those which are less than three years old are liable to VAT at the standard rate (see Appendix 1). Land and the sale and lease of commercial buildings which are more than three years old are exempt from VAT unless the person selling the building has exercised an option to charge it.

> **Insight**
> VAT on commercial property can amount to a considerable sum, so before purchasing land or buildings for your business you need to find out whether VAT will be charged on the price and if so whether you can reclaim it in full or part.

Selling business property

At a future date you may decide to sell your business premises. This could be because you are moving to a new building or because you are disposing of the whole business (see Chapter 13). The most significant tax issue when you sell property used in your business is calculating your capital gains tax liability.

CAPITAL GAINS TAX

Sales of any business real estate can give rise to a capital gain if you sell the land or the building for more than you originally paid for it. If the sales proceeds are less than you paid to acquire the property you will have made a capital loss which can be deducted from any future capital gains you make (see Chapter 5: Capital losses). An Example showing a capital gain tax calculation on the disposal of shop premises is included in Chapter 1.

When working out the capital gain on the disposal of business premises there are two important points to remember:

▶ *If you trade as a limited company the gain will be reduced by indexation allowance. Capital gains tax is paid as part of the company's corporation tax liability.*
▶ *If you are a sole trader or a partner, you will only be able to claim entrepreneurs' relief if the sale is part of the disposal of all or part of your business as a going concern (see Chapter 1). Sales of assets in isolation do not qualify for this relief.*

DEFERRING YOUR CAPITAL GAIN

If selling your business premises has resulted in a capital gain you may be able to reduce it by deducting any capital losses you have made on the previous disposal of other assets (see Chapter 5). There are also two ways of deferring capital gains tax:

▶ Rollover relief. *You can claim this relief if you invest in another qualifying asset one year before the sale or up to three years afterwards. The new asset does not have to be used in the same business. You do not have to buy replacement land and buildings but this is the most likely investment you will make because the other qualifying assets are fixed plant and machinery, ships, aircraft, hovercraft, satellites, space stations and spacecraft, goodwill, milk and potato quotas, fish quota, farming payment entitlement under the single payment scheme and Lloyd's syndicate rights! If you trade as a limited company you cannot roll over your gain into goodwill or quotas.*
▶ Enterprise Investment Scheme deferral relief. *You can claim this relief if you invest in shares in a company qualifying for the Enterprise Investment Scheme one year before the disposal of your premises and up to three years afterwards.*

RENTING OUT UNWANTED PROPERTY

Instead of selling your business premises you may decide to let all or part of the property to a tenant. Any rents you receive are taxable income and liable to income tax if you trade as a sole trader or partner, or corporation tax if you operate as a limited company. You will be able to deduct any expenses you incur in connection with the letting when working out your taxable profits. Tax-deductible expenses include mortgage or loan interest, repairs, insurance, legal costs, and if you pay them rather than the tenant, business and water rates and utilities.

10 THINGS TO REMEMBER

1 *Businesses often start off based at the proprietor's home and later progress to rented or purchased business premises. Working from home and renting or buying business premises all have tax consequences.*

2 *If you own your home and base your self-employed business there you should be careful which expenses you claim as you could have to pay capital gains tax when you sell the property. It may be simpler to claim a 'use of home allowance'.*

3 *Repairs are tax-deductible but improvements are not because they are capital expenditure. It can be difficult to distinguish 'repairs' from 'improvements' so you may require advice if you are making a substantial claim for repairs in your accounts.*

4 *If you work from home you may be liable for business rates if members of the public visit you there or if you have altered part of the premises to accommodate your business.*

5 *As long as you have not used any part of your home exclusively for business purposes there will be no capital gains tax to pay when it is sold.*

6 *When you purchase business premises you cannot claim an income tax or corporation tax deduction for the cost of purchasing the building except in the unusual situation that you qualify for a capital allowance. You do however receive capital gains tax relief for the expenditure when you come to sell the property.*

7 *Capital allowances (the annual investment allowance or writing down allowances) are available for certain features integral to a building such as electrical and water systems.*

8 *If you finance the purchase of business premises with a mortgage or loan tax relief is available for the interest* *payments but no tax relief is available for repayment of the capital sum borrowed.*

9 *When considering the purchase of property you need to take into account all the costs of the transaction including stamp duty land tax and VAT.*

10 *When you sell business property you are likely to owe capital gains tax. This may be deferred by making a suitable alternative investment.*

9

VAT

In this chapter:
- *what is VAT?*
- *when do I need to register?*
- *cars*
- *the different VAT schemes*
- *trading overseas*

VAT (short for Value Added Tax) is the principal tax that most small businesses have to deal with on a daily basis. A VAT registered enterprise must account for VAT on its transactions, make entries for it in its accounting records and use this information to make regular returns of VAT collected and paid out to HM Revenue and Customs. If you are not yet VAT registered you must monitor your sales in case you have to register for VAT in the future. Failing to register on time can be very expensive.

Many business people learn how to account for VAT and prepare their own returns but if you undertake more complex transactions you may require professional advice. These include the purchase of property, vehicles and businesses, and trading overseas. Knowing when to seek advice will prevent you making potentially costly mistakes.

For further information see
www.hmrc.gov.uk/vat/start/introduction.htm.

What is VAT?

VAT is a tax on consumer expenditure. It is charged by VAT registered businesses on the goods and services that they sell in the UK. Other business transactions such as imports and acquisitions from EU countries also attract VAT and these are dealt with under special rules (see Complications). In return for collecting VAT, businesses are rewarded by being able to deduct the VAT they pay to others. This means that they pay less VAT to HM Revenue and Customs as a result. It is the private consumer who bears the full cost of VAT because they are not VAT registered. This is illustrated by a case study.

Case study

Melissa's business makes machine parts. She sells £10,000 worth to Nathan. As she is VAT registered she adds VAT at 17.5% to the sales price and invoices Nathan £11,750. Melissa will pay HM Revenue and Customs VAT of £1,750.

Nathan makes air-coolers. He is also VAT registered. He sells £30,000 worth of coolers to Omega, a supermarket chain. He adds VAT of £5,250 (£30,000 × 17.5%) to the sale and charges his client £35,250. Nathan will pay HM Revenue and Customs £5,250 less the £1,750 that he paid to Melissa for the parts, making his net payment £3,500.

Omega is VAT registered. It sells the air-coolers in its stores for £50 each including VAT on each one of £7.45 (£50 × 17.5/117.5). It will pay HM Revenue and Customs £7.45 for each unit it sells after deducting the £5,250 it paid to Nathan.

Pat is a member of the public. She visits her local Omega store and purchases an air-cooler for £50. Included in the price is £7.45 of VAT. As she is not a VAT registered business she cannot recover the £7.45 from anyone.

Rita also purchases a machine. She is a self-employed therapist and buys the cooler to use in her practice room. She is not VAT registered and as a result cannot reclaim the £7.45 she pays.

Simon buys a machine too. He runs the village store and needs a cooler for his shop. He is VAT registered and as a result can reclaim the £7.45 he pays in VAT on the machine when he completes his next VAT return.

IMPORTANT POINTS TO LEARN ABOUT VAT

The case study illustrates a number of important issues about VAT.

▶ *VAT is charged on some goods at 17.5% (20% from 4 January 2011). There are two other VAT rates, 5% and 0% (see What is the rate of VAT?).*

▶ *VAT registered traders have to charge VAT on their sales. They do this by adding VAT to the cost of the goods or services. If the VAT rate is 17.5%, an item which is sold for £100 will cost the buyer £117.50 when VAT is added (£100 × 1.175%). The £100 before VAT is added is called the amount 'net' of VAT. The VAT is £17.50 and the total price inclusive of VAT (£117.50) is known as the 'gross' amount.*

▶ *Retail goods are sold at a VAT inclusive price (for example the coolers at £50) so you will frequently need to work out how much VAT is included in these items. It is tempting to think that you do this by multiplying £50 by 17.5%. This is not the case as the £50 is the VAT inclusive sum. You work out the VAT on a 'gross' figure by multiplying the total price by 17.5 and dividing it by 117.5. You can also multiply the total by 7 and divide the answer by 47 which will give you the same result. Check that you understand this calculation and practise these sums on your calculator. For example if you purchase an item which costs £1,000, the VAT included in the price is £148.93 (£1,000 × 7/47). If you purchase something which costs £1,175, the VAT is £175 (£1,175 × 17.5/117.5).*

- *VAT charged on sales of goods and services is known as 'Output' VAT. The VAT you can recover on the goods and services you buy in, is known as 'Input' VAT (see Records and VAT returns).*

If you are not VAT registered, VAT will have only a small impact on your business. You will not add any VAT to your sales and you do not need to separately identify the VAT on your expenditure (see Chapter 4: Problem areas – VAT). There is no VAT to pay to HM Revenue and Customs. If you are VAT registered the situation, as we have already seen, is entirely different.

When do I need to register for VAT?

You can register for VAT in two main circumstances:

- *When your sales (known as 'taxable supplies') reach a certain threshold (see Appendix 1). This is called 'compulsory' registration.*
- *If your sales are less than the registration threshold in Appendix 1, you can register voluntarily if you are running a commercial venture. This is known as 'voluntary' registration.*

You also have to compulsorily register for VAT if you take over a VAT registered business from someone else (unless you intend to trade below the VAT threshold) and in certain situations when you trade with other countries.

For further details see www.hmrc.vat/start/register/index.htm.

COMPULSORY REGISTRATION

If the value of your sales at the end of any period of 12 months (or shorter period) exceed the registration threshold, you must register for VAT within 30 days unless one of the exceptions applies. If you expect your sales in the next 30 days to exceed the limit, you must also register. When working out your 'sales' for the purpose of VAT registration, you ignore any exempt supplies (see What is the rate of VAT?) and in some cases sales of any capital assets (equipment, cars etc.). Different rules apply if you carry out all or part of your business overseas or if you dispose of land or buildings. In these situations you may need to seek professional advice to determine the correct time to register.

If you fail to register on time you will be liable to a penalty. This varies according to the length of time you delayed registering but will usually be between 5% and 15% of the net VAT due. In addition you will have to account for VAT on all the sales you have made since exceeding the threshold.

Insight

If you fail to register for VAT on time you may face financial difficulties if you cannot recover the VAT that you owe from your customers. You must therefore keep a close eye on your sales income, particularly if you are trading close to the registration threshold.

Example

Bernadette is a freelance computer trainer. She starts in business on 1 June 2008 but does not want to register for VAT voluntarily. Her sales for the 17 months to 31 October 2009 are as follows:

Month	Sales £	Cumulative sales for the previous 12 months £
June 2009	6,000	6,000
July 2009	5,000	11,000
August 2009	4,000	15,000
September 2009	10,000	25,000
October 2009	5,000	30,000
November 2009	7,000	37,000
December 2009	4,000	41,000

(Contd)

Month	Sales £	Cumulative sales for the previous 12 months £
January 2010	5,000	46,000
February 2010	3,000	49,000
March 2010	3,500	52,500
April 2010	2,000	54,500
May 2010	4,000	58,500
June 2010	4,000	56,500
July 2010	18,000	69,500
August 2010	6,000	71,500
September 2010	9,000	70,500
October 2010	8,000	73,500

Bernadette's sales for the 12 months to 31 August 2010 exceed the VAT registration threshold (see Appendix 1). As a result she must notify HMRC that she needs to VAT register by 30 September 2010 and start adding VAT to her sales from 1 October 2010. She cannot claim exception from registration (see Exceptions) as all her sales are standard-rated (see What is the rate of VAT?) and her sales turnover looks set to remain above the VAT deregistration limit (see Appendix 1). If Bernadette does not realize that she needs to register until 31 October 2010 she will incur a late registration penalty.

If you are not VAT registered it is a good idea to add a cumulative sales column to your accounting records as Bernadette has done so that you can keep track of the sales for the previous 12 months. You will then know when the time has come to register.

Insight

The dates that you use to work out when you need to VAT register are based on a 12-month period calculated to the end of the month. It is not related to the tax year or your accounting period.

Exceptions

There are some circumstances where even if your taxable supplies exceed the VAT registration threshold you may not necessarily have to register for VAT:

▶ *Your sales are wholly or mainly zero-rated (see What is the rate of VAT?);*
▶ *You expect your future sales to be below the VAT deregistration limit (see Appendix 1). In this circumstance, you must still notify HMRC that you have exceeded the limit.*

If all your supplies are exempt (see What is the rate of VAT?) you cannot register for VAT (although there are exceptions to this rule mainly connected with supplies of land and buildings and financial services).

Business splitting

It is not possible to avoid compulsory VAT registration by dividing your business into several parts and claiming that each is an autonomous business, for example that a dry-cleaning chain consisting of three shops is really three separate businesses. Many people have tried this and it usually fails.

Voluntary registration

If you have only recently started to trade and your sales have not yet reached the VAT registration threshold, you can register for VAT voluntarily. If you have yet to make any sales, HMRC will want to see evidence that you are in business, such as copies of contracts, details of purchases, planning permission etc.

Reasons why you might want to register voluntarily include:

▶ *So that you can recover VAT on the goods and services you purchase. These costs may be significant in the early days of your business.*
▶ *PR – it makes your business seem more established and significant.*

If you sell direct to final consumers (usually members of the public) who cannot recover the VAT on the goods or services they buy from you, you should think carefully before registering for VAT voluntarily as you may have to pay the VAT out of your selling price and could be worse off by registering.

Example

Trevor starts in business as a self-employed hairdresser. He is not VAT registered and charges £40 for a cut and blow-dry. Two years later he exceeds the VAT registration threshold and must compulsorily register for VAT. He has two options, either he can still charge his customers £40 and account for VAT of £5.96 (£40 × 7/47) out of each cut giving him £34.04 instead of his previous £40, or he can raise his prices and charge customers £47 for the same service (£40 × 1.175). Trevor still gets £40 per cut with HMRC taking £7. Whether Trevor can do this depends on the local competition.

Once he is VAT registered Trevor can off-set the VAT he pays to his suppliers and on the other goods and services he buys against the VAT that he has to pay over to HM Revenue and Customs. This is unlikely to fully compensate him if he is unable to increase his prices and he may be worse off being VAT registered. Trevor needs to understand how VAT works when he is planning his business so that he can price his services realistically taking into account all the taxes he might have to pay over the first few years of the business. He should seek advice about VAT registration at an early stage.

FORMS

You need to register for VAT online at www.hmrc.gov.uk/vat/start/register/how-to-register.htm. HM Revenue and Customs will usually notify you that you have been VAT registered within one month. You will then receive a VAT number which must be included on all your sales documentation such as invoices and bills (see VAT invoices). Sometimes HM Revenue and Customs make additional checks in connection with your VAT application to prevent fraud.

If they do, your registration can take anything up to three months to process. Even though your application is delayed you must still account for VAT to HM Revenue and Customs from the registration date you have selected but you must not show VAT as a separate item on your invoices. To avoid losing out you should increase the price of your invoices by the amount of the VAT and explain why you are doing so to your customers. When your VAT number is issued you should then reissue your invoices showing your VAT registration number and VAT at the appropriate rate. If your VAT registration application is delayed beyond one month you may want to seek professional advice.

Once registered, there are a number of schemes which you may have to or will want to take advantage of (see Special schemes).

CLAIMING BACK VAT BEFORE REGISTRATION

You can reclaim VAT on items purchased for your business in the three years before registration if you have proof of the VAT you paid (for example an invoice or receipt with a VAT number) and you keep a list of the items and the VAT claimed with your VAT account (see Records and VAT returns). The items must still be in existence at the date of registration so you cannot reclaim the VAT on consumables such as fuel, utilities or phone bills.

What is the rate of VAT?

One area that VAT-registered businesses often find difficult to understand are the different rates of VAT and how they are applied to individual goods and services.

There are currently three VAT rates (see Appendix 1):

▶ *Standard rate: 17.5% (20% from 4 January 2011);*
▶ *Reduced rate: 5%; and*
▶ *Zero rate: 0%.*

In addition some goods and services have no VAT on them because they are:

▶ *Exempt from VAT;*
▶ *Not supplied by a VAT registered person;*
▶ *Supplied overseas.*

The law which sets out which items are subject to which rate of VAT is contained in Schedules 7A, 8 and 9 of the Value Added Tax Act 1994.

▶ *Schedule 7A sets out the reduced rate supplies;*
▶ *Schedule 8 shows zero-rated supplies; and*
▶ *Schedule 9 lists those items which are exempt from VAT in the UK.*

The following table summarizes the main items which are charged to VAT at 0%, the 5% reduced rate, or are VAT-exempt. Everything else is standard-rated, ie VAT is charged on it at 17.5% (20% from 4 January 2011). The list below is only intended as a general guide. For each item listed there are many detailed conditions, exceptions set down in the legislation and aspects which have been considered by the courts. For example, take the apparently simple statement 'food', listed as being zero-rated. Food does not include (amongst others) confectionery, crisps, hot take-away meals or food consumed in restaurants, all of which is liable to standard-rate VAT. Over the years, the courts have had to consider the VAT treatment of very specific food items including jaffa cakes, tea cakes and different types of crisp!

Reduced rate	Zero rate	Exempt
Domestic fuel or power	Food	Land
Installation of energy-saving materials	Sewerage and water	Insurance

Reduced rate	Zero rate	Exempt
Grant-funded installation of heating equipment, security goods or gas supply	Books	Postal services
Women's sanitary products	Talking books for the blind	Betting gaming and lotteries
Children's car seats	Construction of buildings	Finance
Certain residential conversions	Protected buildings	Education
Certain residential renovations and alterations	International services	Health and welfare
Contraceptives	Transport	Burial and cremation
Smoking cessation products	Caravans and houseboats	Subscriptions to trade unions, professional and other public interest bodies
	Gold	Sports, sporting competitions and physical education
	Bank notes	Disposal of works of art and antiques from historic houses
	Drugs, medicines and aids for handicapped persons	Fund raising events by charities and other bodies

(Contd)

Reduced rate	Zero rate	Exempt
	Imports and exports	Cultural services such as admissions
	Children's clothing and shoes and certain protective clothing such as cycle helmets	Supplies of goods where input tax cannot be recovered
		Investment gold and gold coins

Further help and advice on the rates of VAT can be obtained from the National Advice Service on 0845 010 9000 between 8.00 am and 8.00 pm, Monday to Friday or refer to www.hmrc.gov.uk/vat/forms-rates/rates/goods-services.htm.

It is important to understand the difference between zero-rated VAT and exempt from VAT. In the case of zero-rated supplies, you charge VAT to your customers at 0% which entitles you to recover any VAT you have been charged by your suppliers from HM Revenue and Customs. If you make exempt supplies you cannot register for VAT and therefore cannot recover VAT on your purchases from HM Revenue and Customs. Sometimes you will sell something that consists of two elements which are treated differently for VAT purposes. Here you have to decide whether what you are supplying consists of clearly identifiable parts or whether it is one supply. You will probably require advice to be sure and may also need to confirm your treatment with HM Revenue and Customs.

Insight

If you supply some goods or services which are exempt and some which are taxable, you will be able to recover some of your input VAT from HM Revenue and Customs, but it is likely to be restricted under what are known as the partial exemption rules.

Records and VAT returns

Once you are VAT registered you have to complete regular VAT returns to calculate the VAT that you need to pay over to HM Revenue and Customs. If your sales turnover is over £100,000 a year, or if you are newly VAT registered, you have to file your returns and pay your VAT electronically. From 2012 almost all VAT returns are likely to be filed online. VAT returns are completed every three months (quarterly) unless you use the annual accounting scheme (see Special schemes) or you regularly receive VAT refunds because you sell zero-rated goods or services. Different businesses have different VAT return dates. If you have a preference for a particular series of dates you should advise HM Revenue and Customs when you register.

VAT returns must be filed within 30 days of the return date together with any payment due. If you pay your VAT electronically you have an extra seven days' credit. If you are late sending in the form (or paying over the VAT) twice or more within a year you will be fined (surcharged) unless you have a reasonable excuse for making a late payment. The amount of the surcharge depends on how many times you have been late. If the fine is below a minimum set by HM Revenue and Customs they do not collect it. For further information see HMRC Notice 700/50 'Default surcharge' and www.hmrc.gov.uk/vat/managing/problems/penalties.htm.

Insight

If your sales turnover is £150,000 or less, HM Revenue and Customs will offer you help to complete your VAT returns on time and only if you continue to file late returns will they then penalize you.

To complete the VAT return form, you need to keep records of the VAT on your income and your expenses. For details of how to maintain suitable accounting records see

www.hmrc.gov.uk/vat/managing/returns-accounts/accounts.htm
and the Teach Yourself book *Small Business Accounting*.
It does not matter whether your records are computerized
or kept manually provided that they show the information
that HM Revenue and Customs require (see Chapter 2).
In addition to your usual accounting records you must also
keep a VAT account showing how you have worked out
the entries on your VAT return. You must keep your
accounting records safely for at least six years. Failure to
comply with the record keeping requirements could cost you
a penalty.

VAT INVOICES

It is important to raise accurate VAT invoices once you are VAT
registered. These have to show specific information as detailed in
the following list.

Information to be shown on a VAT invoice
- ▶ *Your name and address;*
- ▶ *Your VAT registration number;*
- ▶ *Customer/client's name and address;*
- ▶ *Date the invoice was issued and 'tax point' if different (see Complications);*
- ▶ *Unique reference number (for example the bill number);*
- ▶ *Description of the goods sold or services provided;*
- ▶ *For each type of goods the quantity supplied;*
- ▶ *The unit price of the goods or services;*
- ▶ *The rate of VAT;*
- ▶ *The amount excluding VAT, the VAT and the total invoice value.*
- ▶ *Details of any cash discount offered.*

If you are a retailer you may provide a less detailed invoice for
sales of less than £250 (including VAT).

For further information see www.hmrc.gov.uk/vat/managing/
charging/vat-invoices.htm.

VAT RETURNS

The VAT return requires you to enter the VAT on your sales (outputs) and deduct VAT on your purchases (inputs) to arrive at the VAT you owe HM Revenue and Customs. If your input VAT exceeds your output VAT, you will receive a VAT repayment.

You also have to enter the total of your sales (net of VAT) and the total of your purchases (net of VAT) on the form. HM Revenue and Customs use these figures to check the accuracy of your return and for statistical purposes. The output VAT when divided by your net sales should not exceed the maximum VAT rate (17.5% or 20% from 4 January 2011). You can also use this simple sum to check the accuracy of your return. In many cases the output VAT divided by net sales should come to exactly 17.5% (20% from 4 January 2011). If not you should consider the reason why. Maybe you have made exempt or zero-rated sales or sales to another EU country? Is this usual and if so are you confident that no VAT should have been charged on the sale?

The same calculation applies to your input VAT. The input VAT when divided by your net purchases and expenses should not be more than 17.5% (20% from 4 January 2011). The resulting calculation is likely to be less than 17.5% or 20% because some items you buy will not have VAT on them (see What is the rate of VAT?) or you may also be partially exempt (see Complications).

Finally, the VAT return requires you to enter details of EU sales and purchases (see Trading with the European Union).

Further information about completing your VAT return can be found at www.hmrc.gov.uk/vat/managing/returns-accounts/completing-returns.htm.

Insight

It is worthwhile checking the ratios of output tax to net sales and input tax to net purchases each time you complete a return. Doing so can stop you making an innocent error and may prevent a VAT inspection.

OUTPUT VAT

Recording the output VAT on your income is relatively straightforward. You usually do this by keeping a list of your sales invoices or till totals together with the output VAT. You have a choice as to whether to draw up this list based on actual sales (invoices) or on a cash basis (see Special schemes). Most small businesses pay over their VAT on a cash basis. It is important to remember that even though you use the cash basis for your VAT returns, your accounts cannot be prepared in this way. They must be drawn up using generally accepted accounting principles which means including all your invoices (whether paid or not) and the value of any uncompleted work (see Chapter 4). This disparity of treatment means that you will need to adjust your accounting records to arrive at the correct figures for your VAT returns if you use the cash accounting scheme. You need to find a convenient way to do this, so that you do not omit any entries.

In addition to adding VAT onto your sales, you have to charge VAT on all your taxable supplies. This includes the sale of equipment (not necessarily cars) and private fuel (see Complications – Cars).

INPUT VAT

Your accounting records must include a separate column for VAT on your expenditure. When you prepare your VAT return you will either take into account the VAT on bills you have paid or on bills you have received depending on whether or not you use the cash accounting scheme (see Special schemes).

You can reclaim input VAT on your expenditure including direct costs, overheads and purchases of equipment provided that:

▶ *The expense is not zero-rated or exempt from VAT (see What is the rate of VAT?).*
▶ *The supplier is VAT registered.*
▶ *You obtain a valid VAT receipt.*

▶ *The expense is not one where there are special rules, for example if you are partially exempt (see Complications).*

DEALING WITH HM REVENUE AND CUSTOMS

If you make an innocent mistake involving VAT of less than £10,000 when completing a VAT return but you correct it voluntarily on a subsequent return within four years, you will not be penalized and no interest will be charged. Errors involving VAT of more than £10,000 and careless and deliberate mistakes must be notified to HM Revenue and Customs and may be liable to penalties and interest. For further information see www.hmrc/gov.uk/vat/managing/problems/corrections/correct-mistakes.htm.

If you fail to make a VAT return, HM Revenue and Customs will issue an estimated assessment of your liability.

Periodically HM Revenue and Customs will want to inspect your VAT records. They do this by assessing the risk that you have underpaid VAT based on your previous records, your VAT returns and the business sector you are in. Sometimes HMRC carry out combined inspections to check other aspects of your affairs at the same time, for example PAYE or corporation tax but they will usually inform you in advance that they are going to do this.

If you disagree with HM Revenue and Customs on any matter, you can appeal to the First-tier Tribunal.

Complications

When dealing with your VAT affairs there are any number of potential complications that you may encounter. This section highlights the principal ones. The VAT implications for business premises are dealt with in Chapter 8 and the sale of businesses in Chapter 13.

CARS

You cannot recover VAT on the purchase of a car in most circumstances, although you can reclaim it on the cost of a van. You can reclaim the VAT on a car if you run a taxi, driving school, car hire business, retail motor outlet or leasing business. If you lease a car for use in your business, you can usually only reclaim 50% of the VAT on the leasing charges.

When you sell a car you do not have to charge VAT on the sale if you did not claim back any VAT when you bought the vehicle. If you did reclaim VAT, you have to charge or account for output VAT on the sale proceeds. If you deal in second-hand cars you will probably account for VAT in accordance with the Second-hand scheme (see Special schemes).

Private fuel also causes complications. If you are a sole trader or a partner who drives a car, you have to disallow part of the input VAT by using the private scale charges based on the car's carbon dioxide emissions set out in Appendix 1. If your mileage is low, it may not be worthwhile claiming back any of the VAT but you have to adopt this treatment for all business vehicles. In most cases you will reclaim the VAT on your fuel in full but include as output VAT the appropriate scale charge. If you drive a van, you should disallow VAT on the private use of the vehicle by reference to the percentage of your private mileage compared to the total miles you have driven.

As far as other motor expenses are concerned, you can reclaim VAT on repairs and maintenance but insurance is exempt from VAT and no VAT is charged on car tax. For further information see www.hmrc.gov.uk/vat/managing/reclaiming/motoring.htm.

ENTERTAINING

You cannot recover VAT on business expenditure although you can reclaim it on staff welfare and necessary subsistence. For further details see www.hmrc.gov.uk/vat/managing/reclaiming/entertainment.htm.

BAD DEBTS

If you do not use the cash accounting scheme and a customer does not pay you for the goods or services you have supplied, you can reclaim the output VAT you have paid over to the HM Revenue and Customs once the debt is six months old. For most small businesses it is preferable to use the cash accounting scheme (see Special schemes) because you automatically obtain relief for any bad debts.

If you fail to pay a supplier for any reason you should not claim back the VAT, or if you do you should repay it to HM Revenue and Customs within six months.

For further information see www.hmrc.gov.uk/vat/managing/reclaiming/bad-debts.htm.

SUBSTANTIAL CAPITAL EXPENDITURE

If you spend £50,000 or more on computer equipment (excluding VAT) or £250,000 (excluding VAT) or more on land, buildings, civil engineering works or refurbishments, you have to account for VAT on these items in accordance with the 'capital goods scheme'. This means that you cannot claim all the VAT at once; instead, the VAT is recovered over five years (computers and leases of less than ten years) or over a ten-year period. For further details refer to www.hmrc.gov.uk/vat/managing/reclaiming/capital-assets.htm.

PARTIAL EXEMPTION

Partial exemption means that you sell some goods or services which are exempt and some which are not. If your input VAT on the expenditure relating to your exempt sales is less than 50% of your total input VAT and it is also £625 or less a month on average, you can claim back all your input VAT. If you do not meet these conditions your input VAT is restricted by special rules. If you are a partially exempt trader you should refer to www.hmrc.gov.uk/vat/managing/reclaiming/partial-exemption.htm.

TIME OF SUPPLY

The date on which you supply goods or services is known as the 'tax point'. You need to identify it so that you can include the date on your invoices (see VAT invoices) and to enable you to account for VAT if you do not use the cash accounting scheme. The date of supply is usually the earliest date of these three points in time:

- *when goods are supplied or the services performed; or*
- *the date of the invoice; or*
- *the date of payment.*

If you bill your customers within 14 days of supplying goods or services then this later date is the tax point unless the customer pays you beforehand. If your services are supplied continuously, the tax point is the date of the invoice, or if earlier the date that your customer pays you.

For further details see www.hmrc.gov.uk/vat/managing/returns-accounts/tax-points.htm.

INTERNATIONAL TRADE

Imported goods from outside the European Union (EU) are liable to VAT at the time of import. When you prepare your VAT return, you can claim a credit for the VAT you have already paid. If you regularly import goods from outside the EU, you can join a deferment scheme which enables you to pay customs duty and VAT on a monthly basis.

If you export goods to a country outside the EU you can zero-rate the sale if you have sufficient proof that the goods have left the country such as Customs' control. You will probably use an agent to handle your overseas freight. If you are not sure where the goods are going to, you must charge VAT.

Trading with the European Union (EU)
If you import goods from a European Union country the rules differ from those relating to imports and exports from other countries. Firstly purchases and sales of goods between EU member

states are not treated as imports and exports but as 'arrivals' and 'dispatches'.

If you sell goods to a VAT-registered EU customer, the goods are zero-rated (but special rules apply to new transport including cars). You must state the customer's VAT number on your invoice and you also have to complete and submit an EC sales list to HM Revenue and Customs each quarter.

The principal difficulty with EU exports is obtaining proof that the goods have left the UK because within the EU there are no Customs barriers. HM Revenue and Customs advise that you should retain some or all of the following documents as proof that goods have been transported abroad:

- ▶ *Orders and correspondence with your customer;*
- ▶ *Sales invoice and shipping note;*
- ▶ *Details of freight charges and insurance;*
- ▶ *Confirmation of receipt and evidence of payment; and*
- ▶ *Transportation documents.*

If you make dispatches above £250,000 or have arrivals above £600,000 a year you also have to complete a monthly statistical declaration called an Intrastat return.

If you sell goods to any other EU customer you must add UK VAT as usual. If you sell by mail order you have to comply with the 'distance-selling' rules. These require that when your mail order sales in another EU country reach a specified threshold (about £70,000 but it depends on the country), you must register for VAT in that country and charge its rate of VAT to your customers instead of UK VAT.

If you buy goods (have arrivals) from other EU countries costing more than the VAT registration threshold (see Appendix 1), you have to register for VAT, regardless of whether or not you would otherwise have to do so. When you come to complete your VAT return you must account for output VAT on your arrivals but you can usually deduct an equal amount as input tax. Even though there is no additional VAT cost to you, you cannot just ignore these transactions.

PROVIDING SERVICES OVERSEAS

If you provide services rather than sell goods overseas, you will require professional help to work out the VAT treatment as this depends on the nature of the services you supply and where you supply them. The rules do not just affect whether or not you charge VAT on your invoices but also how much VAT you can recover. The rules are extremely complicated and they are not the same as those for goods. Making a mistake here could be expensive.

For further information on international trade and VAT see www.hmrc.gov.uk/vat/managing/international/index.htm.

Insight

As a general rule if you have not encountered a particular transaction before, you should always check what you have to do, either with HM Revenue and Customs or your adviser.

Special schemes

There are a number of special VAT schemes. Three are general schemes and you do not have to be in a specific line of business to use them. You will however need to meet a number of other conditions. These schemes are the:

- ▶ *Cash accounting scheme;*
- ▶ *Annual accounting scheme; and*
- ▶ *Flat-rate scheme.*

For further information see www.hmrc.gov.uk/vat/start/schemes/basics.htm.

CASH ACCOUNTING SCHEME

The most important of the special schemes as far as small businesses are concerned is the cash accounting scheme. Under cash accounting you pay over the VAT on your invoices when you are paid by your customers giving you automatic bad debt relief if a customer does not pay you. You reclaim VAT when you pay your suppliers.

To join the scheme your sales turnover (excluding VAT) must be no more than £1.35 million a year. You must also be up to date with your VAT returns and payments and not have been convicted of a VAT offence or charged a penalty for VAT evasion in the last year. You cannot use cash accounting for hire purchase and similar transactions where payment is either deferred or in advance. You have to leave the scheme if your annual turnover exceeds £1.6 million. For further information see www.hmrc.gov.uk/vat/start/schemes/cash.htm.

ANNUAL ACCOUNTING SCHEME

You can apply to complete just one VAT return a year under the annual accounting scheme (form VAT 600AA). You cannot however pay your VAT once a year. You have to agree a provisional liability with HM Revenue and Customs which you pay in nine monthly instalments. The annual return has to be submitted within two months of the annual accounting scheme year end together with a balancing payment if necessary. You also have the option to pay quarterly if it suits your business better. Annual accounting is not suitable if you receive regular VAT refunds.

You can join the annual accounting scheme if your turnover (excluding VAT) is £1.35 million or less. You have to leave when your turnover reaches £1.6 million (excluding VAT). You can use the annual accounting scheme in conjunction with other schemes except the flat-rate scheme. For further information see www.hmrc.gov.uk/vat/start/schemes/annual.htm.

FLAT-RATE SCHEME

This scheme offers you an entirely different way of accounting for VAT than this chapter has so far described. Instead of calculating your output and input VAT and paying over the difference to HM

Revenue and Customs, you apply a flat-rate percentage (depending on your business sector) to the VAT-inclusive value of all your sales (including those that are exempt, zero-rated or charged at a reduced rate). The only exception is if you buy equipment costing more than £2,000 when you can claim back the VAT in the usual way.

To join the scheme you must have an annual turnover of up to £150,000 (excluding VAT). Having joined, if your turnover exceeds £230,000 you must usually leave the scheme. You cannot use the scheme if you also use the second-hand scheme or capital goods scheme and you cannot account on a cash-basis when using this scheme. For further information see www.hmrc.gov.uk/vat/start/schemes/flat-rate.htm.

There are also specific schemes for businesses in certain trade sectors including retailers, dealers in second-hand goods and tour operators.

RETAILERS

If you are a retailer you have to account for your VAT under one of HM Revenue and Customs' retail schemes, see www.hmrc.gov.uk/vat/start/schemes/retail.htm.

SECOND-HAND GOODS

If you buy and sell second-hand goods such as antiques, collectables, works of art, cars, caravans etc., you only have to account for output VAT on your profit margin, that is the difference between what you sell the item for and your purchase costs. Where you use this scheme, your invoices must not show any VAT and as a result your customers cannot reclaim any VAT.

If you are charged VAT when you buy an item, you can recover input VAT in the usual way but you must then charge VAT on the full sales price.

For further information see www.hmrc.gov.uk/vat/start/schemes/margin.htm.

TOUR OPERATORS

If your business buys in and resells travel and accommodation you can use the tour operator's margin scheme (TOMS for short). The scheme enables VAT to be accounted for on travel supplies without you having to register and account for VAT in each EU country where the services and goods are enjoyed. The rules are complicated and you are likely to require specialist advice if you operate in this field. For further information see VAT Notice 709/5 'Tour operator's margin scheme'.

Cancelling your VAT registration

You can cease being VAT registered if your turnover falls below a set threshold (see Appendix 1). This is set slightly lower than the registration threshold. You can however remain registered if you want to and you are trading commercially.

If you want to de-register, you must tell HM Revenue and Customs within 30 days of the date you want your VAT registration to stop and complete form VAT 7. You will need to complete a VAT return to the date you have chosen and pay over any outstanding VAT.

There are special rules regarding any business equipment or assets you own at the date of de-registration. If their value is more than £6,714 (£6,000 from 4 January 2011) (£1,000 worth of VAT) and you claimed VAT on them when you purchased the items, you have to pay VAT on their value, unless you are de-registering because you are transferring your business to someone else as a going concern.

For further information see
www.hmrc.gov.uk/vat/managing/change/change.htm.

10 THINGS TO REMEMBER

1 *One of the most expensive mistakes that businesses make is failing to register for VAT at the appropriate time. This is usually the end of any month in which the turnover from all your business activities in the previous 12 months exceeds the VAT registration threshold (see Appendix 1).*

2 *You can reclaim VAT on items purchased for your business in the three years before registration if you have proof of the VAT you paid such as an invoice or receipt containing a VAT number.*

3 *There are three main rates of VAT: standard – 17.5% (20% from 4 January 2011); reduced – 5%; zero – 0%. Some good and services carry no VAT because they are exempt (this is different from zero rate), not supplied by a VAT registered person or supplied overseas.*

4 *Once every three months (unless you are in the annual accounting scheme) you have to file a VAT return detailing the VAT on your sales (outputs) and deducting the VAT on your purchases (inputs). You pay HMRC the difference between your outputs and your inputs unless your inputs exceed your outputs when you receive a VAT refund.*

5 *Most small businesses are better off using the cash accounting scheme. This means that you only pay over VAT when you have received the money from your customers and when you have paid your suppliers. This differs from the way in which you prepare your accounts for income tax purposes.*

6 *The cash accounting, annual accounting or flat-rate schemes do not affect the amount of VAT you charge your customers.*

7 *If you offer customers a cash discount, you should only charge VAT on the discounted amount.*

8   *You should familiarize yourself with the rules for claiming input VAT on cars to avoid making mistakes.*

9   *If you trade overseas you should learn which countries are in the European Union and those which are not as the rules differ. You also need to understand that the rules for goods and services are not the same. In most cases if there is an international dimension to your business you will require professional help.*

10 *There are special VAT schemes for retailers, those dealing in second-hand goods and tour operators.*

10

Pensions and insurance

In this chapter:
- *paying pension contributions*
- *employers*
- *maintaining your state pension entitlement*
- *different types of insurance policy*

This chapter looks at the tax implications of paying into pensions and insurance policies. Saving for your retirement through a pension scheme is largely a matter of personal preference but as paying pension contributions either for yourself or your employees is one of the principal ways of reducing your tax bill we consider the rules in some detail. This chapter also considers how you can improve your state pension. Tax relief on staff pensions is considered in Chapter 4.

Pensions are a complex subject and you will require impartial advice from a regulated financial adviser.

Paying into your own pension

Many business people decide to save for their retirement by paying regular sums into a pension. This section looks at the rules governing tax relief on pension contributions and the tax consequences on retirement. It also highlights ways of making your contributions more tax-effective and indicates how pensions can assist you to finance the purchase of business property.

HOW MUCH CAN I PAY INTO A PENSION?

Unless you are a high earner, you can contribute as much as you like to a pension and the premiums will qualify for tax relief. Tax relief on contributions is restricted by two factors:

▶ *A lifetime allowance capping the value of contributions you make throughout your life (see Appendix 1); and*
▶ *An annual allowance restricting the amount you can contribute to a pension each year (see Appendix 1).*

Example

Daniel is a solicitor approaching retirement. His profits (net relevant earnings) are £80,000 and his marginal tax rate is 40%. He pays a one-off pension contribution of £80,000 in 2010/11. This is permitted as it is less than the annual allowance. He is entitled to basic rate tax relief at source of 20% on the payment plus higher rate relief claimed through his tax return on the difference between the higher rate of tax (40%) and the basic rate (20%) provided that the contribution and all the other pension contributions that he has made in his life do not exceed the lifetime allowance (see Appendix 1).

HOW MUCH TAX RELIEF DO I QUALIFY FOR?

You can get tax relief on sums you contribute to your pension up to the following limits:

▶ *£3,600 a year (if your annual profits are between £0 and £3,600);*
▶ *100% of your income (if your annual profits exceed £3,600) until your income reaches the annual allowance (see Appendix 1).*

Sums paid in excess of the annual allowance attract a tax charge.

All contributions are paid to the pension company after deducting basic rate tax relief (see Appendix 1). This means that if you agree to pay £200 per month into a pension you will actually pay the pension company £160 per month (£200 less basic rate tax relief). The pension company will recover basic rate tax of £40 per month from HM Revenue and Customs and invest it in your fund. If you do not pay tax at the higher or additional rate this is the end of the story.

If you pay tax at the higher or additional rate you are entitled to further tax savings calculated on the difference between the highest rate of tax and the basic tax rate. You must claim this tax relief through your self-assessment tax return, or if you are employed through your tax coding.

Example

Clare is a self-employed film and television producer. Her profits are £50,000 a year, she pays 40% tax and pension contributions of £5,000 a year. Clare pays the pension company £4,000 net of basic rate tax relief of 20% and they reclaim £1,000 from HM Revenue and Customs. She claims higher rate relief in her tax return of £1,000 (40% − 20% = 20% × £5,000). Clare's total tax relief is £2,000 and the £5,000 invested in her pension costs her just £3,000.

Future restrictions on tax relief

The government will restrict the tax relief given to pensions from 6 April 2011. This may be achieved by restricting the annual allowance to the range £30,000– £45,000 (see Appendix 1). Alternatively, relief may be restricted for individuals with an annual income of £150,000 or more.

To prevent people trying to obtain additional tax relief before these rules take effect a special tax charge applies to individuals who change their normal pattern of pension contributions, have an annual taxable income of at least £130,000 and make total pension contributions of £20,000 or more a year.

CLAIMING HIGHER RATE TAX RELIEF

One mistake that people make when claiming additional tax relief on their pension contributions is to claim it on the wrong amount. The following example illustrates how you should claim.

Example

Gordon makes self-employed profits as a marketing consultant of £50,000 a year and pays 40% tax on the highest part of his income. He decides to pay pension contributions of £4,200 a year (£350 per month). Each month he pays the pension company £280 (which is £350 less a deduction for 20% basic rate tax relief). When he comes to complete his self-assessment return he is unsure whether to claim the additional relief on £350 per month or £280.

Gordon should claim relief on the amount he pays before deducting tax relief (i.e. on £4,200 a year or £350 a month). This is known as the gross amount. He will be entitled to a tax saving in his return of £840 (£4,200 × 20%). 20% is the difference between 40% (higher rate tax) and 20% (basic rate tax). If Gordon only enters £280 per month on his return he will miss out on £168 of tax relief per year.

You can check your tax relief in the following way:

▶ *If you pay 40% tax you are entitled to tax relief on your pension contributions of 40%.*
▶ *This means that a contribution of £100 per month attracts relief of £40 and costs you £60.*
▶ *You pay the pension company £80 (£100 less £20 basic tax relief).*
▶ *You claim further relief through your self-assessment return saving you an extra £20 per month.*
▶ *The total tax saved on a contribution of £100 is therefore £40 (£20 + £20).*

LOW EARNERS

If you make low profits or losses and pay little or no tax you may
wonder why you receive tax relief on your pension contributions.
The good news is that even if you are a non-taxpayer you are
still entitled to basic rate tax relief deducted at source on your
contributions. This makes paying into a pension tax-effective for
lower earners – if you can afford the premiums.

Example
Betty is a self-employed counsellor making annual profits of around
£3,000 a year. As her income is less than her personal allowance
she is a non-taxpayer. Betty can pay pension contributions of up to
£3,600 and obtain basic rate tax relief on the payments.

PAYING A PENSION FOR SOMEONE ELSE

If you cannot afford to make pension contributions someone else
could pay them on your behalf. If they do you are still entitled to
receive basic rate tax relief on the contributions.

If your business is doing well you may be able to afford to pay pension
premiums for other members of your family such as a non-working
spouse, partner or your children. Contributions receive basic rate
tax relief irrespective of your income or theirs as long as they fall
within the limits set out in 'How much tax relief do I qualify for?'

Example
Andy is a successful businessman paying a top rate of tax of 40%.
He contributes £3,600 a year into a pension policy for his 10-year-old

grandson Sean. Sean is entitled to basic rate tax relief, so Andy only has to pay £2,880 to the pension company. The pension company reclaims tax of £720 from HM Revenue and Customs and invests it in Sean's policy. Even though Andy pays 40% tax, he cannot claim any further tax relief.

DIRECTOR/SHAREHOLDERS

The amount you can pay into a pension and receive tax relief on depends on your income (net relevant earnings), the annual allowance and the lifetime allowance. Net relevant earnings and income are not the same, for example share dividends are excluded from net relevant earnings. This means that if you are a shareholder/director remunerated partly by a salary and partly by dividends, you need to calculate how much salary you require each year to make your desired level of pension contributions.

FINANCING YOUR PENSION WITH HIGHER RATE TAX RELIEF

If you have an established business making profits above the higher rate tax threshold (see Appendix 1) you can fund your pension more tax-effectively by limiting your pension premiums to those which obtain higher rate tax relief.

Case study

Edgar runs an electrical retail outlet. His annual profits are usually in the range £45,000–£50,000. His aim is to pay annual pension premiums to reduce his profits to the basic rate tax threshold. As a result he obtains higher rate relief on all the sums he invests in his pension.

The following table illustrates how much Edgar should pay into his pension in 2008/09 and 2009/10 to optimize his tax savings.

(Contd)

Year	Profits (A)	Higher rate threshold (B)	Personal allowance (C)	Amount above which higher rate tax is due B + C (D)	Optimum pension premium A – D (E)	Tax relief (E × 40%)
	£	£	£	£	£	£
2008/09	48,000	34,800	6,035	40,835	7,165	2,866
2009/10	49,000	37,400	6,475	43,875	5,125	2,050
Total					**12,290**	**4,916**

Edgar should restrict his pension contributions to £7,165 in 2008/09 or £5,125 in 2009/10 because any additional sums will only receive basic rate tax relief and not higher rate tax relief.

Over two years Edgar invests £12,290 in his pension. As he has obtained higher rate tax relief on the entire sum contributed it has only cost him £7,374 (£12,290 – £4,916) to obtain £12,290 of pension benefits (60% of the sum invested). If he had paid £12,290 into his pension in either 2008/09 or 2009/10, he would only have obtained basic rate tax relief on the 'excess' £5,125 or £7,165, so making the same contribution would have cost him either £1,025 or £1,433 more than arranging his contributions in this way.

Insight

It is almost impossible to calculate a pension premium to this degree of accuracy but if you maintain good business records, you (or your adviser) should be able to estimate a suitable one-off premium towards the end of the tax year which will more or less maximize your tax relief.

SELF-ADMINISTERED PENSION SCHEMES

If you have an established business and you would like a greater degree of control over where your pension fund is invested, you might consider a self-invested scheme such as a Small Self-Administered Scheme (SSAS) or a Self-Invested Personal Pension (SIPP). The range of investments attracting tax relief excludes residential property and items such as classic cars, art and antiques. Self-administered schemes can be tax-effective if you are considering the purchase of commercial property for your business or if you want to transfer ownership of an existing commercial property to a pension scheme. There are many detailed rules which must be followed and restrictions on how much the scheme can borrow to finance the purchase of property. You will require specialist advise if you want to explore this option further.

PENSION MORTGAGES

If you are purchasing a property for use in your business or domestically, you could consider a pension mortgage. The sum borrowed will eventually be repaid by the tax-free lump sum from the policy (see Retirement). For this to be a viable option you need to have a sufficiently high and stable level of income, preferably be a higher rate taxpayer and be prepared to sacrifice some of your income in retirement to repay the mortgage. You will require professional advice to determine whether this is a suitable means of financing the purchase.

RETIREMENT

Even though retirement is probably a long way off it is important to understand what you will get for your pension contributions and when.

The minimum age at which you can draw your pension is 55 although if you suffer from ill-health it may be possible to retire sooner. The later you decide to retire the more your pension will be worth as the contributions will be invested for a longer period of time. If you are paying into a pension for children, you should note that the earliest the fund can be accessed is when they reach age 55.

Up to 25% of your pension fund can be taken as a tax-free lump sum. The sum is restricted to a maximum of 25% of the lifetime allowance (see Appendix 1). Alternatively you have the option of taking no lump sum and a higher pension.

Between the ages of 55 and 75 most people choose to take their pension (which is taxed under PAYE). If you do not want to take your pension, for example because annuity rates are low, you have the option to draw income from the fund instead. There are also various types of pension that you can take depending on your health and family circumstances and you will probably require advice.

By age 75 most people will have taken their pension but even at this age it is possible not to take an annuity but rather to choose an 'alternatively secured pension' instead. Once again each option has tax consequences and you should seek professional advice.

Insight

The date you choose to receive your pension does not have to coincide with the date you receive your state retirement pension and you can continue to run your business and receive a pension at the same time.

DEATH BENEFITS

When taking out a pension it is possible to use the policy to provide for your dependants if you die. Subject to various limits they could receive a lump sum or a pension. As the contributions receive basic and higher rate relief (depending on your income), this is more tax-effective than taking out separate term life assurance (see Insurances).

Employers and pensions

If you employ five or more people in your business (including any company directors) you need to offer them access to a registered pension scheme but you do not have to contribute to their pensions. You will require advice about the options available. If you decide to set up your own pension scheme you must contribute to it in order for it to be registered with HM Revenue and Customs and qualify for favourable tax treatment.

CONTRIBUTIONS

Contributing to employee and directors' pensions is usually a good way to incentivize your staff as well as being tax-effective for the following reasons:

There are no tax or National Insurance consequences as the payments do not count as a perk (see Chapter 7).

The contributions reduce your business profits so you receive tax relief on the contributions.

You may be able to eliminate your taxable profits by paying additional pension contributions. If the contributions turn a profit into a loss, you can claim loss relief (see Chapter 5). Tax relief for irregular contributions of more than £500,000 has to be spread over up to four years.

LIFE INSURANCE

Insuring the lives of your employees in case they die whilst they are working for you can be arranged through a pension scheme. Lump sums paid out in the event of a death up to the value of the lifetime allowance are tax-free.

State pension

In spite of what has been said in the previous sections about the need to provide your own pension or a pension for your employees, the state pension is still a significant source of income in retirement.

To be entitled to a state pension you, or your spouse/civil partner, need to have paid sufficient National Insurance contributions (or received credits) during your working life. When you receive it, the state pension is taxable income.

IMPROVING YOUR STATE PENSION

You can improve your state pension particularly in the years coming up to retirement in the following ways:

▶ *Pay missing National Insurance contributions but this does not benefit everyone so you should take advice.*
▶ *If you have a period of time when you do not run your business or work because you are caring for children or a disabled person for 20 or more hours per week you are entitled to a weekly credit.*
▶ *Consider deferring the date when you start to receive your state pension. As a reward for deferring for at least 12 months, your weekly pension is increased or you can choose to receive a one-off taxable lump sum instead. This can be claimed in the year when you first receive your pension, or in the following year.*

STATE SECOND PENSION

The State Second Pension or S2P replaced the State Earnings Related Pension or SERPS in 2002. If you are an employee or director, S2P and SERPS increase your state pension by an earnings-related addition. Some people can contract out of S2P and make their own pension provision. Your employer may arrange for you to be contracted-out as part of a company scheme. Whether contracting-out is a good idea depends on how much you earn and your age. You may need to seek advice about whether this is a good idea for you.

Insurances

This section reviews the tax treatment of a range of different insurance policies. Not all insurance premiums are tax-deductible and in some cases even where a deduction could be claimed, it may be advisable not to. Some types of insurance taken out to cover your staff are treated as a perk whilst others are not. In other words before taking out any kind of insurance, you should consider the tax consequences for your business and staff.

GENERAL INSURANCE

Insurance premiums paid to cover loss, theft or damage are tax-deductible against your business profits on the following types of policy (amongst others):

▶ *Buildings and contents insurance;*
▶ *Stock loss and goods in transit;*
▶ *Motor insurance;*
▶ *Employee and public liability insurance;*
▶ *Loss of profits;*
▶ *Professional indemnity;*
▶ *Other business risks such as libel or breach of copyright.*

Fee protection insurance to cover accountancy costs in the event of an enquiry by HM Revenue and Customs is not tax allowable (see Chapter 2).

Sums you receive from an insurance company for a claim may be taxable trading receipts (for example claims for lost stock or loss of profits). In some cases they will be capital (for example to replace a vehicle) and will affect a claim for capital allowance (see Chapter 6). In other circumstances the insurance pay-out may result in a capital gain (for example where a building is destroyed).

SICKNESS INSURANCE

If you take out a policy to provide an income or a lump sum in the event that you are injured or fall ill, you may claim a tax deduction for the premiums in your business accounts but if you do, any sums paid under the policy whilst you are sick become taxable income. If you do not claim a tax deduction for the premiums, sums paid out do not count as taxable income. Similar rules apply to policies taken out to insure against periods of unemployment. Group sickness policies taken out to insure against staff illness do not usually give rise to a benefit in kind charge.

MEDICAL INSURANCE

There is no tax relief available on your own private medical insurance premiums. If you provide this perk for your staff they will pay income tax on the cost of the premiums and the business will incur a Class 1A National Insurance charge (see Appendix 1). You can claim a tax deduction in your accounts for the cost of providing the private medical cover and the associated National Insurance.

No benefit in kind or National Insurance charge arises on medical insurance taken out to cover employees for business trips overseas.

DIRECTORS' LIABILITY INSURANCE

If you are a company director there is no benefit in kind tax or National Insurance charge if the company takes out directors' liability insurance for you. This is the case whilst you are employed and for up to six years after you leave the company. The company can claim a deduction in its accounts for the cost of the premiums. If you have to pay your own directors' liability insurance, you can claim an income tax deduction in your tax return.

KEY EMPLOYEE/DIRECTOR INSURANCE

You can insure for loss of profits arising from the death or illness of a key employee or director. The premiums are usually tax-deductible. Any sums paid under the policy are treated as taxable income.

MORTGAGE ENDOWMENT POLICIES

If you are financing the purchase of a commercial or domestic property with an endowment policy, you cannot claim a deduction for the premiums in your business accounts. This is because in most cases the sum paid out when the policy matures is tax-free. If you redeem an endowment policy before the expiry of its term and you are a higher or additional rate taxpayer you may face an unexpected tax charge. If you are considering cashing in a policy early you should seek professional advice as keeping it going may be more tax-effective.

LIFE INSURANCE

There is no tax relief on policies taken out to insure your own life (except for some policies taken out before 14 March 1984). Lump sums paid out under a term assurance policy are usually tax free. If you include term assurance in a pension policy tax relief is given on the premiums. Death benefits for your staff in case they die whilst they are working for you can also be included in a pension scheme.

10 THINGS TO REMEMBER

1 If you are an employer and you contribute to your employees' pensions the cost is a tax-deductible business expense. If you pay into your own pension the premiums are not deducted in your accounts but you are given tax relief on your contributions by the pension company or by claiming relief in your tax return.

2 Tax relief is available on pension contributions at the basic rate or, if you pay tax at the higher or additional rates at these rates. If you pay tax at the 40% rate £1,000 of pension contributions will usually cost you only £600 after tax relief.

3 From 6 April 2011 tax relief on pension contributions is restricted. In most cases you cannot circumvent this restriction by paying additional pension premiums before that date.

4 Tax relief on pension contributions is limited by the lifetime allowance and the annual allowance (see Appendix 1).

5 Directors/shareholders remunerated partly by a salary and partly by dividends need to calculate how much salary they require each year in order to make their desired level of pension contributions.

6 You can pay into a pension for someone else such as a non-working spouse, civil partner, child or grandchild and still obtain basic tax relief on the premiums.

7 When you come to retire the minimum age at which you can take a pension is 55. You can take some of your pension as a tax free lump sum and some as an annuity taxed under PAYE, or you can take all the pension as an annuity.

8 The state pension is taxable income. To be entitled to it you (or your spouse/civil partner) need to have paid sufficient

National Insurance contributions (or received credits) during your working life.

9 Most business insurance is a tax deductible expense. Special rules apply to insurance for professional fees to help you in the event of a tax enquiry or investigation.

10 No tax relief is available on private medical insurance premiums for a sole trader or partner. If you take out personal insurance for sickness or injury you can claim a tax deduction but if you do any sums paid out under the policy become taxable income.

11

Incorporating a business

In this chapter:
- *changing from being self-employed to a limited company*
- *transferring the business tax-effectively*
- *the advantages of running a business with share capital*

Many people start a business as a sole trader (or a partnership) but as it grows they wonder if they should change it into a limited company. Sometimes this will be because of government incentives, for example companies being taxed at a lower rate than individuals. In other cases becoming a limited company (incorporation) is desirable because the business has expanded, greater risk is involved or external investment is required. It is worthwhile revisiting parts of Chapter 3 before reading this chapter so that you understand the tax differences between unincorporated businesses and limited companies.

When incorporating a business, the assets and liabilities belonging to the sole trader are transferred to a limited company. There are three main stages to the transfer and each has tax implications:

▶ *Closing down the self-employment – see Chapter 12.*
▶ *Starting up a new limited company – this is dealt with in Chapter 3.*
▶ *Structuring the transfer to minimize capital gains tax – we look at this in detail here.*

The tax legislation recognizes that incorporating an existing self-employment does not create an entirely new business; instead the original business continues in a different form. As a result you are permitted to transfer assets, losses, capital allowances and your VAT registration between the two entities as long as you meet various conditions.

Incorporation is complicated and unless your business is very small with minimal assets, you are likely to require professional advice so that you do not pay tax unnecessarily.

When is the best time to incorporate?

You need to select a suitable date to incorporate. From an income tax point of view there is little benefit in one date over another because there is no scope to manipulate your self-employed profits so that some of them are not taxed but it might be beneficial to incorporate in a year when you have all your capital gains tax annual exemption available (see Appendix 1).

Insight
In most circumstances commercial reasons should govern your choice of incorporation date unless the end of the tax year is approaching and delaying incorporation for a month or two does not inconvenience you.

Closing down your self-employment

When you started your self-employment there were four tax-related things that you had to do:

▶ *Register to pay Class 2 National Insurance.*
▶ *Advise HM Revenue and Customs that you were in business.*
▶ *Set up a PAYE scheme for your employees (if you have any).*
▶ *VAT register (if appropriate).*

As you are now ceasing to be self-employed and incorporating your business, you have to reverse these registrations or modify them.

NATIONAL INSURANCE

From your chosen incorporation date, you must notify the National Insurance Contributions Office (NICO) that you are no longer self-employed and liable to pay Class 2 National Insurance. You should also contact your bank and cancel your direct debit.

As a company director you will now pay employee's Class 1 contributions and the company will pay employer's Class 1 contributions on your salary, bonuses and perks but not dividends (see Chapter 1).

INCOME TAX

You must inform the tax office that deals with your tax affairs that you are no longer self-employed (the address and phone number will be on your tax form or other correspondence). You will then complete your accounts to the date that you cease the self-employment. You can claim overlap relief against your final profits if your original accounting year end was any date other than 31 March or 5 April (see Chapter 12). You must also follow special rules when valuing your stock, claiming losses and calculating capital allowances.

You should ensure that you have sufficient personal resources to be able to pay your final income tax bills. Once the company is formed you cannot withdraw money from it unless you have funds available on your director's loan account or you are paid a salary, bonus or dividend.

After the end of the tax year in which your final self-employed accounting period falls, you will no longer complete the self-employed (or partnership) pages of the tax return. You will in future complete the employment pages because you are now a company director.

When you incorporate a business one of the key decisions you have to make is to decide how much of the value of your self-employment to treat as share capital in the new company and how much to leave available as a director's loan account (see Minimizing your capital gains tax).

....

Insight

The division between share capital and director's loan account in the new company should allow for any self-employed tax bills so that you do not lock too much money into the company as share capital only to find yourself in financial difficulties because you cannot pay your income tax.

....

PAYE SCHEME

You must inform the tax office dealing with your PAYE scheme about the transfer of your old business to the limited company. They will arrange to transfer your scheme to the company if you comply with various conditions.

VAT REGISTRATION

You can ask HM Revenue and Customs to transfer your VAT registration (including the VAT registration number) from your self-employment to the company. You do this by completing form VAT 68, application form VAT 1 and agreeing to certain conditions. Alternatively, you can cancel your existing VAT registration by completing form VAT 7 and apply for a new registration number by completing form VAT 1.

Three aspects of your affairs have special rules on incorporation. These are:

▶ *stock (see Chapter 4);*
▶ *losses (see Chapter 5); and*
▶ *capital allowances (see Chapter 6).*

STOCK

Any stock you have on hand at the date of incorporation will be transferred to the company. You can choose the value at which this transfer takes place. You could use market value. This will usually create a larger profit in your final self-employed accounts and a smaller one in the company. Alternatively, you can elect within two years of incorporation for the stock to be transferred at its cost, or the amount paid by the company for the items if this is more. This will usually give you a lower profit in your self-employed accounts and a higher one in the company.

> ### Insight
> The stock valuation that you choose to use will depend on factors such as the profit profile of the business, whether there are unused losses and the respective tax rates applying to the company and the self-employment.

LOSSES

If you have trading losses accumulated during your period of self-employment which you were carrying forward to use against future trading profits, you will now have to re-think what happens to them. You have three possible options:

▶ *To use them against your income in the year of the loss or the previous year (if you are in time to make this claim and you have income against which the losses can be used);*
▶ *To use them in a terminal loss claim;*
▶ *To carry them forward against your director's fees and dividends from the company. You cannot deduct the loss from the company's profits.*

> ### Insight
> In order for losses to be used against director's fees and dividends you must transfer your self-employed business to the company in return for shares (not cash or a director's loan account) which you must still own when you claim the loss relief.

CAPITAL ALLOWANCES

You cannot claim the annual investment allowance, first year allowances or writing down allowances in your final self-employed accounts. The company can claim writing down allowances on the value of the assets transferred to it but not annual investment allowance or first year allowances. These restrictions on your capital allowance claims mean that where possible the company should buy any assets on which you can claim annual investment allowance or first year allowances.

When a business ceases a balancing allowance or charge may arise when 'pooled' assets are disposed of (see Chapters 6 and 12). When you incorporate, you have the option of transferring such assets to the company at their tax written down value. As a result there will be no balancing allowance or charge in your final self-employed accounts. You have to elect for this treatment to apply within two years of the transfer.

Starting a limited company

Some aspects of incorporating an existing self-employment are just as they would be if you had started trading as a limited company from the outset. This means that:

▶ *You must notify HM Revenue and Customs about the formation of the company and pay corporation tax on your profits (see Chapter 3: Notifying HM Revenue and Customs).*
▶ *You have to operate PAYE on your directors' and employees' salaries. If you have asked your tax office to transfer your existing PAYE scheme to the company you have satisfied this requirement (see Closing down your self-employment). If you do not have a PAYE scheme, you will need one now even if you are the company's only employee/director as you must operate PAYE and National Insurance on your salary and perks.*

- *You need to register for VAT. If you have transferred your VAT registration from the unincorporated business you will have complied with your VAT obligations (see Closing down your self-employment). If you are not VAT registered, you should reconsider whether you need to register (see Chapter 9).*

Minimizing capital gains tax

You learned in Chapter 1 that capital gains tax is charged on the profit you make when you sell or otherwise dispose of your capital assets. When you incorporate a self-employed business or partnership this is what you are doing. You are disposing of personally owned capital assets by transferring them to a limited company. You may have to pay capital gains tax as a result.

Fortunately capital gains tax is not charged on all your assets. It only applies to the transfer of freehold or leasehold business premises, plant and machinery attached to the building and goodwill (see Goodwill). Stock, debtors, money in the bank and other cash investments, and liabilities such as creditors, loans and overdrafts are not liable to capital gains tax. Equipment on which you have claimed capital allowances is not liable to capital gains tax provided that the individual items are valued at less than £6,000.

GOODWILL

Goodwill can cause complications on incorporation. Basically goodwill is the difference between what your business is worth and the value of its identifiable assets such as buildings, equipment and stock. The amount it is worth depends on the type of business you run, your turnover and profits, clients, brands, reputation and the skills and management abilities of yourself and your staff. HM Revenue and Customs distinguish between personal and business goodwill but consider that a sole trader supplying their own services with few staff has no goodwill associated with the business. This is a mixed blessing. On the plus side if there is no goodwill you cannot owe capital gains tax on it. On the negative side, you cannot use the goodwill to create a director's loan account in the company and you will not be able to claim corporation tax relief on it.

Insight

HM Revenue and Customs review goodwill calculations carefully. When you incorporate an existing self-employment or partnership you should always have your business professionally valued so that the new company can be structured in the most tax efficient way.

Case study

Monty started a security business on 1 November 2003 as a sole trader. He decides to incorporate the business on 31 October 2010. The business is valued at £500,000 made up as follows:

	£
Freehold office (acquired 1 November 2003 for £175,000)	350,000
Equipment (no items worth more than £6,000)	50,000
Goodwill	75,000
Stock	50,000
Debtors	40,000
Bank balance	35,000
Loans	−100,000
	500,000

Monty does not have to pay capital gains tax on the transfer of the equipment, stock, debtors, cash and loan to the company. Capital gains tax is due on the freehold office and goodwill. The loan cannot be deducted from this value even if it is used to finance the

(Contd)

purchase of the building. Monty, a higher rate tax payer, has no costs to deduct from the goodwill as he started the business from scratch but he is entitled to entrepreneurs' relief (see Chapter 1) because he is disposing of a business as a going concern which he has owned for more than a year. No annual exemption is available because Monty has already used this against other personal capital gains.

Monty's capital gains tax calculation goes like this:

2010/11	£
Freehold office – value 31.10.10	350,000
Freehold office – cost 1.11.03	–175,000
	175,000
Goodwill	75,000
Taxable gains	250,000
Capital gains tax at 10% (£250,000 × 10%)	**25,000**

It will cost Monty £25,000 to transfer the assets from his self-employment to a limited company. This liability would be higher if he had not been in business for at least one year so that he qualifies for entrepreneur's relief. If you are in this situation, it could be worthwhile deferring incorporation for a few months assuming that it makes commercial sense to delay.

There are several other things that Monty could do to reduce his capital gains tax liability.

Do not transfer the office
Monty could retain ownership of the office and either rent it to the company or let it use it free of charge. If he charges the company rent he will pay income tax at his highest rate on the rental income but not National Insurance. He could reduce the income tax charge by taking out a mortgage on the property. The interest on the loan is then deducted from the rental income along with any other property expenses he incurs before income tax is calculated.

There are other reasons for Monty to keep hold of the property. If he transfers the office to the company he will also have to pay stamp duty land tax on the transfer. This will amount to a further £10,500 (£350,000 × 3%). The transfer may also have VAT implications.

If Monty does not transfer the office to the company, he will only owe capital gains tax on the goodwill. This amounts to £7,500 and is calculated as follows.

2010/11	£
Goodwill	75,000
Taxable gain	**75,000**
Capital gains tax at 10% (£75,000 × 10%)	**7,500**

Monty may be happy to pay the capital gains tax of £7,500 and doing so will enable him to credit £75,000 (the value of the goodwill) to his director's loan account with the company – at a tax rate of only 10%. This is explained in more detail later in the chapter (see Director's loan account).

If Monty does not want to pay this amount of capital gains tax he has further options available to him.

Claim gifts relief on the goodwill
The gain on the goodwill cannot be cancelled but it can be deferred (completely or partially) by claiming 'gifts relief'.

If Monty wants to defer almost the whole of the gain on the goodwill he should charge the company a nominal sum for it, for example, £100, giving rise to a capital gains tax liability of £10. This means that he has 'gifted' the company £74,900 (£75,000 – £100) by charging it less than the goodwill is worth. The disadvantage is that he only has £100 credited to his loan account rather than the full £75,000.

If Monty decides on this option he must claim gifts relief in his tax return.

(Contd)

The company can claim corporation tax relief when it writes off goodwill over its useful life. There is therefore an advantage in Monty selling the goodwill to the company for another amount up to £75,000. For example, if Monty was to charge the company £30,000 for the goodwill, claiming gifts relief of £45,000 (£75,000 – £30,000), his capital gains tax liability would only be £3,000, he would have £30,000 credited to his director's loan account and the company could claim corporation tax relief on the purchase of the goodwill for £30,000. This has two advantages over claiming a higher amount of gifts relief:

- *It gives Monty a bigger credit to his director's loan account (or payment) for the work he has put into the business up to the point of incorporation; and*
- *The company has a higher value of goodwill on which to claim corporation tax relief and a greater value to off-set against any future capital gains.*

Director's loan account

It is unlikely that the company will have the resources to pay Monty for the goodwill at the date he incorporates. As a result the amount owed by the company is usually credited to a director's loan account. Creating a loan account will enable Monty to withdraw the equivalent of his salary against it each month until the balance has been used up (but he must not overdraw it). This means that he should not need to take a salary during this period, saving the company employer's National Insurance and himself higher rate income tax depending on the amount of money that he needs to live on.

Claim incorporation rollover relief

Monty also has the option of deferring the gain on the property and goodwill through incorporation rollover relief. You should be familiar with the expression 'rollover relief' from Chapters 1 and 8. Where you meet the relevant conditions this relief is given automatically. In other words you do not need to claim it as long as you qualify for it.

To be eligible for rollover relief, you must transfer all the assets from your self-employment to the company (you can exclude any bank balances). All other assets such as cars, equipment, stock and debtors must be transferred. In return you will receive shares in the company.

Returning to Monty's original gains on the office building and goodwill; in exchange for transferring all his assets (excluding the bank balance) to the company, he receives 465,000 £1 shares in the company. He no longer has a capital gains tax liability because the gains are 'rolled over'.

	£
Value of business	500,000
Cash excluded	−35,000
Shares 465,000 £1 shares	465,000
Gain on office and goodwill (£350,000 − £175,000 + £75,000)	−250,000
Capital gains tax cost of 465,000 £1 shares	**215,000**

When Monty comes to sell his shares, instead of deducting £465,000 from the sale proceeds, he can only deduct less than half this value, i.e. £215,000. He will therefore have a higher gain in the future because he did not pay any capital gains tax when he incorporated the company. He may however be able to defer the gain again.

Pitfalls
There are three pitfalls to watch out for when claiming incorporation rollover relief.

1 *All the assets (apart from the bank balances) must be transferred to the company including cars. Many people prefer to own their car privately rather than transfer them into the company to avoid a benefit in kind charge (see Chapter 7: Taxing perks). You cannot do this without losing rollover relief. One way*
(Contd)

round this difficulty is to take the car out of the business well before you incorporate.

2 *Your investment in the company is locked up as share capital. You may want a greater degree of flexibility than this provides with some of the value of your business credited to a director's loan account so that you can draw against it when the company has the available resources. For example, instead of receiving 465,000 shares Monty might choose to receive 279,000 £1 shares and have £186,000 credited to his loan account. This means that only 60% (£279,000 divided by £465,000) of the £250,000 gain can be rolled over. This will result in a capital gains tax liability on the remaining 40%. Monty may consider that the capital gains tax of £18,600 is worth paying for the benefit of having access to £186,000. Alternatively, he may decide to allocate the balance between shares and his loan account so that the resulting gain is covered by his capital gains tax annual exemption.*

3 *Make sure that structure of the company does not jeopardise a future claim to entrepreneurs' relief (you will need to take professional advice).*

ENTERPRISE INVESTMENT SCHEME DEFERRAL RELIEF

There is a further option for deferring a gain on incorporation. Whether or not you can take advantage of it depends on the nature of your business. The Enterprise Investment Scheme (EIS) gives income tax and capital gains tax relief for certain investments by some people in suitable companies.

Insight

You will require specialist advice if you are considering deferring a gain through Enterprise Investment Scheme deferral relief as there are myriad conditions for the investment, the investor and the company to comply with.

The advantage of running a business with share capital

Irrespective of how you structure the transfer of your self-employment to the company, some of the investment you have accumulated in the business will become share capital in the company. Running a business with a share capital gives you new options to attract investment and reward yourself and your staff as follows.

1 *You can pay dividends to shareholders. Dividends are not liable to National Insurance but if you pay income tax at the higher rates you may have additional tax to pay (see Chapter 1 and Appendix 1). Paying a large dividend and a small salary may not be tax effective as HM Revenue and Customs can block any tax advantage by rules known as 'IR35' and the 'MSC' legislation (see Chapter 3).*

2 *Your spouse or civil partner, or other family members can own shares in the business and receive dividends on them. If you pay dividends to divert income which is really yours to someone else, usually a spouse, partner or child under 18 because they pay tax at a lower rate than you do, the income may be treated as if it still belonged to you and you could be taxed on it under what is known as the 'settlements legislation' (see Chapter 3).*

3 *External investors are more likely to want to invest in your business if they can become shareholders and as a result have a say in the business affairs under company law. Depending on the nature of your business, you may be able to structure it so that you are a 'qualifying company' for the purposes of the Enterprise Investment Scheme. This means that investors may be able to obtain income tax and capital gains relief on their investment as long as various conditions relating to the company, the investor and the shares are met. You will need professional advice.*

4 Trading through a limited company enables you to reward your staff with shares, or options to buy shares in the company. If these are awarded through a scheme approved by HM Revenue and Customs, the shares receive favourable tax treatment. The approved schemes are:

▷ Share incentive plans (SIPs);
▷ Enterprise management incentives (EMI);
▷ Save As You Earn (SAYE) schemes;
▷ Company share option plans (CSOP).

Each scheme has many detailed rules about the organization and structure of the company, the employees that can participate and the nature and extent of the shares or options involved. Directors can only participate if they own or control (including with other people such as a spouse or civil partner) less than 25% (in some cases 30%) of the company's shares.

Insight

If you are interested in rewarding staff and directors with shares you will need professional help to set up the scheme. You should be aware that all share schemes will involve you in additional administration.

10 THINGS TO REMEMBER

1 There is no easy way to tell whether or not you will save tax by trading as a limited company rather than a sole trader or partner. It all depends on the profits of the business, how much you retain in the business as working capital and the amount you pay yourself as salary and dividends. Your adviser could prepare comparative calculations to ascertain which option will minimize your tax bill but as your profits and the tax rates change annually: the best option in one year will not necessarily be so in another. Transferring your business to a limited company should usually be because of commercial factors, for example increased risk or the need for external investment.

2 When you incorporate, you have to close down your self-employment (or partnership) and start up a new company. You will transfer assets, registrations, losses and capital allowances from one to the other.

3 Freehold and leasehold land and buildings and goodwill are the most likely assets to give rise to a capital gains tax liability when you incorporate but there are several ways to help you to minimize your capital gains tax bill such as claiming gifts relief or incorporation rollover relief.

4 Another way to eliminate a gain on land or a building is not to transfer it to the company but owning the asset personally prevents the gain on other assets such as goodwill from being rolled over.

5 The value of assets transferred to a limited company can be credited to your director's loan account, paid to you in cash, or formed into share capital. The advantage of share capital is that the business has a stronger balance sheet. The disadvantage is that you cannot easily get your hands on the money (selling private company shares depends on you finding an independent investor willing to buy them). You

cannot draw money from the company against the value of your shares but you can withdraw a loan account as long as the business has the resources to enable you to do so. Your bank and other financiers will sometimes stipulate that your investment must be tied up in the business as share capital.

6   The main advantage of claiming gifts relief to defer a capital gain is that the consideration does not have to be treated as share capital, which it does if you claim incorporation rollover relief.

7   Gifts relief must be claimed on your tax return (use Helpsheet IR295). Rollover relief is given automatically without the need for you to make a claim.

8   If you claim rollover relief, the issue of shares on incorporation must be reported to HM Revenue and Customs on form 42 by 7 July following the tax year in which the shares are issued. This form may also need to be completed at other times if you make changes to your shares, for example if you issue new ones. You will require help to complete it.

9   If you have more than one business you could defer some of your gains by claiming rollover relief against an investment in assets in that venture rather than the new company (see Chapters 8 and 13).

10 Forming a limited company is straightforward but running and getting rid of one is not.

12

....

Closing a business

In this chapter:
- *closing down your self-employment*
- *closing down a company*
- *VAT de-registration*
- *redundancy payments*

In Chapter 3 we looked at the tax consequences of starting up your
business. We now consider what happens when you close it down.
There are many reasons why a business closes such as retirement,
failure to make a profit and personal reasons. A business may also
be shut down because it is incorporated (see Chapter 11) or sold to
a third party (see Chapter 13).

The closure process depends on whether you have been running an
unincorporated business (sole trader or partnership) or a limited
company. Closing down an unincorporated business is relatively
straightforward. Closing a company is more complicated because
unless it is solvent and its affairs very simple, it can only be closed
by a formal liquidation.

Closing down an unincorporated business

We considered the procedure for closing down a self-employment
or partnership in Chapter 11. This chapter looks at how your
business is taxed in the final years.

CESSATION DATE

The first thing to decide is a date for the business to cease. Over the lifetime of your business all your profits are taxed so you cannot reduce your taxable profits by choosing one date over another.

ALLOCATING PROFITS TO TAX YEARS

In Chapter 4, you learned that there are special rules for taxing business profits when a business starts. There are also special rules for taxing profits when a business ceases. The way in which they operate depends on the date you stop trading and your last accounting year end. Sometimes the rules for the opening and closing years overlap if you are only self-employed for a short period.

Examples

Cora, who has been self-employed for many years, retires on 30 September 2009. Her accounting year end was previously 31 March. Her 2009/10 self-assessment will be for the period 1 April 2009 to 30 September 2009.

Derek has been self-employed for ten years preparing accounts to 31 October each year. He stops being self-employed on 31 December 2009. When he drew up his first accounts, he was taxed twice on the same profits because his year end is a date other than 31 March or 5 April. This created overlap profits of £5,000. His trading profits are as follows:

- *Year to 31 October 2008*   £30,000
- *1 November 2008–31 December 2009 (14 months)*   £25,000

His taxable profits are:

Tax year	Accounting period	Profits £
2008/09	Year to 31 October 2008	**30,000**
2009/10	1 November 2008–31 December 2009 (14 months)	25,000
	Less: Overlap profits	–5,000
	Taxable profit	**20,000**

··

Insight

Depending on your accounting date and the date you cease your self-employment you may find that more than 12 months worth of profits are taxed in your final tax year but if you are entitled to overlap relief this reduces your profits.

··

Edwardo prepares accounts to 31 May and has overlap profits of £2,000. He ceases self-employment on 31 December 2009. His trading profits as are follows:

▶ *Year to 31 May 2008*   £15,000
▶ *Year to 31 May 2009*   £10,000
▶ *1 June 2009–31 December 2009 (7 months)*   £ 5,000

His taxable profits are:

Tax year	Accounting period	Profits £
2008/09	Year to 31 May 2008	**15,000**
2009/10	Year to 31 May 2009 (12 months)	10,000
	1 June 2009–31 December 2009 (7 months)	5,000
	Less: Overlap profits	–2,000
	Taxable profit	**13,000**

If Edwardo's overlap profits had been £20,000 instead of £2,000 he would have made a loss of £5,000 (see Losses).

Flo prepares accounts to 31 August and ceases self-employment on 30 April 2010. She has overlap profits of £10,000. Her trading profits as are follows:

- ▶ *Year to 31 August 2008* £ 20,000
- ▶ *1 September 2008–30 April 2010 (20 months)* £ 15,000

Her taxable profits are:

Tax year	Accounting period	Profits £
2008/09	Year to 31 August 2008	**20,000**
2009/10	Year to 31 August 2009 (12 months) £15,000 × 12 months/20 months	**9,000**
2010/11	1 September 2009-30 April 2010 (8 months) £15,000 × 8 months/20 months	6,000
	Less: Overlap profits	−10,000
	Loss	**−4,000**

As Flo has no accounting date ending in 2009/10, a year's worth of profits from her final accounts are taxed in that year. The balance of eight months is taxed in 2010/11. There is no choice about when Flo can deduct the overlap relief – it can only be deducted from the final tax year. Flo has various options for using her loss (see Chapter 5).

OVERLAP RELIEF

Overlap profits were created when you first started to be self-employed because you chose to prepare your accounts to a date other than 31 March or 5 April (see Chapter 4). You may have already used some of your overlap profits if you changed your year end. Any overlap relief that is left over can be deducted from the taxable profits of your final self-employed year. You will know how much your overlap profits are because each year you have to enter them on the self-employment pages of your tax form.

Insight

If you have a year end other than 31 March or 5 April and no overlap profits, this is probably because you made a loss in your first accounting period.

STOCK

When you stop being self-employed, you may have left-over stock. You cannot ignore it for tax purposes and must value it accurately. If you take it from the business for your own use, you must value it at market price. If you sell it to someone connected to you (a spouse, civil partner or relative) it must usually be valued at its sale price or its cost, whichever is the highest amount.

CAPITAL ALLOWANCES

You cannot claim writing down, annual investment or first year allowances in the year that you cease your business. It is also quite probable that you will take some assets (such as your car) out of the business when you stop trading. These assets must be taken out of the capital allowance calculation at their market value (not tax written down value). The same rule applies if you sell the assets to someone connected with you such as your spouse, civil partner or relation.

LOSSES

If you make a loss in your final year it is calculated in the usual way. It may be increased by overlap relief giving you a bigger loss to claim if you are a sole trader or a partner (see Overlap relief). Loss claims when you cease in business are covered in detail in Chapter 5.

INCOME AND EXPENSES INCURRED AFTER THE FINAL ACCOUNTING PERIOD

After you have closed down your business, you may unexpectedly receive income or incur expenses relating to the business. For example you may receive payment for a debt that you had previously written off in your accounts as an irrecoverable bad debt. These items cannot be ignored. 'Post-cessation receipts' (as such income is called) are either treated as taxable income in the year you receive them, or if you are a sole trader or partner and you receive the income within six years of ceasing the business, you can ask for it to be treated as the income of the year when you stopped trading. You will want to do this if it results in you paying less tax, for example because you had unused losses in that year or a lower income than the current year. To opt for this treatment you must enter the income and state the tax year concerned on the additional information pages of the tax return (see Questions 15 and 16 'Other UK income') in the year you receive the money and file the form on time. You do not need to alter the tax form for the year you ceased in business.

If you incur certain expenses (known as 'post-cessation expenses') within the seven years after ceasing your business, you can deduct them from:

▶ *post-cessation receipts (if you have any); or*
▶ *your other income and gains for the year in which they arise.*

To obtain a tax deduction for post-cessation expenses you must claim them by the second 31 January filing date following the tax year in which you incurred the expense (so for 2010/11 by 31 January 2013). The type of expenses that you can claim as post-cessation expenses are:

▶ *The costs of remedying defective work;*
▶ *Damages;*
▶ *Associated legal and insurance costs;*
▶ *Bad debts and debt recovery costs;*
▶ *Professional indemnity insurance.*

Closing down a limited company

The tax consequences of closing down a company are more complicated than the cessation rules for a self-employment or partnership. The degree of complexity depends on whether the company is solvent, in administration or liquidation. Administration and liquidation are formal arrangements under company law for winding up a company.

STRIKING-OFF A COMPANY

The simplest way to get rid of a limited company that you no longer need is to have it 'struck-off' the register of companies. You can only do this if you obtain HM Revenue and Customs approval. Their consent will usually be given if you have filed the company's final accounts and returns and settled the outstanding corporation tax, PAYE and VAT (or provide an undertaking to do so). It is usual to have paid out the majority of any remaining profits by way of a dividend before applying to HM Revenue and Customs to strike the company off the register.

A capital gain could arise on the distribution of the final profits in the company but it depends on the original cost of the shares, the amount of the payment and the availability of the annual exemption. You should take professional advice before striking-off a company.

Insight

For a company with no outstanding debts apart from amounts owed to director/shareholders, HM Revenue and Customs will usually agree that any funds remaining in the company can be distributed to its shareholders without income tax consequences if the sums involved are small.

FORMAL ARRANGEMENTS

If your company is insolvent (or it has complicated affairs) you will only be able to close it down by a formal liquidation. In such cases dealing with the tax authorities on company matters is taken out of your hands as they are dealt with by the liquidator (or administrator).

The principal concern for you as a shareholder is with regard to capital gains tax. If you make a gain on a capital sum paid out on liquidation you will need to take advice about the reliefs available to you.

VAT de-registration

If you cease your business you have to de-register for VAT from the date you stop trading by completing form VAT 7. You will then be sent a final VAT return to complete.

In your final return you may have to account for VAT on any unsold stock and on assets such as equipment, vans (but not most cars), computers, furniture etc. You should normally value the items at the price you would expect to pay for them in their present condition. If their value is £6,714 or less (£6,000 or less from 4 January 2011) you do not have to account for VAT (the official limit is £1,000 or more of VAT). You must keep a list of all these items irrespective of whether you have to pay VAT on them. If you use a VAT scheme you may have to follow additional procedures, and barristers have to account for their outstanding fees in accordance with special rules. If HM Revenue and Customs are satisfied with your application for de-registration you will receive official confirmation of de-registration on form VAT 35. HM Revenue and Customs may inspect your records before finalizing your de-registration application.

From the date that you de-register you must not charge VAT. In some limited circumstances however you can reclaim VAT for up to three years after de-registration on:

▶ *Irrecoverable bad debts (if you did not use the cash accounting scheme).*

> *Professional invoices, for example from your solicitor or accountant provided that the services relate to the period when you were VAT registered.*

To reclaim this VAT you must complete form VAT 427 and send it together with the original invoices to HM Revenue and Customs Accounting Adjustments (VAT 427 team).

For further information on VAT de-registration see www.hmrc.gov.uk/vat/managing/change/cancel-reclaim.htm.

Closing down your PAYE scheme

In addition to notifying the HM Revenue and Customs department handling your PAYE scheme that you have ceased trading, you will need to undertake the following:

> *Pay employees up to their leaving date including any entitlement to holiday pay;*
> *Issue employees with a form P45 (see Chapter 7);*
> *Pay redundancy pay (see Redundancy payments);*
> *Complete all outstanding end of year returns P35, P11Ds etc. (see Chapter 7);*
> *Pay all outstanding PAYE and National Insurance, including Class 1A and Class 1B contributions.*

Insight

Before they close down your PAYE scheme HM Revenue and Customs may conduct a final PAYE inspection to make sure that there are no outstanding issues or liabilities so you need to maintain good payroll records.

REDUNDANCY PAYMENTS

If you lay-off your staff because you are closing down your business you will be liable to pay them statutory redundancy (paid at a set rate) if they have been employed by you for two or more years since the age of 18. If you are self-employed or a partner you are not entitled to receive statutory redundancy if you close the business but if you are a company director working under an employment contract you may be eligible for a payment. For further information about redundancy refer to the Business Link website (see Appendix 4).

Redundancy payments are not liable to income tax or Class 1 National Insurance but unpaid wages, bonuses and holiday pay are taxed under PAYE in the usual way. If you provide counselling services and retraining for redundant employees this perk is tax-exempt (see Chapter 7).

Should you decide to pay your employees a termination payment of more than the statutory minimum, they will not have to pay income tax and employee's Class 1 National Insurance on it, and you will not have to pay employer's Class 1 National Insurance as long as they had no contractual entitlement to the payment and the package you give them is £30,000 or less. You will require professional advice, particularly if you want to pay a termination payment to a company director.

10 THINGS TO REMEMBER

1 *Closing down an unincorporated business is straightforward. Closing down a company is more complicated. In most cases a company can only be closed by a formal liquidation.*

2 *The first thing to decide is your cessation date. If you are self-employed you may save tax by choosing to end the business in one tax year rather than another especially if your income has fallen.*

3 *If your accounting date is other than 5 April or 31 March you may be entitled to overlap relief. This will reduce your taxable profits in your final tax year so don't forget to claim it.*

4 *When you close down a self-employment or partnership you have to tell HM Revenue and Customs that the business has ceased.*

5 *You should ensure that you cancel your Class 2 National Insurance direct debit from the date you stop being in business.*

6 *You cannot claim writing down, annual investment or first year allowances in the year that you cease your business.*

7 *There are special rules for taxing income received and expenses incurred after your final accounting period.*

8 *If you are VAT registered you must de-register for VAT and complete a final VAT return. Remember to account for VAT on stock and assets if they are worth more than £6,714 (£6,000 from 4 January 2011).*

9 *If you have employees make sure that you pay them all outstanding pay including holiday pay, and redundancy and termination pay if appropriate.*

10 *You will need to complete all outstanding PAYE forms and then arrange to close down your PAYE scheme.*

13

Selling a business

In this chapter:
- *selling shares or assets?*
- *will you receive cash or shares for the business?*
- *reducing capital gains tax*

In the last two chapters we looked at the tax consequences of the disposal of your business by transferring it to a limited company and closing it down or liquidation. In this chapter we consider the tax consequences of the ultimate disposal – sale to a third party. Selling a business is complicated and this is a time when you will need professional help.

What are you selling?

When you come to sell your business, the first thing to ask yourself is 'what are you selling?' The answer depends on whether you are self-employed, in partnership or a limited company. The tax consequences for sole traders and partners are relatively straightforward. Selling a limited company is more complicated because you can sell either the individual assets or the entire company by selling its shares.

SOLE TRADERS

If you operate as a sole trader you cannot sell the 'business' because legally there is nothing to sell as there is with a limited company. You can however sell all the individual business assets such as land, buildings, equipment, goodwill (such as your client list) and stock. In some situations you might decide to incorporate your self-employment in order to sell it (see Chapter 11).

Insight

If you are going to incorporate your business prior to a sale you need to plan ahead because you will minimize your capital gains tax liability if you are incorporated for more than a year before the sale.

The tax consequences of selling your self-employed assets are as follows:

▶ *Land, buildings, plant fixed to a building, goodwill and intangible assets such as patents, licences, rights and designs are all liable to capital gains tax (see Chapter 11). You have to work out the gain on each item individually, deduct the cost of acquiring the asset and the purchase and sale costs and then claim any reliefs to which you are entitled such as entrepreneurs' relief (see Chapter 1 for an example of the calculation).*

▶ *Equipment on which you have claimed capital allowances is not liable to capital gains tax unless the selling price for an individual item is £6,000 or more. 'Chattels' relief will reduce any gain that does arise. If you have a balance brought forward on a capital allowances pool you will include the proceeds from the sale of equipment in your final capital allowance calculation which will give you either a balancing allowance or a balancing charge (see Chapter 6).*

▶ *Income from the sale of stock will be included in your final trading accounts and is liable to income tax.*

▶ *If you sell your debts there is no capital gains tax to pay. If you receive less than the debts are worth you will include a deduction for bad debts in your final trading accounts.*

▶ *If you are not selling the business as a going concern you may have to charge VAT on some of the assets (see Company).*

Once you have sold the assets to a third party, you will close own your business along the lines described in Chapter 12. Any asset with a balance on a capital allowance pool that you keep for yourself, such as a car, must be valued at its market value and included as a disposal in the final capital allowance calculation.

A tax effective sale agreement

Balancing your requirements with those of the buyer can be difficult. As the seller you will probably want an agreement which allocates a greater proportion of the sale proceeds to those assets which are liable to capital gains tax (principally property) rather than those that have income tax consequences. Although there is little difference between the rates of capital gains tax and the basic rate of income tax, you will save tax by having gains rather than income because you may be able to claim entrepreneurs' relief. In some circumstances you can also defer paying tax on your gain (see Reducing capital gains tax).

On the other hand the buyer will prefer to allocate higher values to goodwill (if they trade as a limited company), equipment and stock rather than property because they can obtain tax relief on these items in the first accounting period after the purchase. They will not receive tax relief on the sums they invest in land and buildings until they sell the property.

Insight

HM Revenue and Customs may challenge the division of the sales proceeds between the various assets. You will require professional help to agree the allocation of the sales price so that it is acceptable to you, the purchaser and the tax authorities.

PARTNERS

A partnership may sell its assets or the individual partners may sell their share in the partnership. If a partnership sells its assets to a third party, the tax consequences are the same as they are for a sole trader, with each partner being liable for capital gains tax on their share of the partnership property and goodwill.

Any payment received for the sale of stock and work-in-progress is adjusted in the final partnership accounts and the disposal of equipment with a brought forward pool value is included in the final capital allowances computation. The partnership is then closed down (see Chapter 12).

A more common scenario is for a partner (or partners) to sell all or part of their partnership share to their existing partners or a new partner joining the partnership. The tax consequences are then as follows:

▶ *If you leave a partnership and the partnership continues in business without you, the withdrawal of your investment in the partnership (your capital account) has no capital gains tax consequences unless the partnership assets such as land, buildings and goodwill are revalued and you are given a share of the profit resulting from that revaluation.*
▶ *If you continue as a partner but you reduce your profit share by selling it to an existing or new partner, you will have a capital gains tax liability if land, buildings and goodwill are revalued. Capital gains tax is due irrespective of whether you withdraw the revaluation profit or the new partner's contribution, or whether it remains invested in your capital account in the partnership.*

COMPANY

If a company wants to sell its business it has two options:

▶ *to sell its assets (as would be the case where a sole trader sells up); or*
▶ *for all the shareholders to agree to sell their shares (here the purchaser takes over all the company's assets and liabilities including the tax liabilities).*

The vendor will usually prefer to sell shares because this minimizes their capital gains tax liability (see Case study).

The purchaser often prefers to buy assets because it is usually more straightforward without the risk of taking on all the company's liabilities. An asset sale has the following tax advantages for them:

▶ *Capital allowances can be claimed (see Chapter 6);*
▶ *A tax deduction can be claimed on the write-off of the goodwill (assuming that the purchaser is a company);*
▶ *The assets may be a suitable reinvestment in a claim for rollover relief (see Reducing capital gains tax).*

If however the purchaser can be persuaded to buy shares, they will obtain two tax advantages:

▶ *Stamp duty on the acquisition of shares is less than the cost of stamp duty land tax on the purchase of land and buildings.*
▶ *No VAT is charged on the sale of shares.*

In some circumstances the vendor may prefer to sell assets instead of shares where:

▶ *It has trading losses which can be off-set against the gains (see Chapter 5);*
▶ *It can claim rollover relief.*

Insight

The vendor (seller) and the purchaser (buyer) may have different objectives in the sale negotiations and what will be tax advantageous to one party is likely to be to the detriment of the other. These differences will need to be reconciled if a tax effective sale is to result.

VAT

VAT on the sale of a business is notoriously complex. If you sell an entity as a going concern (i.e. a new owner takes it over and operates it without major changes), you do not have to charge VAT on the sale. If the business is not sold as a going concern, you must charge VAT on the assets, including goodwill, stock and equipment and some cars. As far as property is concerned, sometimes you must charge VAT even if you are selling the business as a going concern. HM Revenue and Customs' view of whether you have sold a business as a going concern may differ from your own and many cases end up being considered by the First-tier Tribunal.

Insight

It is essential to take professional advice about the correct VAT treatment on the sale of your business because if you get it wrong the amount you receive for the sale could be significantly reduced if you have to pay VAT out of the proceeds.

Case study – shares or assets?

The following case study illustrates the tax that will be saved where a company sells shares rather than assets.

FF Ltd has been trading since March 2002. It owns freehold premises included in its accounts at £300,000 and has net current assets of £200,000. Its share capital is £50,000 and it has reserves of £450,000.

GG Ltd, a competitor, wants to buy the business and offered FF Ltd £750,000 for it in October 2010. This sum is divided as follows: property and goodwill £550,000 and net current assets £200,000. FF Ltd wants to know how much tax it will owe depending on whether it sells shares or its assets.

SHARES

	£
Offer by GG Ltd to buy the shares from the shareholders of FF Ltd	750,000
Cost of shares	–50,000
Gain	700,000

(Contd)

	£
Capital gains tax at 10% (assuming entrepreneurs' relief is available)	70,000
Amount received by shareholders of FF Ltd (£750,000 – £70,000)	**680,000**

ASSETS

	£	£
Assets in accounts		500,000
Increase in value of property and goodwill	250,000	250,000
Indexation allowance on the £300,000 cost of property (approximately)	–72,000	
Gain	178,000	
		750,000
Corporation tax on gain (assumed rate 22.47% × £178,000)	–40,000	–40,000
Distributed to the shareholders when the company ceases trading (£750,000 – £40,000)		**710,000**
Cost of shares		–50,000
Gain		660,000
Capital gains tax at 28% (assuming the higher rate applies and no further reliefs are available) (£660,000 × 28%)		184,800
Amount received by the shareholders of FF Ltd (£710,000 – £184,800)		**525,200**

If FF Ltd sells its assets and is then liquidated, the shareholders receive £154,800 less than they would do if the company sold its shares without selling the assets first. This is because on an asset sale capital gains tax is charged twice:

1 *On the increase in value of the premises (as corporation tax); and*

2 *On the shareholders when the company makes a capital distribution (as capital gains tax).*

If GG Ltd is aware of the comparative tax advantage to FF Ltd of a share sale, it may use this information to negotiate a reduced price for the shares. Alternatively, if GG Ltd only wants to buy the assets, it may be persuaded to pay a higher price to cover FF Ltd's extra tax costs. Insofar as the sales proceeds are allocated to goodwill and equipment, GG Ltd will be able to claim corporation tax relief on the write-off of the goodwill and capital allowances on the equipment (see Assets) and these tax savings may go some way to off-setting the higher price that FF Ltd will expect from an asset sale.

Will you receive cash or shares?

When you sell a company you need to agree what you will receive in return and when you will receive it. The most straightforward option is for the purchaser of the company to pay you in 'cash'. This means that you receive payment on the agreed sale date and that is the end of the matter. Your tax liability is calculated as shown in the Case study according to whether you have sold shares or assets. If you sell your business for cash to be paid in the future, conditional on the company's ongoing business performance, you will still have to pay capital gains tax. Working out when this liability arises and valuing the sales proceeds in this case is more complicated.

If you agree to sell the shares in your company to another company there is an alternative to being paid in cash – you can trade your shares for shares in the purchasing company. This is called a share for share arrangement or a paper exchange. You can also exchange shares for loan stock. The advantage of agreeing to a paper exchange is that you do not dispose of your shares for capital gains tax purposes until you sell the new shares. When you come to sell the new shares at a future date you will deduct the amount you originally paid for the old shares in calculating your capital gain.

Most people selling a business prefer to receive cash for it straight away and usually consider shares to be a risky option (unless they are quoted on the stock exchange). A compromise deal is often reached to sell shares in your company partly in exchange for cash and partly for shares in the purchasing company. The part you receive in cash is liable to capital gains tax whilst the gain on the paper exchange is deferred until the new shares are sold.

Example

Hannah the director/shareholder of HH Ltd agrees to sell the company to II Ltd. She receives cash of £1,000,000 and shares in II Ltd valued at £1,000,000 in return for her shares in HH Ltd which originally cost £100,000 four years ago. Her capital gains tax position is as follows:

	Cash(£)	Shares(£)
Sales proceeds	1,000,000	1,000,000
Cost of shares – divided 50:50	–50,000	50,000
Gain	950,000	
Capital gains tax at the 10% entrepreneurs' relief rate assuming that the shares qualify (£950,000 × 10%)	**95,000**	

Hannah has no capital gains tax liability on the £1 million she is paid in shares in II Ltd. She will however have to pay capital gains tax when she sells these shares. At that point she can deduct £50,000 as the cost of the shares in II Ltd. This is half the original cost of £100,000 and not the £1 million that they were worth at the date of exchange.

EARN-OUT

If as part of the sale agreement you are to have a continuing involvement in the business, you may not receive all the shares straight away. Some of them may be held back and only transferred to you if the company's performance meets expectation. This is called an 'earn-out'. The value of the earn-out is treated as part of the shares being exchanged so once again no capital gains tax is due until the new shares are sold.

Insight

If the earn-out arrangement with the purchaser stipulates that you will receive shares for personal performance they will be liable to income tax and National Insurance as employment earnings.

Reducing capital gains tax

If the sale of your business results in a capital gains tax liability, there are several ways to reduce or defer it.

CHECK YOUR ENTITLEMENT TO ENTREPRENEURS' RELIEF

You will save capital gains tax if you are eligible for entrepreneurs' relief (see Appendix 1). This was discussed in outline in Chapter 1. Entrepreneurs' relief is not available on all business disposals. Broadly, to qualify for relief on the sale of shares you must meet three conditions for at least a year before the disposal:

▶ *You need to own at least 5% of the ordinary shares in the company and have 5% of the voting rights;*
▶ *You must be an employee or officer of the company (although you do not have to work full-time); and*
▶ *The company must be a trading company. Determining whether a company qualifies as a trading company is not as straightforward as it may seem.*

CLAIM ROLLOVER RELIEF

Rollover relief works like a rolled over lottery jackpot but instead of the prize being deferred, the date when you have to pay capital gains tax is rolled over to a future date. To qualify you must reinvest in new assets. The assets you sell and the replacement assets must be 'qualifying assets' and you must make the reinvestment during the year before the sale or up to three years afterwards. You do not need to use the new assets in the same business and you can sell one type of asset and reinvest in another. The usual qualifying assets are land, buildings and fixed plant and machinery (for a full list see Chapter 8). Goodwill is a qualifying asset only if you are a sole trader or partner. If you only reinvest part of the proceeds, the gain may be only partly rolled over, or not rolled over at all as the following Example illustrates.

Example

When James sells his business, he disposes of all his assets including retail premises for £350,000, making a gain on the property of £200,000. A year after selling his business he invests £375,000 in a freehold restaurant building and goodwill. The gain is deferred by being rolled over.

	£
Gain on retail premises	200,000
Rollover relief (no restriction because all the sales proceeds are reinvested)	−200,000
Immediately chargeable gain	−
Cost of restaurant premises and goodwill	375,000
Rolled over amount	−200,000
Revised cost of restaurant and goodwill for capital gains tax	**175,000**

When James comes to sell the restaurant his gain will include the gain from the retail premises but he may be entitled to rollover that gain too.

If James only reinvests £300,000 in the restaurant the calculation goes like this:

	£
Gain on retail premises	200,000
Rollover relief (restricted because £50,000 of the sales proceeds are not reinvested)	−150,000
Immediately chargeable gain before reliefs	**50,000**
Cost of restaurant premises and goodwill	300,000
Rolled over amount	−150,000
Revised cost of restaurant and goodwill for capital gains tax	**150,000**

If James only reinvests £100,000 in the restaurant, he has not reinvested any of the gain.

	£
Gain on retail premises	200,000
Rollover relief (restricted because £250,000 of the sales proceeds are not reinvested)	−
Immediately chargeable gain before reliefs	**200,000**
Cost of restaurant premises and goodwill	**100,000**

Insight

If you only reinvest part of the sales proceeds in new assets, rollover relief is restricted. As a result it may not necessarily give you the capital gains tax benefit you expect.

CLAIM ENTERPRISE INVESTMENT SCHEME DEFERRAL RELIEF

You can claim Enterprise Investment Scheme deferral relief if you invest in shares in a company qualifying for the Enterprise Investment Scheme one year before the disposal of your premises and up to three years afterwards. There are many detailed rules relating to this relief and you are likely to require professional advice.

Using professionals

Selling a company is complex and you will need to engage experienced advisers to help you. You will usually need both an accountant and a solicitor. They will usually undertake the following for you:

▶ *Assist you to negotiate the sale agreement with the purchaser.*
▶ *Determine your future role (if you are to have one).*
▶ *Calculate your capital gains tax liabilities and tell you when they are due to be paid.*
▶ *Suggest ways to minimize your capital gains tax liability.*
▶ *Advise whether or not you should charge VAT on the sale.*
▶ *On a share sale, provide the purchaser with financial information so that they can check out the company's liabilities (including to all the various taxes). This is called the 'due diligence' process.*
▶ *On a share sale, negotiate with the purchaser regarding the indemnities and warranties they require concerning the company's tax liabilities.*
▶ *Draw up the sale document.*
▶ *Make the necessary conveyances of land and buildings and deal with the stamp duty land tax.*
▶ *Liaise with HM Revenue and Customs regarding any contentious issues.*

10 THINGS TO REMEMBER

1 *A sole trader cannot sell their business but they can sell the individual business assets. A capital gains tax liability may arise on the sale of land, buildings, goodwill and intangible assets such as patents and designs.*

2 *A partner will usually sell all or part of their partnership share to their fellow partners. Capital gains tax is due on the value of the revalued assets regardless of whether the profit is withdrawn or left invested in the partnership.*

3 *If you sell a limited company you need to decide whether you are selling shares in the company or the company's assets. An asset sale will usually have tax advantages for the purchaser but the vendor will generally prefer to sell shares. A means has to be found of balancing the interests of both parties.*

4 *If you sell shares in your company to another company, instead of being paid cash for the sale you can be paid wholly or partly in shares in the purchasing company. This has the advantage of deferring some of your capital gains tax liability until the shares are sold but it is a riskier option.*

5 *If you continue to be involved in the business after it is sold, some of the shares you have received in payment may be held back to a future date. This is known as an 'earn-out'. No capital gains tax is due until the shares are sold.*

6 *If you have a capital gains tax liability on the disposal of your business check out your entitlement to entrepreneurs' relief.*

7 *You may be able to defer a gain on the disposal of a business by investing in qualifying assets such as land and buildings and claiming rollover relief.*

8 *You can also defer a capital gain by investing in shares in a company qualifying for the Enterprise Investment Scheme.*

9 VAT on the sale of a business is complex. If the business is sold as a going concern no VAT is due but HMRC's view of what is a going concern may differ from your own. Many cases end up being considered by the First-tier Tribunal.

10 You will need to engage experienced advisers to help you sell your business.

14

Passing on a business

In this chapter:
- *giving away your business*
- *what happens to my business when I die?*
- *making a will*

We have already looked at two ways of disposing of your business – closing it down and selling it. In this chapter we consider a third option – passing it on to someone else such as your children or other relatives. We also consider the tax consequences for your business when you die and look at the inheritance tax reliefs available for business and agricultural property. Irrespective of whether you want to hand over the reins while you are still alive or continue working until you die, you will need professional advice to minimize the inheritance tax on your estate.

When you die your executors have to pay inheritance tax on the value of your estate above a certain threshold including the value of your business (see Appendix 1). If however you are entitled to business or agricultural property relief there may be no inheritance tax to pay on the business or farm.

Insight

If you are unsure whether inheritance tax will be charged on your estate you should refer to the calculations in Chapter 1, bearing in mind that inheritance tax depends on the nature of your assets, who you leave them to and your marital status.

Giving away your business

At some stage in your life you may decide that you want to retire from your business and pass it over to someone else, usually your children or someone from the next generation. Although this transaction has both capital gains tax and inheritance tax consequences, in most cases there will be no immediate capital gains tax charge because of 'gifts relief' (see Gifts relief) and there will be no inheritance tax to pay if you are entitled to business or agricultural property relief (see Inheritance tax).

When you transfer your business to your children or other relatives, it has to be commercially valued because it is being transferred to a 'connected' person (see Appendix 3). Valuing small businesses is subjective and the amount you think the business is worth and the value that HM Revenue and Customs place on it could differ significantly.

Insight

If you claim gifts relief HMRC usually accept your valuation without protracted negotiations but may query it if the person you give the business to later sells it. As this may be many years down the line it is important to keep detailed records.

If you give your business to your spouse or civil partner the business is transferred for capital gains tax purposes at its cost so there is no gain and no loss. For inheritance tax, the business is usually transferred to a spouse or civil partner at its commercial value but there will be no inheritance tax to pay provided that they are from the UK (domiciled). If your spouse or civil partner is not UK domiciled you can only transfer assets worth £55,000 to them free of inheritance tax (see Chapter 1).

GIFTS RELIEF

Although you need to value your business, most gifts of business assets do not attract an immediate capital gains tax charge because you can claim gifts relief to defer the gain until the recipient sells the business. Details of how gifts relief is calculated can be found in Chapter 11.

The principal assets eligible for gifts relief are:

▶ *Business assets (including agricultural property) used in a self-employment or partnership; and*
▶ *Shares in or assets used by a trading company in which you own at least 5% of the shares.*

You have to claim gifts relief in your tax return (see HMRC's Helpsheet 295).

INHERITANCE TAX

Providing that you live for seven or more years after transferring your business, there will be no inheritance tax to pay. This kind of transfer made during your lifetime is called a 'potentially exempt transfer' because there potentially may be tax to pay but it all depends on a number of factors. If you die within seven years of transferring your business, inheritance tax may be due on the transfer.

Insight
Whether or not inheritance tax is due on a potentially exempt transfer depends on its value, other gifts made in the seven-year period and the value of your nil rate band (see Appendix 1).

If you are entitled to 100% business or agricultural property relief no inheritance tax will be charged on the potentially exempt transfer (see What happens to your business when you die?). This relief can be jeopardized if the person you give the property to disposes of it before you die or the property ceases to meet the conditions to qualify for the relief. If you are not entitled to 100% business or agricultural property relief, any inheritance tax due on the transfer will be reduced if you live for three or more years after making the gift. If you claimed gifts relief, any inheritance tax which becomes due on the gift can be taken into account in working out the gain on an eventual sale of the business.

There are other tax consequences to giving away your business while you are alive depending on whether you operate as a sole trader, partner or company.

- ▶ **Sole trader:** *If you give away a business you have previously run as a sole trader you will simply pass over some or all of the business assets (including property, equipment, goodwill and stock) and then close down your self-employment. All the income tax considerations relevant to closing down a self-employment will apply to you (see Chapter 12).*
- ▶ **Partner:** *If a partner gives away his or her partnership share and/or capital account, the partnership will continue without needing to be closed down. Where just one partner remains they will operate from then on as a sole trader.*
- ▶ **Company:** *If you are a director/shareholder of a small limited company, you will usually pass control of your business to your heirs by giving away your shares. The company will continue trading.*

What happens to my business when I die?

Dying 'in-the-saddle' is something that few business people want to think about but it is vital to plan in advance to minimize inheritance tax and so that your business passes to your chosen successor. This means that you need to make a will (see Making a will).

DYING WITHOUT A WILL

If you die intestate (without making a will) your estate will go to your dependants and relatives in accordance with strict rules. This may jeopardize the smooth running of your business and may mean that it has to be sold.

Insight

It is possible to 'vary' an intestate estate within two years of your death by a formal variation (see Appendix 3) so that the assets pass in a different way. Everyone who would inherit under the intestacy must agree to the change and this is not always easy to achieve.

RUNNING THE BUSINESS UNTIL IT CAN BE PASSED ON

If you are a sole trader or the sole director/shareholder of a company, when you die there may be no one to run your business. You need to plan for this in advance by appointing suitable executors in your will such as the eventual beneficiaries and a solicitor or accountant. If the business has a viable existence without you, the executors will run the business from the date of your death to the date when probate is obtained so that the business can either be sold or passed on in accordance with the instructions in your will. If the business cannot continue without you, the executors will close it down. Either way if you are a sole trader, the business ceases on your death (see Chapter 12). If you are a partner or a director in a larger company, the business will probably continue after you die without the involvement of the executors. They will however need to liaise with the partnership or company to arrange for your capital account or director's loan account to be repaid to your estate. Depending on what is stipulated in any shareholder agreement, they will either sell or retain your shares. The executors are responsible for preparing estate accounts and tax returns for the administration period.

If you have insured your own life the executors will claim on the policy and pass the proceeds to the nominated beneficiaries. If the policy forms part of your estate the proceeds are liable to inheritance tax. If the policy is written in trust, there may be no inheritance tax to pay on the proceeds but the trust will be liable for inheritance tax and other taxes. If your spouse, civil partner or business partner has insured your life or your company has 'key-man' insurance, they will also make claims. The tax consequences are covered in Chapter 10.

CAPITAL GAINS TAX

Your business, partnership share or shareholdings have to be valued when you die but this is for the purposes of inheritance tax, not capital gains tax as there is no capital gains tax to pay when you die.

INHERITANCE TAX

If you bequeath everything to your spouse or civil partner (assuming that they are domiciled in the UK) there will be no inheritance tax to pay on your estate. Leaving everything to a spouse or civil partner results in your nil rate band (see Appendix 1) being unused. This unused proportion can be used to increase the nil rate band of your surviving spouse or civil partner when they die in due course (see Chapter 1). If you bequeath assets up to the value of the inheritance tax nil rate band to your children or other relatives no inheritance tax will be due but your surviving spouse or civil partner's nil rate band will either then not be increased, or only uprated by a smaller percentage. If your estate exceeds the nil rate band and you do not bequeath assets to a spouse or civil partner, inheritance tax will be due unless you are entitled to business property relief or agricultural property relief on your business or agricultural assets. In some circumstances a trust will be advantageous but you will need professional advice.

Business property relief

Your self-employed business, a partnership share or shares in an unquoted company may qualify for 100% business property relief. Bequests of partnership assets (property, equipment, goodwill etc.) or assets used by a company which you control, are eligible for 50% business property relief, as are shares in a quoted company which you control.

To qualify for business property relief:

▶ *you must have owned the business, shares or assets throughout the previous two-year period; and*
▶ *your business must not be principally concerned with holding investments or dealing in property or shares.*

Agricultural property relief

Most agricultural property (including a farmhouse) is entitled to 100% agricultural property relief. Agricultural property relief is sometimes denied if the land is not used for 'agriculture' for example where a farm has diversified. Where agricultural property relief does not apply, business property relief may be due instead.

To qualify for agricultural property relief:

▶ *you must have occupied the property for the purposes of agriculture throughout the previous two years; or*
▶ *you must have owned the property for seven years with either you or someone else farming it throughout that period.*

Making a will

If you have a business of any kind you should make a will and review it at least every couple of years in case there have been changes in legislation or your business operations. You will need to re-make your will if you marry, form a civil partnership or divorce. Should your will turn out to be unsuitable or tax-ineffective for any reason, it can be changed by a formal variation within two years of your death provided that all the beneficiaries agree to the changes.

10 THINGS TO REMEMBER

1 *Planning for your succession is an emotive subject but many businesses fold because the proprietor has devoted insufficient time to planning their succession and ensuring that the business qualifies for business or agricultural property relief.*

2 *If you give away your business during your lifetime you may be entitled to claim gifts relief. This will defer the tax on the gain until such time as the recipient sells the business.*

3 *Gifts relief is available on the assets used in an unincorporated business and shares in, or assets used by, a trading company in which you own at least 5% of the shares.*

4 *Provided that you live for seven or more years after transferring your business there is no inheritance tax to pay.*

5 *If you die within seven years of transferring your business inheritance tax may be due on the transfer depending on a number of factors.*

6 *If you leave your business to your spouse or civil partner on your death no inheritance tax will be due but this may not necessarily be the most tax effective thing to do.*

7 *Business or agricultural property relief may save your estate inheritance tax providing that you qualify for it. To do so you must have owned the business, shares or assets throughout the previous two-year period and your business must not be principally concerned with holding investments or dealing in property or shares.*

8 *In some circumstances a trust will be advantageous to planning the succession of your business.*

9 *A regularly reviewed will and professional advice are essential to minimizing your inheritance tax liability.*

10 *If you die without making a will your estate will go to your relatives and dependents in accordance with the strict rules of intestacy. This may not be what you wanted to happen and it could jeopardize the future viability of your business.*

Putting it all together

In this chapter:
- *tax in the early years of a new business*
- *important dates and forms*
- *avoiding pitfalls*

We have now looked at all the different taxes that affect a small business from formation to closure and you should have an understanding of how the UK tax system operates. If you are planning a new venture, you should appreciate that your tax will differ depending on whether you trade as a sole trader or limited company. If you are already running a small business, you will have considered the tax consequences of major investments such as buying equipment and taking on employees.

▶ *This chapter brings together many of the themes in the book as a case study. It highlights how tax affects a small business as it develops, which forms have to be completed and how to avoid costly mistakes.*

Nina's Kitchen

Meet Nina, she used to work as a PR consultant but left her job 18 months ago when she had her first baby. She is a keen cook and enjoys making chutneys and pickles which she gives away to friends and family. Recently they have been asking her for extra jars and even paying her for them. In June 2009 Nina took a stall at a local farmers' market and sold almost all her jars of chutney, taking £500. She then had a stall at a craft fair and sold another £300 worth of stock. Inspired by her success she approached some local shops and now has orders for a further 500 jars which she plans to make over the coming month.

Starting to trade

Until Nina started selling her chutneys and pickles to the public she was not trading. Even when she was occasionally paid for a jar of her condiments, she simply had a cookery hobby. Now she is trading more regularly what was once a hobby has become a business. Like many small business people, Nina has been rather overtaken by events and she has probably become a self-employed business even though this was not necessarily her original intention.

Insight

Irrespective of what she intends to do with the business at a later date, Nina must notify HM Revenue and Customs within three months of the date she started to be self-employed (probably when she went to the farmers' market in June 2009) otherwise she could be fined.

Nina completes HM Revenue and Customs form CWF1 'Becoming self-employed and registering for National Insurance Contributions and/or tax' which can be downloaded from www.hmrc.gov.uk/forms/cwf1.pdf or completed by calling the Self-Employed Registration Helpline on 0845 915 4515.

Refer to Chapter 3 for further information.

Getting organized

Since we last met up with Nina she has made sure that she complies with all the necessary planning and hygiene rules laid down by her local authority and she has taken out public and product liability insurance. She has also started to keep records on a computer spreadsheet recording her income and expenses. She files all her receipts in a box file in case she or the tax authorities need to refer to them at a later date.

Nina decides not to register for VAT because she is unsure how long she will be running the business for. She decides to pay Class 2 National Insurance and not to opt for a small earnings exception to preserve her state pension entitlement.

Nina and her husband who is employed as an engineer earning £25,000 a year claim Child Tax Credit, so she informs HM Revenue and Customs about her new business. As the couple receive only the family element of the award their claim is not affected.

Refer to Chapters 2 and 3 for further information.

Buying new equipment

Nina is finding it increasingly difficult to transport her produce in her small hatchback car so she decides to exchange it for a larger estate model. In November 2009 she buys a second-hand vehicle costing £6,000. She trades-in her old car for £2,000 and she finances the balance with a bank loan repayable over three years. Nina also buys a new fridge for her business at a cost of £550 and various items of kitchen equipment (pans, funnels, food processor etc.) costing £500. She makes a note to claim capital allowances on these items (see Claiming capital allowances)

Refer to Chapter 6 for further information.

Tax return time

Nina has now been in business for a year. She has been sent her first tax return to complete. Nina needs to decide on a suitable date to prepare her first accounts to. She is tempted to prepare them for a year to 31 May 2010 but in the end decides to keep her affairs simple by preparing accounts for the ten-month period 1 June 2009 to 31 March 2010.

Refer to Chapter 4 for further information.

Nina's accounting spreadsheet shows the following totals:

1 June 2009–31 March 2010	£
Sales	15,400
Jars and labels	−1,500
Ingredients	−2,800
Fridge	−550
Stall hire and entry fees	−650
Insurance	−300
Telephone	−420
Car costs	−5,400
Computer, office and administration	−525
Bank charges	−85
Advertising	−330
Car loan	−705
Nina	−5,000

STOCK

Unfortunately Nina forgot to count her stock of chutneys and pickles on 31 March 2010 because she did not know that she would use that date as her accounting year end. She therefore counts the unsold chutney at 31 May 2010 and finds that she has 500 jars in stock. Nina works out that she made 700 jars of chutney and sold 600 of them in April and May 2010 so she must have had 400 jars in stock at her year end. She sells each jar for £4 and she estimates that each one costs £1 to make. She values her stock at cost as this is less than the sales price, so her stock of finished produce is £400. Nina also works out that she took delivery of a new consignment of empty jars shortly before her year end at a cost of £420. Her total stock is therefore £820.

> ## Insight
> Your accounts must include an adjustment for opening and closing stock, that is the stock you had on hand at the beginning and the end of the accounting period. It is valued according to set rules at the lower of its cost and its selling price.

Adjusting the accounting records for tax purposes
Nina examines her accounting records in more detail and finds that:

- *Her insurance policy expires in August 2010. She therefore deducts £125 from her costs because five months' worth of the costs relate to the next tax year (£300 × 5 months/12 months).*
- *She receives a phone bill in April 2010 which relates to her previous accounting year so she includes a further £70 of telephone costs.*
- *Nina realizes that her car costs include both her vehicle running costs of £1,400 and the net cost of buying the new car, i.e. £4,000 (£6,000 cost – £2,000 trade-in). The car itself cannot be written off in the year in which she buys it because it is a capital purchase. Capital allowances can be claimed instead. Nina works out that she has used the vehicle 60% of the time for work purposes and 40% of the time for private journeys. She therefore reduces her car running costs by £560 (£1,400 × 40% = £560).*
- *Nina's car loan includes loan repayments of £555 and interest of £150. Nina realizes that she cannot claim a tax deduction for the loan repayments because this is also capital expenditure.*
- *Nina takes £500 each month from the business for her personal expenditure. These sums are her drawings and she*

cannot claim tax relief on them. She also takes one jar of chutney each week for personal use. She therefore adjusts her accounts by £172 (43 weeks at £4 per jar) for these items.

Refer to Chapter 4 for further information.

USE OF HOME ALLOWANCE

Nina works from home. She has not yet included anything in her accounting records for her home costs even though her gas and electricity bills have increased since she has been in business. Nina estimates that her costs of working from home are £5 per week (£215 for the 10 months). She decides not to include a deduction for part of the mortgage because she does not want to jeopardize the capital gains tax exemption on the family home.

....

Insight

One way to avoid the issue of capital gains tax when you run a business from home is to claim a 'use of home allowance' and deduct a few pounds per week or month instead of claiming a proportion of your domestic bills.

....

Refer to Chapter 8 for further information.

CLAIMING CAPITAL ALLOWANCES

Nina's accounting records include four items of capital expenditure:

- ▶ *The new car costing £6,000 and emitting 150g/km of carbon dioxide;*
- ▶ *The sale of the old car for £2,000 (it was worth £2,400 when she started the business);*
- ▶ *A fridge costing £550; and*
- ▶ *Kitchen equipment costing £500.*

Nina works out her capital allowances as follows.

Description	Equipment pool (£)	Single asset car pool (60% business) (£)	Private use (40%) (£)	Allowances (£)
Assets introduced		2,400		
Disposal of car		−2,000		
Balancing allowance		−400	160	240
Additions	1,050	6,000		
Annual investment allowance: (100%)	−1,050			1,050
Writing down allowance: 20% × 10 months/12 months		−1,000	400	600
Value carried forward to the next accounting period	0	**5,000**		
Capital allowances				**1,890**

> ### Insight
> As the accounting period is less than 12 months long, the annual investment allowance limit is reduced to £83,333 (£100,000 × 10/12). This does not affect Nina as her capital expenditure is only £1,050 in the period in question.

Refer to Chapter 6 and Appendix 1 for further information.

INCOME AND EXPENDITURE

Nina now prepares her income and expenditure account and enters the details on the self-employment pages of the tax return.

Income and expenditure 2009/10	Disallowable expenses (£)	Total income/ expenses (£)	Calculations
Turnover (takings, fees, sales or money earned)		15,400	
Cost of goods bought for resale or goods used		−3,480	Purchase of jars, labels and ingredients £1,500 + £2,800 − Closing stock £820
Gross profit (not shown on the tax return)		**11,920**	
Car, van and travel expenses	560	1,400	Motor expenses £1,400 − disallowable private use £560
Rent, rates, power and insurance		1,040	Stall hire £650 + use of home allowance £215 + insurance £175 (£300 paid in advance £125)

(Contd)

Income and expenditure 2009/10	Disallowable expenses (£)	Total income/ expenses (£)	Calculations
Telephone, fax, stationery and other office costs		−1,015	Telephone £490 (£420 + bill received after the year end £70) + computer, office and administration costs £525 = £1,015
Advertising and business entertainment		−330	
Interest on bank and other loans		−150	Loan interest not capital repayments
Bank, credit card and other charges		−85	Bank charges
Net profit		**7,900**	
Disallowable expenses (additions to net profit)		560	Private motor expenses
Goods taken for own use		172	
Capital allowances		−1,890	See capital allowance calculation
Taxable profit		**6,742**	Amount on which Nina pays income tax

Nina's sales are less than the VAT registration threshold (see Appendix 1) and her affairs are straightforward. She can therefore complete the short version of the self-employed pages of the tax return if she wants to. As her annual sales are also less than £30,000 she also has the option of entering her total expenses (rather than the individual items) on the form.

....

Insight

Even though Nina does not have to provide HM Revenue and Customs with comprehensive details of her expenses she may still want to provide the full information so that the tax authorities have a better understanding of her business.

....

Refer to Chapter 4 for further information.

WORKING OUT THE TAX LIABILITY

Nina checks through her tax return and as she has no other sources of income and no other deductions to claim, she can now work out how much income tax she owes on her taxable profit.

Income tax liability 2009/10	£
Taxable profit	6,742
Personal allowance	−6,475
Income subject to income tax	**267**
Tax at the basic rate: 20% ×£267	53.40
Class 4 National Insurance: £6,742 − £5,715 = £1,027 × 8%	82.16
Nina's total income tax and Class 4 National Insurance	**135.56**

Refer to Chapters 1 and 4 for further information.

SUBMITTING THE TAX RETURN

Nina submits her tax return on 31 July 2010 using the paper form sent by HM Revenue and Customs. As this is before 31 October 2010 her return is filed on time. HM Revenue and Customs will work out her tax liability and confirm Nina's calculation.

Insight

If Nina fails to submit her paper tax return by 31 October 2010 she will have to file the return electronically. The final date for filing a 2009/10 return online is 31 January 2011. If she files after this date she will incur a penalty.

Refer to Chapter 2 and Appendix 2 for further information.

PAYING TAX

Nina pays her income tax and Class 4 National Insurance on 11 January 2011. This is before the due date of 31 January 2011 so she avoids paying interest.

Nina is pleased to see that she does not need to pay any tax on account of her potential tax liability for 2010/11 because her total tax bill for 2009/10 is less than £1,000.

Refer to Chapter 2 and Appendix 2 for further information.

Moving on

We now catch up with Nina at the beginning of April 2011. She has just counted her stock so that she can prepare accurate accounts for the year to 31 March 2011 in due course. Her business is thriving thanks to good PR and she has just signed a contract to supply three spicy chutneys to a well-known food emporium for their Christmas 2011 range. As she will have to increase production significantly to meet the new order, she decides to rent a unit on an industrial estate at a cost of £6,000 a year. She spends £10,000 on kitchen units, appliances and equipment which she finances with a further bank loan.

Nina will be able to claim a tax deduction for the rent, business and water rates, power, insurance and security. She will be able to claim annual investment allowance for the cost of fitting out the unit provided that the individual items qualify as either plant or machinery.

Refer to Chapters 6 and 8 for further information.

Taking on staff

Nina needs to take on staff to fulfil her Christmas order so she recruits a cook, two part-time assistants and an office administrator to process orders and deliveries. Each member of staff is paid a basic salary of more than the National Minimum Wage with the promise of a bonus when the order is fulfilled. Nina decides to use an agency to administer her payroll and pay her employees each month.

Nina obtains a form P45 from three of the employees and sends these to the agency together with their pay and bank details. One assistant cook does not have a P45 so Nina asks her to complete a form P46 instead.

At the end of the month, the agency produces payslips for each employee and tells Nina how much to pay them. They also inform her how much PAYE and Class 1 employee's and employer's National Insurance to pay to HM Revenue and Customs by the 19th of the following month.

Insight
Nina will obtain a tax deduction for the employees' gross salaries and employer's National Insurance. She can also claim a tax deduction for the cost of recruiting the employees and the payroll agency fees.

Refer to Chapters 4 and 7 and Appendix 2 for further information.

VAT registration

Nina's sales have not yet reached the VAT registration threshold but she knows that they will do so within the next few months when she invoices her Christmas sales. She therefore decides to register for VAT voluntarily from 1 July 2011.

Nina completes HM Revenue and Customs form VAT 1 online which she accesses from the VAT Online Registration Service by following the links from www.hmrc.gov.uk/vat/index.htm. Nina reads the literature and checks with the National Advice Service on 0845 010 9000 that chutney is a zero-rate supply because it is food. She learns that because all her sales are zero-rated that she will be entitled to VAT repayments, as a result there is no benefit to her to join either the cash or annual accounting schemes.

Nina belatedly realizes that she could have registered for VAT when she started her business and reclaimed the VAT on her purchases but she is not too dismayed when she realizes that she can reclaim the VAT on items she still owns back to the date she started in business because it was less than three years ago. She therefore makes a list of all her kitchen equipment and stock on hand at 1 July 2011. She locates the original invoices so she can include the items on her first VAT return.

Nina alters the way that she keeps her accounting records. She now needs to make additional entries to record the VAT on her purchases.

Refer to Chapter 9 for further information.

Completing the first VAT return

Nina asked HM Revenue and Customs to allocate her VAT returns for calendar quarters so that they coincide with her accounting year end. Her first VAT return is due for the three-month period

1 July 2011–30 September 2011 and must be submitted by 31 October 2011. During the first week of October, she completes the return online and is pleased with the refund she is owed.

Refer to Chapter 9 for further information.

Completing the second tax return

In November 2011 Nina has not yet completed her tax return for the year to 5 April 2011. She must file the return electronically by 31 January 2012. She therefore prepares her accounts to 31 March 2011 and enters the details on the return. The entries are similar to the previous year. Nina is pleased to see that her profit has nearly doubled but she is concerned about her tax liabilities.

In due course HM Revenue and Customs confirm that she owes income tax and Class 4 National insurance for 2010/11 of £1,360. All the tax is due on 31 January 2012. She also learns that because this liability is more than £1,000, she has to pay the same sum again as two payments on account for the tax year 2011/12 (£680 on 31 January 2012 and £680 on 31 July 2012).

Insight

As Nina needs to pay tax of £2,040 on 31 January 2012 (£1,360 + £680) she mentally notes that when she is paid for her Christmas orders she must put some of it aside to pay the tax before she takes extra drawings.

Refer to Chapters 2 and 4 and Appendix 2 for further information.

Rewarding staff

By the end of November 2011 Nina's Kitchen has fulfilled its Christmas orders and as promised Nina pays her staff a bonus.

She tells the payroll agency how much to add to their usual pay. They calculate how much PAYE and National Insurance must be deducted and tell Nina how much extra to pay each employee.

Insight

Nina has forgotten that she would have to pay employer's National Insurance on top of the bonuses. As a result it costs her more than she anticipated. She can however deduct both the bonuses and employer's National Insurance as a business expense.

Nina takes her employees out for a seasonal meal to thank them for their hard work. The bill for the evening comes to £300. As this is less than £150 per head, Nina can deduct these costs as a business expense and there is no tax to pay on the perk.

Refer to Chapters 4 and 7 for further information.

An established business

We next meet Nina in late April 2012. Her business is still thriving. She has a repeat order for Christmas 2012 from the food emporium and now makes regular sales to two large department stores. She is also planning a range of anti-pasti.

Completing employer end-of-year returns

Nina has to file an employer end-of-year return for the year to 5 April 2012 consisting of a form P35 and a form P14 for each member of staff. The payroll agency completes the forms for her and she issues her employees with forms P60 showing the details of their pay, tax and National Insurance before the end of May. None of her employees has received any perks so she does not complete forms P11D and P9D.

Refer to Chapter 7 and Appendix 2 for further information.

PAYE inspection

In July 2012 HM Revenue and Customs come to inspect Nina's PAYE records. She obtains monthly printouts from the payroll agency which she makes available to the officer. He discusses her business operations and checks her bank payments. He tells her that she should have reported details of the office expenses she reimburses to her administrator on a form P11D because she does not have a dispensation in force. Nina therefore completes the form P11DX 'Dispensation of expenses payments and benefits in kind' to apply for a dispensation so that she does not have to report non-taxable benefits in kind in the future.

Refer to Chapter 7 for further information.

Completing the third tax return

Nina completes her third tax return to 5 April 2012 in August 2012. Apart from the fact that her profits have increased significantly, she has no further difficulties with the numbers. She wonders whether she can obtain a tax deduction for some of her childcare costs but learns that her own childcare costs are not a tax-deductible expense.

HM Revenue and Customs advise Nina that she owes a balancing tax payment for 2011/12 of £5,200 after deducting the two payments of £680 she paid on account. This tax is due to be paid on 31 January 2013. In addition Nina owes payments on account for 2012/13 of £3,280 per instalment, making her 31 January 2013 payment a total of £8,480 (£5,200 + £3,280).

Refer to Chapters 2, 3 and 4 and Appendix 2 for further information.

Paying a pension

Nina is concerned about her rising profits and increased tax bills. She has read that paying into a pension can save tax, so she consults a financial adviser who recommends that she starts paying £250 per month into a pension. Nina is pleased to learn that she only has to pay the pension company £200 each month and that they reclaim £50 per month from the tax authorities and pay it into her pension.

Refer to Chapter 10 for further information.

Paying a sick employee

In September 2012 Nina's cook falls ill and she has to pay her part-time assistants to cover his work. She notifies the payroll agency of the changes to her employees' pay and her cook's sickness. They calculate how much statutory sick pay (SSP) he must be paid and work out how much of the SSP Nina can recover against the monthly PAYE and National Insurance she pays to HM Revenue and Customs.

Refer to Chapter 7 and Appendices 1 and 2 for further information.

Loss

We meet Nina again in March 2013. Things have not been going well for her. Her new anti-pasti range has not been the success she hoped for and an expensive advertising campaign in a gourmet food magazine produced no new customers. She calculates that she has made a loss of £6,000 and is keen to submit her tax return to 5 April 2013 as quickly as possible to claim tax relief for it. First of all she needs to reduce the tax she is paying on account so that she does not have to pay income tax of £3,280 on 31 July 2013.

Nina sees that she has two possible ways to get tax relief for her loss:

▶ *As the loss is in the fourth tax year of her business (2012/13), she can claim relief against her income of the three previous tax years but she must claim it against the earliest year first (2009/10).*
▶ *Alternatively, she can claim the loss against her profits for the previous tax year (2011/12).*

In 2009/10 Nina's profits were only £6,742 and her tax bill £135.56. She will waste her personal allowance to claim the loss against this year and she will only receive a tax refund of £135.56 because that is all the tax she paid in that year. She will therefore choose to use the loss against her income of the previous tax year 2011/12 by making a 'Section 64 claim'. This will probably give her a tax refund of £1,680.

Refer to Chapters 2 and 5 for further information.

Completing the fourth tax return

Nina completes her fourth tax return to 5 April 2013 in May 2013. Her loss must be entered in the box 'Loss from this tax year set-off against other income for 2011/12'. Nina must also provide details of the claim she is making in the 'any other information' box on the form. HM Revenue and Customs will then refund the tax from 2011/12. Nina will also receive a tax refund for 2012/13. The £3,280 she paid on account of her tax liabilities for 2012/13 on

31 January 2013 will be returned to her as she owes no tax at all for that year.

Nina also has to enter details of her pension on the tax return this year. As she has made a loss there is no further tax relief to claim. Her annual contributions are less than £3,600, so are within the permitted limits in spite of the loss.

Refer to Chapters 2, 3, 5 and 10 for further information.

Where next?

It is time to leave Nina. Her business has now been running for nearly five years and like many new ventures she has had her share of misfortune. During this time Nina has developed a basic knowledge of tax and business. With a reliable customer base she could continue running her self-employment for many years. She may alternatively consider expansion and incorporation, selling the business or closing it down. Whatever the future holds for Nina's Kitchen, Nina is now aware of the tax consequences that can occur at each stage in the development of her business.

10 THINGS TO REMEMBER

1 *You should start keeping records of your business transactions as soon as you start trading. If you register for VAT you will probably need to make changes to the way that you keep your records.*

2 *If you claim Child or Working Tax Credits, remember to notify the relevant department about your new business as it could affect your entitlement.*

3 *Chose a convenient and practical date to prepare your accounts to.*

4 *Remember to count any stock on hand at your year end and make a note of amounts owed to you by your debtors and by you to your creditors. Your accounting records will probably need to be adjusted for tax purposes.*

5 *If you take goods from your business for your private use or consumption you must account for these items as drawings at their market value.*

6 *Purchases of equipment costing up to £100,000 (£25,000 from April 2012) per year are eligible for the 100% annual investment allowance.*

7 *Cars used privately as well as for business are treated differently from other equipment and vans when working out your capital allowances claim.*

8 *Paper tax returns have to be filed by the 31 October falling after the end of the tax year. You can file online returns until the following 31 January. Late-filed forms attract a penalty.*

9 *PAYE and National Insurance deducted from your employees must be paid over to HMRC by the 19th of the following month.*

10 *Apply for a dispensation so that you do not have to report employee or director's non-taxable benefits in kind.*

Appendix 1: rates and allowances

The following tables summarize the tax rates, allowances and thresholds for the 2009/10 tax year (6 April 2009 to 5 April 2010) referred to throughout the book. The figures for 2008/09 are also included. Where figures have already been announced for 2010/11 and later tax years these are also provided.

Annual changes

Many of the allowances and thresholds change each year so if you are reading this book in 2011 and want to make tax calculations for 2010/11 (or a subsequent tax year) you will need to update the figures. There are columns for the years 2010/11 and 2011/12 to enable you to do this. Most of the numbers do not change dramatically from year to year unless a particular tax is radically overhauled, there is a change of government or a need to raise more tax. Generally allowances and thresholds rise annually by the rate of inflation or the increase in earnings. Tax rates change less often and they frequently stay the same for many years.

Updating the tables

The annual increases in personal allowances and National Insurance are first announced in the Chancellor's autumn Budget statement. All other rates, allowances and thresholds are usually given in the spring Budget. National newspapers often print details of these or they can be accessed from HM Revenue and Customs website under www.hmrc.gov.uk/rates/index.htm (Rates and Allowances).

Once you have located the new rates, allowances and thresholds for the relevant tax year, you should enter the numbers in the grid supplied and use them in your calculations.

Income tax

Income is taxed at different rates according to whether it is:

▶ *Dividend income;*
▶ *Interest; or*
▶ *Another source of income such as self-employed and partnership profits, employed earnings or rental income.*

The rates of tax applicable to each source of income are applied to a slice or band of your taxable income (that is income after deducting personal allowances and other reliefs such as losses). If you have multiple sources of income including dividends and interest, the dividends are treated as if they are the top slice, then interest as the next slice and finally all the other sources. It is therefore possible for you to pay tax at six different tax rates in 2010/11 – 10%, 20%, 32.5%, 40%, 42.5% and 50%.

INCOME BANDS

	2008/09	2009/10	2010/11	2011/12
Income band	£	£	£	£
Band 1 (starting rate for savings) (Note 1)	0–2,320	0–2,440	0–2,440	
Band 2 (basic rate)	0–34,800	0–37,400	0–37,400	
Band 3 (higher rate)	Over 34,800	Over 37,400	37,401–150,000	
Band 4 (additional rate) (Note 2)	Not applicable	Not applicable	Over 150,000	

Note 1: The starting rate band applies if your employment income or self-employed profits are less than the limit, to the interest received in the tax year that is less than the limit. It does not apply to self-employed profits or earnings.

Note 2: The additional rate of tax applies from 6 April 2010 onwards.

The rate bands change annually and can be updated from www.hmrc.gov.uk/rates/it.htm.

RATES

You now need to look up the rate of income tax which corresponds to Band 1, 2, 3 and 4. The tax rates depend on the type of income you receive.

SELF-EMPLOYED AND PARTNERSHIP PROFITS, EMPLOYED EARNINGS, RENTAL INCOME

	2008/09	2009/10	2010/11	2011/12
Income band	%	%	%	%
Band 1 (starting rate for savings)	Not applicable	Not applicable	Not applicable	
Band 2 (basic rate)	20	20	20	
Band 3 (higher rate)	40	40	40	
Band 4 (additional rate)	Not applicable	Not applicable	50	

INTEREST

	2008/09	2009/10	2010/11	2011/12
Income band	%	%	%	%
Band 1 (starting rate for savings)	10	10	10	
Band 2 (basic rate)	20	20	20	
Band 3 (higher rate)	40	40	40	
Band 4 (additional rate)	Not applicable	Not applicable	50	

DIVIDENDS

	2008/09	2009/10	2010/11	2011/12
Income band	%	%	%	%
Band 1 (starting rate for savings)	Not applicable	Not applicable	Not applicable	
Band 2 (basic rate)	10	10	10	
Band 3 (higher rate)	32.5	32.5	32.5	
Band 4 (additional rate)	Not applicable	Not applicable	42.5	

PERSONAL ALLOWANCES

A basic annual personal allowance is available to UK resident adults and children. British Citizens living abroad and some other people from overseas are also eligible.

Higher allowances are paid to those who are aged 65 and over and aged 75 or more. These higher allowances are reduced to the level of the basic personal allowance if your income exceeds a certain limit. From 6 April 2010 the basic personal allowance is progressively and completely withdrawn if your annual income is above £100,000.

Married couples and those in civil partnerships born before 6 April 1935 are eligible for the tax reduction for married couples and civil partners. This allowance is reduced where your income exceeds an income limit but it cannot be reduced to less than a stated minimum. The allowance is usually given to the husband or partner with the higher income but can also be claimed by a wife or the other civil partner, or shared equally.

	2008/09	2009/10	2010/11	2011/12
Description of the allowance	£	£	£	£
Basic personal allowance aged under 65 (restricted where income over £100,000 from 2010/11)	6,035	6,475	6,475	7,475
Personal allowance aged 65–74 (depending on income, see income limit)	9,180	9,490	9,490	
Personal allowance aged 75 and over (depending on income, see income limit)	9,180	9,640	9,640	
Blind person's allowance	1,800	1,890	1,890	
Tax reduction for married couples and civil partners born before 6 April 1935 (aged under 75 and depending on income, see income limit)	6,535	6,865	Not applicable	Not applicable
Tax reduction for married couples and civil partners born before 6 April 1935 (aged 75 and over and depending on income, see income limit)	6,625	6,965	6,965	
Married couple's allowance born before 6 April 1935 (minimum amount irrespective of income)	2,540	2,670	2,670	
Income limit for age-dependent personal allowances and the tax reduction for married couples and civil partners	21,800	22,900	22,900	

Personal allowances are deducted from your income before you pay tax. This means that they save you tax at the highest rate you pay, so the basic personal allowance will save a basic rate taxpayer £1,295 (£6,475 × 20%) and a higher rate taxpayer £2,590 (£6,475 × 40%) in 2009/10 and 2010/11. If you pay income tax at the 50% additional rate you are not entitled to a personal allowance.

The tax reduction for married couples and civil partners only saves you tax at the 10% rate of tax, so for those born before 6 April 1935 and aged 75 and over, it is worth a maximum tax saving of £696.50 (£6,965 × 10%) in 2009/10 and 2010/11.

Personal allowances change annually and can be updated from www.hmrc.gov.uk/rates/it.htm.

ENTERPRISE INVESTMENT SCHEME (EIS)

	2008/09	2009/10	2010/11	2011/12
Maximum investment	£500,000	£500,000	£500,000	
Rate of tax relief	20%	20%	20%	
Share-holding period	3 years	3 years	3 years	

These figures may not necessarily change each year. For further information see Chapters 3, 11, and 13 and www.hmrc.gov.uk/eis/part1/1-2.htm.

Capital gains tax – individuals

RATES

	2008/09	2009/10	2010/11	2011/12
	%	%	%	%
18% rate (Note 1)	18	18	18	

(Contd)

	2008/09	2009/10	2010/11	2011/12
28% rate (Note 2)	Not applicable	Not applicable	28	

Note 1: From 23 June 2010 the 18% rate of capital gains tax applies to individuals whose capital gains and income are less than the upper limit of the basic rate income tax band (see Income bands). For 2008/09 and 2009/10 this was the only rate of capital gains tax.

Note 2: From 23 June 2010 the 28% rate of capital gains tax applies to gains that are wholly or partly above the upper limit of the basic rate income tax band and to the gains of trustees and personal representatives.

ANNUAL EXEMPTION

The annual exemption is the capital gains tax equivalent of the income tax personal allowance. It is deducted from your gains before the tax is calculated.

	2008/09	2009/10	2010/11	2011/12
Annual exemption	£	£	£	£
Individuals	9,600	10,100	10,100	

This table can be updated by referring to www.hmrc.gov.uk/rates/cgt.htm.

ENTREPRENEURS' RELIEF

If you are eligible for entrepreneurs' relief on the disposal of a trading business or shares in a trading company you pay capital gains tax at 10%. The relief may be claimed by individuals (not companies) up to a lifetime limit of £5 million from 23 June 2010. Between 6 April 2010 and 22 June 2010 the limit was £2 million and between 6 April 2008 and 5 April 2010 it was £1 million.

Capital gains tax – companies

Companies pay capital gains tax as part of their corporation tax bill. They are not entitled to an annual exemption or entrepreneurs' relief but their gains can be reduced by the indexation allowance (see Chapter 1). Gains are added to the company's profits and are taxed at the corporation tax rates.

Indexation tables are published by HM Revenue and Customs and are available on www.hmrc.gov.uk/rates/c_gains_subject_c_tax.htm.

Corporation tax

RATES AND THRESHOLDS

Company profits are taxed at one of two rates depending on whether the company qualifies as a small company because it has profits below the stated threshold. Marginal rate relief eases the transition between the small profits rate of corporation tax and the main rate.

This table can be updated by referring to www.hmrc.gov.uk/rates/corp.htm.

Financial year	2008 – year ended 31 March 2009	2009 – year ended 31 March 2010	2010 – year ending 31 March 2011	2011 – year ending 31 March 2012
Small profits rate	21%	21%	21%	20%
Marginal relief lower limit	£0–£300,000	£0–£300,000	£0–£300,000	£0–£300,000

(Contd)

Financial year	2008 – year ended 31 March 2009	2009 – year ended 31 March 2010	2010 – year ending 31 March 2011	2011 – year ending 31 March 2012
Marginal relief upper limit	£1,500,001 and above	£1,500,001 and above	£1,500,001 and above	£1,500,001 and above
Standard fraction	7/400	7/400	7/400	
Main rate	28%	28%	28%	27%

Inheritance tax

No inheritance tax is charged if the value of your estate is below the level of the nil rate band. Above this limit inheritance tax on death is charged at 40%.

Tax percentage	2008/09	2009/10	2010/11	2011/12
0% (nil rate band)	Up to £312,000	Up to £325,000	Up to £325,000	Up to £325,000
40% (charged on death)	Over £312,000	Over £325,000	Over £325,000	Over £325,000

Note 1: The 0% nil rate band will increase if you 'inherit' the unused portion of the nil rate band of your deceased spouse or civil partner (see Chapter 1).

National Insurance

As outlined in Chapter 1, National Insurance is divided into four classes.

CLASS 1

	2008/09	2009/10	2010/11	2011/12
	Per week £	Per week £	Per week £	Per week £
Lower earnings limit (LEL)	90	95	97	
Upper earnings limit (UEL)	770	844	844	
Upper accrual point (UAP)	–	770	770	
Employee's (primary) threshold (ET)	105	110	110	
Employer's (secondary) limit	105	110	110	

	2008/09	2009/10	2010/11	2011/12
Employees	%	%	%	%
Under employee's threshold	0	0	0	0
Between employee's threshold and upper earnings limits	11	11	11	12
Above upper earnings limit	1	1	1	2
S2P contracted out rebate	1.6	1.6	1.6	
Married women's reduced rate (Note 1)				
Under employee's threshold	0	0	0	0
Between employee's threshold and upper earnings limits	4.85	4.85	4.85	5.85

(Contd)

	2008/09	2009/10	2010/11	2011/12
Above upper earnings limit	1	1	1	2
Employers (Note 2)				
Under employer's limit	0	0	0	0
Above employer's limit	12.8	12.8	12.8	13.8
S2P contracted out rebate – salary schemes	3.7	3.7	3.7	
S2P contracted out rebate – money-purchase schemes	1.4	1.4	1.4	

Note 1: Available only to women married before 6 April 1977 making the required election and who have not subsequently divorced.

Note 2: Including Classes 1A and 1B National Insurance.

CLASS 2

	2008/09	2009/10	2010/11	2011/12
Weekly rates	£	£	£	£
Class 2 contributions	2.30	2.40	2.40	
Share fishermen	2.95	3.05	3.05	
Volunteer development workers	4.50	4.75	4.85	
Annual threshold				
Small earnings exception	4,825	5,075	5,075	

CLASS 3

	2008/09	2009/10	2010/11	2011/12
Weekly rates	£	£	£	£
Class 3 contributions	8.10	12.05	12.05	

CLASS 4

	2008/09	2009/10	2010/11	2011/12
Per year	£	£	£	£
Lower profit limit	5,435	5,715	5,715	
Upper profit limit	40,040	43,875	43,875	

	2008/09	2009/10	2010/11	2011/12
Annual profits or gains	%	%	%	%
Less than lower limit	0	0	0	
Between lower and upper limit	8	8	8	9
Above upper limit	1	1	1	2

The National Insurance tables can be updated by referring to www.hmrc.gov.uk/rates/nic.htm.

VAT

For further information about VAT see Chapter 9. These tables can be updated by following the links from 'VAT' on www.hmrc.gov.uk.

RATES

From	1 April 2008	1 April 2009	1 April 2010	4 January 2011
Rate	%	%	%	%
Standard	17.5	17.5	17.5	20
Reduced	5	5	5	5
Zero	0	0	0	0

The VAT rate was temporarily reduced to 15% for a 13-month period, 1 December 2008 to 31 December 2009.

ANNUAL TURNOVER THRESHOLDS

From	1 April 2008	1 April 2009	1 April 2010	1 April 2011
Rate	£	£	£	£
Registration	67,000	68,000	70,000	
De-registration	65,000	66,000	68,000	
Annual accounting – joining	1,350,000	1,350,000	1,350,000	
Annual accounting – leaving	1,600,000	1,600,000	1,600,000	
Cash accounting – joining	1,350,000	1,350,000	1,350,000	
Cash accounting – leaving	1,600,000	1,600,000	1,600,000	
Flat-rate scheme – joining	150,000	150,000	150,000	
Flat-rate scheme – leaving (Note 1)	225,000	225,000	225,000	

Note 1: The threshold rises to £230,000 from 4 January 2011.

CAR VAT FUEL SCALE CHARGES

The VAT car scale charge to be used in assessing the amount of private fuel is determined by reference to its carbon dioxide emissions. Rates are published for one-, three- and 12-month return periods and can be obtained by contacting the National Advice Service on 0845 010 9000. The tables of rates are updated annually on 1 May.

Stamp duties

STAMP DUTY LAND TAX ON PROPERTY

For further information see Chapter 8. The tables can be updated from www.hmrc.gov.uk/so/rates/index.htm.

Rate bands	2008/09	2009/10	2010/11	2011/12
Purchase price including VAT				
Residential				
Band 1 (Note 1)	£0–£125,000	£0–£125,000	£0–£125,000	
Band 2 (Note 1)	£125,001–£250,000	£125,001–£250,000	£125,001–£250,000	
Band 3	£250,001–£500,000	£250,001–£500,000	£250,001–£500,000	
Band 4	Over £500,000	Over £500,000	Over £500,000	
Band 5 (Note 2)	Not applicable	Not applicable	Not applicable	Over £1 million
Commercial				
Band 1	£0–£150,000	£0–£150,000	£0–£150,000	
Band 2	£150,001–£250,000	£150,001–£250,000	£150,001–£250,000	
Band 3	£250,001–£500,000	£250,001–£500,000	£250,001–£500,000	
Band 4	Over £500,000	Over £500,000	Over £500,000	

Note 1: Purchases of residential property costing between £125,001 and £250,000 by first time buyers between 25 March 2010 and 24 March 2012 come within Band 1. The Band 1 limit is £150,000 instead of £125,000 for residential property in specified deprived areas. It was £175,000 for residential sales between 3 September 2008 and 2 September 2009.

Note 2: Purchases of residential property on or after 6 April 2011 costing more than £1 million come within Band 5.

Now look up the tax rates which apply to each band in the following table.

Rates	2008/09	2009/10	2010/11	2011/12
Purchase price including VAT	%	%	%	%
Residential				
Band 1	0	0	0	
Band 2	1	1	1	
Band 3	3	3	3	
Band 4	4	4	4	
Band 5	Not applicable	Not applicable	Not applicable	5
Commercial				
Band 1	0	0	0	
Band 2	1	1	1	
Band 3	3	3	3	
Band 4	4	4	4	

LEASES

Broadly, for residential properties stamp duty land tax is charged on 1% of the discounted rental value over the lease term where it exceeds the upper limit in Band 1. For non-residential property where the annual rent is more than £1,000 special rules apply. Where the annual rent is less than £1,000 the duty on the premium is the same as the duty on freehold property.

OTHER STAMP DUTIES

	2008/09	2009/10	2010/11	2011/12
Rate	%	%	%	%
Stocks and shares	0.5	0.5	0.5	
Stamp duty reserve tax	0.5	0.5	0.5	

Capital allowances

Type of allowance	2008/09	2009/10	2010/11	2011/12
	%	%	%	%
Writing down allowance (general) (Note 1)	20	20	20	20
Writing down (cars with CO_2 emissions over 160g/km) (Note 1)	–	10	10	10
Writing down (features integral to a building) (Note 1)	10	10	10	10
Writing down (thermal insulation in buildings) (Note 1)	10	10	10	10
Long life assets (Note 1)	10	10	10	10
Annual investment	100	100	100	100
Annual investment – maximum annual limit (Note 2)	50,000	50,000	100,000	100,000
First year (energy efficient and water-saving technologies)	100	100	100	
First year (new electric vans to 31 March 2015)	–	–	100	100
First year (new low emissions cars to 31 March 2013)	100	100	100	100

(Contd)

Type of allowance	2008/09	2009/10	2010/11	2011/12
First year (natural gas, hydrogen and biogas refuelling equipment to 31 March 2013)	100	100	100	100
First year (temporary on plant and machinery)	–	40	–	–
Flat conversion (or 25% writing down allowance)	100	100	100	
Business premises renovation (or 25% writing down allowance)	100	100	100	
Industrial buildings (in the process of being completely withdrawn)	3	2	1	–
Agricultural buildings (in the process of being completely withdrawn)	3	2	1	–
Enterprise Zone (withdrawn from 31 March 2011)	100	100	100	–

Note 1: From April 2012 the 20% rate falls to 18% and the 10% rate becomes 8%.

Note 2: From April 2012 the annual investment allowance maximum annual limit falls to £25,000.

For details of the conditions applicable to each allowance see Chapters 6 and 8.

Employers

For further details see Chapter 7. The following tables can be updated from www.hmrc.gov.uk/paye/statutorypayments.htm.

STATUTORY SICK PAY (SSP)

	2008/09	2009/10	2010/11	2011/12
Weekly rate	£75.40	£79.15	£79.15	
Weekly earnings threshold	£90.00	£95.00	£97.00	
Recovery percentage	13%	13%	13%	

STATUTORY MATERNITY PAY (SMP)

	2008/09	2009/10	2010/11	2011/12
Weekly rate – first 6 weeks	90% of pay	90% of pay	90% of pay	
Weekly rate – next 33 weeks	£117.18 or 90% of pay if lower	£123.06 or 90% of pay if lower	£124.88 or 90% of pay if lower	
Weekly earnings threshold	£90	£95	£97	
Recovery threshold	£45,000	£45,000	£45,000	
Recovery percentage – NIC under threshold	100%	100%	100%	
Compensation rate – NIC under threshold	4.5%	4.5%	4.5%	
Recovery percentage – NIC over threshold	92%	92%	92%	

STATUTORY PATERNITY PAY (SPP)

	2008/09	2009/10	2010/11	2011/12
Weekly rate	£117.18 or 90% of pay if lower	£123.06 or 90% of pay if lower	£124.88 or 90% of pay if lower	
Additional rate	–	–	£124.88 or 90% of pay if lower	
Weekly earnings threshold	£90	£95	£97	
Recovery threshold	£45,000	£45,000	£45,000	
Recovery percentage – NIC under threshold	100%	100%	100%	
Compensation rate – NIC under threshold	4.5%	4.5%	4.5%	
Recovery percentage – NIC over threshold	92%	92%	92%	

STATUTORY ADOPTION PAY (SAP)

	2008/09	2009/10	2010/11	2011/12
Weekly rate	£117.18 or 90% of pay if lower	£123.06 or 90% or pay if lower	£124.88 or 90% or pay if lower	
Weekly earnings threshold	£90	£95	£97	
Recovery threshold	£45,000	£45,000	£45,000	

	2008/09	2009/10	2010/11	2011/12
Recovery percentage – NIC under threshold	100%	100%	100%	
Compensation rate – NIC under threshold	4.5%	4.5%	4.5%	
Recovery percentage – NIC over threshold	92%	92%	92%	

NATIONAL MINIMUM WAGE

	From 1 October 2008	From 1 October 2009	From 1 October 2010	From 1 October 2011
	£	£	£	£
Adults aged 21 and older (22 years until 30 September 2010)	5.73	5.80	5.93	
18–20 year olds and adults attending approved training schemes (21 years until 30 September 2010)	4.77	4.83	4.92	
16 and 17 year olds (Note 1)	3.53	3.57	3.64	
Apprentice rate (Note 2)	Not applicable	Not applicable	2.50	

Note 1: 16 year olds who are no longer of compulsory school age.

Note 2: To apprentices otherwise exempt from the minimum wage. Applicable to apprentices under the age of 19 and those 19 and over for the first twelve months of their apprenticeship.

STUDENT LOAN REPAYMENTS

	2008/09	2009/10	2010/11	2011/12
Earnings threshold	£15,000	£15,000	£15,000	
Percentage repaid	9%	9%	9%	

Repayment is at the percentage specified once a student's earnings reach the earnings threshold.

COMPANY CARS

For further information see Chapter 7, www.hmrc.gov.uk/cars/index.htm. An interactive tool to calculate the tax change on company cars and fuel is available on www.hmrc.gov.uk/calcs/cars.htm.

CO_2 EMISSIONS IN GRAMS PER KILOMETRE (G/KM)

Percentage of car's price taxed	2008/09	2009/10	2010/11	2011/12
10*	120	120	120	120
15*	135	135	130	125
16*	140	140	135	130
17*	145	145	140	135
18*	150	150	145	140
19*	155	155	150	145
20*	160	160	155	150
21*	165	165	160	155
22*	170	170	165	160
23*	175	175	170	165
24*	180	180	175	170

Percentage of car's price taxed	2008/09	2009/10	2010/11	2011/12
25*	185	185	180	175
26*	190	190	185	180
27*	195	195	190	185
28*	200	200	195	190
29*	205	205	200	195
30*	210	210	205	200
31*	215	215	210	205
32*	220	220	215	210
33**	225	225	220	215
34***	230	230	225	220
35****	235	235	230	225

*   add 3% if car runs solely on diesel
**   add 2% if car runs solely on diesel
***   add 1% if car runs solely on diesel
**** maximum charge so no diesel supplement

From 2012/13 all CO_2 emissions will be moved down by 5g/km so that the 10% band applies to cars with emissions up to 99g/km.

Discounts for alternatively fuelled cars are abolished from 2011/12. From 6 April 2010 electric cars are taxed at the rate of 0% (previously 9%).

FUEL CHARGE

	2008/09	2009/10	2010/11	2011/12
Figure used to calculate scale charge	£16,900	£16,900	£18,000	

VANS

For further information see Chapter 7 and www.hmrc.gov.uk/vans/index.htm.

	2008/09	2009/10	2010/11	2011/12
Scale charge	£3,000	£3,000	£3,000	
Fuel charge	£500	£500	£550	

From 6 April 2010 there is no tax charge on electric vans.

AUTHORIZED MILEAGE RATE

Employers can reimburse business mileage driven in the employee's own vehicle up to the following rates without a tax charge arising. To update the table see www.hmrc.gov.uk/rates/travel.htm.

Single rate for all vehicles	2008/09	2009/10	2010/11	2011/12
Cars up to £10,000 miles	40p	40p	40p	
Cars excess over 10,000 miles	25p	25p	25p	
Passenger rate per mile	5p	5p	5p	
Motorbikes	24p	24p	24p	
Bikes	20p	20p	20p	

Where an employee reimburses their employer for the cost of private fuel at a rate not exceeding that stated there will be no benefit in kind charge.

The rates in the following table are updated every six months. The table can be revised by referring to www.hmrc.gov.uk/cars/advisory_fuel_current.htm.

Fuel-only rate	Petrol	Diesel	LPG
Engine size			
From 1 July 2009			
1,400cc or less	10p	10p	7p
1,401–2,000cc	12p	10p	8p
Over 2,000cc	18p	13p	12p

Fuel-only rate	Petrol	Diesel	LPG
From 1 December 2009			
1,400cc or less	11p	11p	7p
1,401–2,000cc	14p	11p	8p
Over 2,000cc	20p	14p	12p
From 1 June 2010			
1,400cc or less	12p	11p	8p
1,401–2,000cc	15p	11p	10p
Over 2,000cc	21p	16p	14p
From 1 December 2010			
1,400cc or less			
1,401–2,000cc			
Over 2,000cc			
From 1 June 2011			
1,400cc or less			
1,401–2,000cc			
Over 2,000cc			

Petrol hybrid cars are treated as petrol cars.

Construction industry

	2008/09	2009/10	2010/11	2011/12
Rate of tax deducted at source	%	%	%	%
Payments to sub-contractors registered with HMRC (standard rate)	20%	20%	20%	
Payments to sub-contractors not registered with HMRC (higher rate)	30%	30%	30%	

Pensions

For further details see Chapter 10.

	2008/09	2009/10	2010/11	2011/12
	£	£	£	£
Lifetime allowance	1,650,000	1,750,000	1,800,000	1,800,000*
Annual allowance	235,000	245,000	255,000	255,000*

*Frozen at this rate up to and including 2015/16. The Government is considering reducing the annual allowance to £30,000–£45,000.

Interest rates

For further details see Chapter 2 and Appendix 2.

Unpaid tax

	From 24 March 2009	From 29 September 2009		
Income tax	2.5%	3%		
Corporation tax	2.5%	3%		

This table can be updated from the information at www.hmrc.gov.uk/rates/interest-late.htm.

Overpaid tax

	2008/09	2009/10	2010/11	2011/12
Income tax	0%	0.5%*		
Corporation tax	0%	0.5%*		

*This rate applies from 29 September 2009.

This table can be updated from the information at
www.hmrc.gov.uk/rates/interest-repayments.htm.

Appendix 2: key dates

The following calendars set out the important dates and deadlines that individuals, employers and companies need to know about. Further details are given in Chapters 2 and 7.

Individuals

TAX RETURNS – DUE DATES

6 April	Beginning of the tax year. Tax returns issued.
31 October	Last date for submitting paper tax returns.
30 December	Last date for submitting your tax return over the Internet if you have a tax underpayment of less than £2,000 which you want to be included in your tax code.
31 January	Last date for submitting electronic returns. Forms filed on-line after this date attract a penalty.
5 April	End of the tax year.
31 July	Further penalties charged on tax returns which should have been filed on 31 January but which are still outstanding.

Income tax and capital gains tax payments – due dates

31 January (payment on account)	1st income tax payment on account due for the current tax year (usually 50% of the previous year's total tax bill).

31 January (balancing payment)	Balancing income tax and capital gains tax payment due for the previous tax year (usually your total tax bill less two payments on account made on the previous 31 January and 31 July).
31 July (payment on account)	2nd income tax payment on account due for the current tax year (usually 50% of the previous year's total tax bill).

Interest and penalties are charged on overdue payments.

Employers

FORMS – DUE DATES

5 April	End of the tax year.
19 May	Date for submitting employer end of year returns including forms P35, P38A and P14.
31 May	Last date to give employees form P60 (summary of salary, tax, National Insurance and other income and deductions).
6 July	Date that forms P9D, P11D and P11D(b) must be submitted to HMRC. Final date to give employees details of their benefits in kind on forms P9D and P11D.
19 July	Class 1A National Insurance due on relevant benefits in kind if paid by cheque. Late payments attract interest.
22 July	Class 1A National Insurance due on relevant benefits in kind if paid electronically. Late payments attract interest.
19 October	Tax due on a PAYE Settlement Agreement (PSA) if paid by cheque.
22 October	Tax due on a PAYE Settlement Agreements (PSA) if paid electronically.

MONTHLY PAYMENT DATES – BY NON-ELECTRONIC MEANS

19 January	HMRC must receive December employer deductions.
19 February	HMRC must receive January employer deductions.
19 March	HMRC must receive February employer deductions.
19 April	HMRC must receive March employer deductions. Interest is due on any unpaid deductions for the previous year.
19 May	HMRC must receive April employer deductions.
19 June	HMRC must receive May employer deductions.
19 July	HMRC must receive June employer deductions.
19 August	HMRC must receive July employer deductions.
19 September	HMRC must receive August employer deductions.
19 October	HMRC must receive September employer deductions.
19 November	HMRC must receive October employer deductions.
19 December	HMRC must receive November employer deductions.

MONTHLY PAYMENT DATES – ELECTRONICALLY

22 January	HMRC must receive cleared funds for December employer deductions.
22 February	HMRC must receive cleared funds for January employer deductions.
22 March	HMRC must receive cleared funds for February employer deductions.
22 April	HMRC must receive cleared funds for March employer deductions. Interest is due on any unpaid deductions for the previous year.
22 May	HMRC must receive cleared funds for April employer deductions.
22 June	HMRC must receive cleared funds for May employer deductions.

22 July	HMRC must receive cleared funds for June employer deductions.
22 August	HMRC must receive cleared funds for July employer deductions.
22 September	HMRC must receive cleared funds for August employer deductions.
22 October	HMRC must receive cleared funds for September employer deductions.
22 November	HMRC must receive cleared funds for October employer deductions.
22 December	HMRC must receive cleared funds for November employer deductions.

QUARTERLY PAYMENT DATES – BY NON-ELECTRONIC MEANS

19 January	Payment date for employer deductions.
19 April	Payment date for employer deductions. Interest is due on any unpaid deductions for the previous tax year.
19 July	Payment date for employer deductions.
19 October	Payment date for employer deductions.

QUARTERLY PAYMENT DATES – ELECTRONICALLY

22 January	Payment date for employer deductions.
22 April	Payment date for employer deductions. Interest is due on any unpaid deductions for the previous tax year.
22 July	Payment date for employer deductions.
22 October	Payment date for employer deductions.

Details of the date that electronic payments must be initialised in order to reach HMRC's bank account by the due date are available on their website.

Late payment penalties are charged if you do not pay the PAYE due each month or quarter on time and in full.

Companies

CORPORATION TAX PAYMENT DATES

Nine months and one day after the end of the company's accounting period unless it is a large company and has to make quarterly payments on account.

CORPORATION TAX RETURN

Returns must normally be filed within 12 months of the end of the company's accounting period. Different dates apply if the accounting period is longer than 12 months.

Appendix 3: glossary

This appendix provides quick definitions of the tax phrases and abbreviations found in the book.

Word or phrase	Description	Further reading
Accrual	Cost incurred in one accounting period relating to an earlier period.	Chapter 15
Administration	Formal way to manage: **1** an insolvent company's affairs and, **2** a deceased person's estate.	Chapters 12 and 14
Agricultural property relief	An inheritance tax relief.	Chapters 1 and 14
Annual allowance	Limit on the amount that you can contribute to a pension each year and still obtain tax relief.	Chapter 10
Annual exemption	Amount of capital gains you can make each year before you owe any capital gains tax.	Chapter 1
Annual investment allowance (AIA)	A type of capital allowance.	Chapter 6
Annuity	Pension.	Chapter 10
Asset	A positive balance in a business such as property, equipment, cars, goodwill, stock, debtors and cash.	Chapters 1, 6, 11 and 14

(Contd)

Word or phrase	Description	Further reading
Beneficiary	Someone benefiting from an inheritance or trust.	Chapter 14
Bequest	Gift in a will.	Chapter 14
BERR (see also BIS)	Department for Business Enterprise and Regulatory Reform.	Chapters 7 and 12
BIS	Department for Business Innovation and Skills	Chapters 7 and 12
Business property relief	An inheritance tax relief.	Chapters 1 and 14
Capital account	Sum owed to a partner by a partnership.	Chapter 14
Capital allowances	Tax allowances given on your business equipment, fixtures in a building and cars.	Chapters 6 and 8.
Capital expenditure	Assets of lasting benefit to the business (usually more than a year).	Chapter 6
Chattels	Personal property or assets.	Chapter 13
CIS	Construction Industry Scheme. Special tax arrangements for workers in the building trade.	Chapter 7
Company share option plan (CSOP)	Tax advantaged share scheme for employees.	Chapter 11

Word or phrase	Description	Further reading
Connected person	You (or your spouse or civil partner's) close relatives (and their spouses and civil partners). Your business partners (and their spouses and civil partners and relatives). Companies controlled by the same person.	Chapters 12 and 14
Director's loan account	Sum owed by a company to a director (it is illegal to overdraw it).	Chapter 11
Dispensation	Formal agreement with HMRC which dispenses with the need for you to report non-taxable perks.	Chapter 7
Domicile	Country in which you have your family roots. Non-domiciled means that your natural home is not in the UK.	Chapter 1
Enquiry	Investigation into your tax affairs by HMRC.	Chapter 2
Enterprise Investment Scheme (EIS)	A scheme enabling people investing in certain small companies to obtain tax advantages.	Chapters 3, 11 and 13
Enterprise Management Incentives (EMI)	Tax advantaged share scheme for employees.	Chapter 11

(Contd)

Word or phrase	Description	Further reading
Entrepreneurs' relief	Relief that may reduce your capital gains tax when you dispose of a business.	Chapters 1, 11 and 13
ET	Earnings threshold for Class 1 National Insurance.	Chapter 7
EU	European Union	Chapter 9
Executor	Person responsible for administering your estate after you die. They may be a professional person such as a solicitor or a relative.	Chapter 14
First year allowance (FYA)	A type of capital allowance.	Chapter 6
FSA	Financial Services Authority.	Chapter 10
GAAP	Generally Accepted Accounting Principles	Chapter 4
Gifts relief	A capital gains tax relief which defers tax on transfers of business assets.	Chapters 11 and 14
Goodwill	The amount that a business is worth over and above the value of its assets. It depends on profits, customers, brands, expertise etc.	Chapter 11
Gross	Total amount before deducting something (often tax or VAT).	Chapters 7 and 9

Word or phrase	Description	Further reading
HMRC	HM Revenue and Customs.	Chapter 2
Incorporation	Forming a limited company.	Chapter 11
Indexation allowance	A capital gains tax relief for companies.	Chapters 1 and 14
Input VAT	VAT on purchases or expenditure.	Chapter 9
Intestate	Dying without making a will.	Chapter 14
LEL	Lower earnings limit for Class 1 National Insurance.	Chapter 7
Lifetime allowance	Limit on the amount you can contribute to a pension over your lifetime and obtain tax relief on the investment.	Chapter 10
LLP	Limited Liability Partnership.	Chapter 3
Liquidation	Formal means of closing down a company, usually when it is insolvent.	Chapter 12
Marginal rate relief	A deduction from a small company's corporation tax liability to bridge the gap between the small company rate of corporation tax and the full rate.	Chapter 1
Net	Amount left after deducting something (often tax or VAT).	Chapters 7 and 9

(Contd)

Word or phrase	Description	Further reading
Net relevant earnings	The measure of your income (excluding dividends) used to calculate how much you can pay into a pension.	Chapter 10
NICO	National Insurance Contributions Office	Chapter 11
Nil rate band	Part of your estate which is free from inheritance tax. Unused nil rate band can be used to increase the nil rate band of a surviving spouse or civil partner.	Chapters 1 and 14
Output VAT	VAT on your sales or income.	Chapter 9
Overlap relief	Profits taxed twice when you start in self-employment because you use an accounting year end date other than 31 March or 5 April. Relief is given when you change your year end or stop trading.	Chapters 4, 5 and 12
PAYE	Pay As You Earn – the system for deducting income tax and National Insurance from employees' and directors' wages.	Chapter 7
Payment on account	Interim income tax payments made on 31 January and 31 July based on your tax bill for the previous year.	Chapter 2

Word or phrase	Description	Further reading
Personal allowance	The amount of income you can earn or receive before you owe any income tax. Certain high income taxpayers are not entitled to a personal allowance.	Chapter1
Plant	Equipment, apparatus and furnishings.	Chapter 6
Pool	A group of assets on which capital allowances are claimed.	Chapter 6
Post-cessation expense	Expenses incurred after closing down a business.	Chapter 12
Post-cessation receipt	Income received after closing down a business.	Chapter 12
Potentially exempt transfer	Inheritance tax term for a gift which may become liable to inheritance tax depending on when you die, the nil rate band for the year in question and other gifts made within a seven year period.	Chapters 1 and 14
Prepayment	Advance payment.	Chapter 15
Probate	An official form giving executors the right to deal with a deceased person's estate.	Chapter 14
PSA	PAYE Settlement Agreement.	Chapter 7

(Contd)

Word or phrase	Description	Further reading
Quoted company	A company that is listed on a stock exchange.	Chapter 14
R&D	Research and development	Chapter 6
Residue	The part of a deceased person's estate that is left over after all the bequests have been paid.	Chapter 14
Rollover relief	A capital gains tax relief which defers a gain arising on the sale of business assets through reinvesting the proceeds in new business assets.	Chapters 1, 8, 11 and 13.
SAP	Statutory Adoption Pay.	Chapter 7
SAYE scheme	Tax advantaged share scheme for employees.	Chapter 11
SDLT	Stamp duty land tax.	Chapter 8
Self-assessment	Tax system under which the taxpayer is responsible for informing HMRC of their tax liabilities and paying their tax by the due date.	Chapter 2.
Self-invested pension scheme (SIPP)	Type of self-directed pension arrangements.	Chapter 10
Settlement	**1** An agreement reached with HMRC about tax owing as the result of an enquiry. **2** A trust.	Chapters 2 and 3
Share incentive plan (SIP)	Tax advantaged share scheme for employees.	Chapter 11

Word or phrase	Description	Further reading
Short-life assets	Equipment expected to last for less than five years.	Chapter 6
Small self-administered scheme (SSAS)	Type of self-directed pension scheme.	Chapter 10
SMP	Statutory Maternity Pay.	Chapter 7
SPP	Statutory Paternity Pay.	Chapter 7
SSP	Statutory Sick Pay.	Chapter 7
Standard-rated	VAT charged on certain items at 17.5%.	Chapter 9
State Second Pension (S2P)	Addition to the state pension based on your earnings.	Chapter 10
Statement of account	Document produced by HMRC showing your tax liability and the payments made to them.	Chapters 2 and 15
Striking-off	Having a company removed from the register of companies.	Chapter 12
Tax credit	**1** A government payment to certain families, low earners and those with disabilities. **2** The tax associated with a dividend. **3** A means of tax relief for certain expenditure incurred by a company (research and development and land remediation).	Chapters 1 and 3

(Contd)

Word or phrase	Description	Further reading
Tax return	Form on which you notify HMRC about your liability to tax.	Chapter 2
Tax year	6 April to 5 April.	Chapter 2
Terminal loss	A loss made in the twelve months before ceasing your business.	Chapter 5
UEL	Upper earnings limit for Class 1 National Insurance.	Chapter 7
Unlisted company	A company whose shares are not quoted on a stock exchange.	Chapter 5
Variation	A formal means of changing a will (or intestacy) within two years of death upon meeting certain conditions.	Chapter 14
VAT	Value Added Tax.	Chapter 9
Writing down allowance (WDA)	A type of capital allowance.	Chapter 6
Zero-rated	VAT charged on certain items at 0%.	Chapter 9

Appendix 4: further information

This appendix tells you how to access additional information about the subjects discussed in this book.

Organizations regulating accountants and tax advisers

Institute of Chartered Accountants for England and Wales (ICAEW). Members are denoted by the letters FCA or ACA – www.icaewfirms.co.uk

Institute of Chartered Accountants of Scotland (ICAS). Members are denoted by the letters CA – www.icas.org.uk

Institute of Chartered Accountants in Ireland (ICAI). Members are denoted by the letters CA – www.icai.ie

Association of Chartered Certified Accountants (ACCA). Members are denoted by the letters FCCA or ACCA – www.accaglobal.com

Chartered Institute of Taxation (CIOT). Members are denoted by the letters CTA, FTII and ATII – www.tax.org.uk

The Association of Taxation Technicians (ATT). Members are denoted by the letters ATT – www.att.org.uk

The Association of Accounting Technicians (AAT). Members are denoted by the letters AAT – www.aat.org.uk

---

Organizations regulating solicitors

The Law Society of England and Wales – www.lawsociety.org.uk/home.law

The Law Society of Scotland – www.lawscot.org.uk

The Law Society of Northern Ireland – www.lawsoc-ni.org

Organization regulating providers of financial services

The Financial Services Authority (FSA) (to be abolished by 2012) – www.fsa.gov.uk

Government departments

HM Revenue and Customs – www.hmrc.gov.uk

Reference sources:

- ▶ *Manuals – www.hmrc.gov.uk/thelibrary/manuals.htm*
- ▶ *Employer Bulletin – www.hmrc.gov.uk/employers-bulletin/index.htm*
- ▶ *Briefs – www.hmrc.gov.uk/thelibrary/customs-briefs.htm*

Inheritance tax – www.hmrc.gov.uk/inheritancetax/

Stamp duty land tax – www.hmrc.gov.uk/so/index.htm

National Insurance – www.hmrc.gov.uk/nic

Valuation Office Agency (business rates) – www.voa.gov.uk/index.htm

Enhanced Capital Allowances – www.eca.gov.uk

The Department for Business Enterprise and Regulatory Reform (BERR) incorporating the Department for Business Innovation and Skills (BIS) – www.berr.gov.uk

The Insolvency Service – www.insolvency.gov.uk

Vehicle Certification Agency (Car CO_2 emissions) –
www.vcacarfueldata.org.uk/index.asp

HM Courts Service (probate) –
www.hmcourts-service.gov.uk/cms/wills.htm

Department for Work and Pensions (DWP) – www.dwp.gov.uk

Advisory services

Business Link – www.businesslink.gov.uk

Citizens Advice – www.adviceguide.org.uk

TaxAid – www.taxaid.org.uk

Community Legal Service – www.communitylegaladvice.org.uk

Employers

The Advisory, Conciliation and Arbitration Services (ACAS) –
www.acas.co.uk

Insolvency

Association of Business Recovery Professionals – www.r3.org.uk

Pensions

The Pensions Advisory Service – www.pensionsadvisoryservice.org.uk

Index